"It's not only here." Tuberski shook his small head. "In isolated towns and forgotten specks on the map whose names veritably ache with a faraway loneliness—the Three Sisters Wilderness, the Yolla Bolly, Devil Bear Gorge—are people, Michael, who will tell you of a giant creature, not man, not ape, whose howls reverberate at night, shrill and high-pitched, like a mortally wounded banshee. They will use their hands to measure footprints seventeen inches long with a stride of eight feet, and they'll point to hidden valleys where no birds sing and no animals go, and the quiet makes the hair on the back of your neck tingle. It's the last American legend, Mikey, and I propose we catch it."

Other TSR® Books

NAKED CAME THE
SASQUATCH

John Boston

NAKED CAME THE SASQUATCH

First Printing May 1993.
Printed in the United States of America.
Library of Congress Catalog Card Number: 92-61088

9 8 7 6 5 4 3 2 1

ISBN: 1-56076-602-6

TSR, Inc.
P.O. Box 756
Lake Geneva, WI 53147
U.S.A.

TSR Ltd.
120 Church End, Cherry Hinton
Cambridge CB1 3LB
United Kingdom

To my dad, Walt Cieplik,
who has been dear friend, advisor, and supporter
since, well, since I can remember.

To Jane Jordan Brown, pal and agent,
my gratitude for your ". . . going the extra mile."

And to my Loretta, aka Leslie Anne Peters,
the good queen of all the cowgirls.
Thanks for the steak, you thing you,
and for the . . . ahem, well, you know.

PART I:

Fenberg didn't believe in monsters, or women.
But he did believe in maniacs.
This was just about a year ago,
before he knew better.

—1—

FENBERG

Two beady orbs, small, dark, and piglike, slid back and forth, searching the lime green hallways for the intruder. Nurse Doris Lagoris heard the noise again.

The rustle of cellophane. It interrupted the silence of the old hospital, and she traced its source to a lone figure in the waiting room. The tall man with the half-smile, half-smirk had been sitting for two hours with his feet propped up on a wooden chair.

It was Fenberg.

Fenberg thoughtfully munched on a cookie. Staring at the old, crinkled, wallet-sized photo protected by yellowed Scotch tape, he fondly regarded the wholesome blonde holding the baby. The child was making a face.

One dead wife. One dead baby. One four-thousand-dollar double funeral in a drizzle. And that was that. Fenberg had long ago resigned himself to the fact that those closest to him were either dearly departed or crazy.

"Marching to the tune of a different drummer," Fenberg preferred.

Fenberg's brother was crazy. Or so the townspeople said. Despite his long walks in the forest, hands behind his back, where he stared at distant horizons and considered what made things tick, there was a darker side to Fenberg's baby brother. Fenberg's sibling liked to roughhouse. He irritated people, and sometimes they tried to hit him with chairs. Or bottles. And once with a banjo. Fenberg's brother had been stabbed eight separate times, poisoned once, and shot at another sixteen. Mostly, people missed. All things considered, Mike's brother was pretty much an indestructible sort, stronger than both Magonogonovitch brothers put together. He actually could bend steel in his bare hands, and he never got cold. But the stories of his fights and county-fair strength paled in comparison to the time Fenberg's brother earned brief national network notice and war-declared-size headlines in *The Basin Valley Bugle* a few years earlier:

31 INJURED IN "SEE 'EM DEAD ZOO BAR & GRILL" MASSACRE

Tuberski Claims They Tripped

Fenberg's brother had legally changed his name to "John Tuberski" many years earlier for career purposes, confirming rural suspicions that Fenberg's brother was crazy because Fenberg's brother didn't have a career.

Tuberski believed in reincarnation. Publicly, Fenberg pooh-poohed the notion of eternal life, but it was secret comfort to believe that his wife and son might come around again as bright, fresh babies with clean slates. Fenberg caught himself examining the faces of the little kids in town, trying to see a light of recognition in the eyes, some familiar gesture.

No.

Nurse Lagoris softly closed the door behind her. She tucked a note into her pocket and eyed Fenberg with suspicion. She felt compassion for the young widower, as nurses and decent people should. Fenberg had lost wife and baby in a hit-and-run accident, and then, a few days later, his mother and father had disappeared without a trace in a plane crash. But that was five Christmases behind Fenberg. In the here-and-now, Nurse Lagoris stood in the silent hallway and watched the newspaper editor walk toward her.

"He's sedated," she said, planting herself between Fenberg

and the doorway to the reporter's room. A woman of intimi-
dating proportions, she sported more chins than a Chinese
telephone book and carried a vague, stale odor masked by
talcum powder.

"How's he feeling?" Fenberg asked. "Is he going to be all
right?"

"He didn't say. And I didn't ask him. He's sedated." Her
voice was husky. Fenberg nodded.

"Did he mention anything before going under?" Fenberg
asked. "Any messages? Does he need anything?"

"Here," said the nurse, reaching into her pocket. "He
wanted you to have this letter."

The hospital was quiet and cool. The lime sherbet hallways
were deodorized by frequent baths of Pine-Sol and ammonia.
Nurse Lagoris watched Fenberg's mouth move as he silently
read the letter. She folded her arms across her rolling, white
chest and finally asked, "Say . . . what happened to that guy,
anyway?"

"He was shot by an Indian," said Fenberg, not looking up
from his reading. The message said:

Dear Mike,
  Sorry about putting you in a bind like this and I want
  you to know this is nothing personal. But I quit.

"Swell," said Fenberg, shifting his weight. The sixth
reporter this year. "Just swell."

  This has nothing to do with my being shot during
  office hours and again, nothing personal. You've been
  more than fair, a friend, and a good guy to work for.
  But since taking this job two months ago, I've been phys-
  ically assaulted by strangers and have had numerous
  pranks perpetrated on me by certain members of your
  family.

"What pranks is he talking about?"
Fenberg turned his head and saw Doris Lagoris reading

over his shoulder. He mentally sifted through some unkind remarks about doughnut-loving nurses, but then reconsidered. After all, someday Fenberg might be stricken, and this *was* the only hospital in town.

"A few months back? The day at the lake?" Fenberg prompted.

Lagoris squinched her face in recollection. "Oh, yeah. I remember now. Poor guy."

"There you go."

There were four Fenberg brothers. Mike was the oldest at thirty-two, with John a year behind. Then came Angry Joe at thirteen. Joe was a sea of angst, an ocean of hormones. He was permanently hostile. Except for Fenberg, no one ever dared ask why. The baby of the family was Clifford. Clifford was six, and he thought he was Norman Bates. It was no secret that Angry Joe and Clifford delighted in terrorizing the frail and cosmopolitan Henry Darich. One sizzling afternoon at the lake, Joe and Clifford replaced the reporter's suntan lotion with Nair. Which rhymes with hair. It denuded Darich. He had no eyebrows, and for several weeks whenever he showered or swam water beaded off Darich like he was a Safeway chicken.

Fenberg continued to read:

> *I despise your brothers and am not at all attracted to a community whose only social graces are drinking to excess, high school football, and a drive-in theater.*
>
> *This is a land frozen in time. I don't know why you stay here.*
>
> > Charmed, I'm sure,
> > Henry Darich
>
> *PS A letter of recommendation would be greatly appreciated.*

Fenberg smiled at the postscript. Darich had been the best reporter he'd had all year. "I'll hate to lose you."

"Huh?"

"Nothing," Fenberg told the nurse. "Make sure he gets

especially good care and anything he asks for." He turned and walked away.

"Hey!" the nurse called out after him. "All those stories you've been running in the paper. Is this another one of your hoaxes, or are you on the level?"

"What do you mean?" asked Fenberg, walking backward.

"Is there *really* a monster out there?" Nurse Lagoris needed to know.

"It's not a monster," said Fenberg. And then, more to himself . . . "It's more like a maniac."

* * * * *

"No. It's a monster," corrected the old Indian. He leaned forward on his cell bunk and slowly rubbed his dry hands together.

Fenberg sat on the cold cement floor opposite, his back against the bars. He doodled on his steno pad. "What makes you think so?"

The jail was institution-white, empty except for the other Indian, Red Dog Rassmussen, in the next cell over.

"Something like this happened before, back when I was a boy. It was after World War I, in the fall. And I remember my father telling me stories, you know, that were handed down." Fenberg occasionally called on Charlie Two Eagles Soaring Johnson for background. Charlie was seven-eighths Alliklik, the rest, Swede. He had a weathered face and knew things.

"I like you, Fenberg. My people like you," said the Indian.

"It's nice to be liked," said Fenberg.

"But I must ask you something that has troubled my heart for a long time," said Charlie Two Eagles Soaring.

Fenberg shrugged. "Go ahead."

"Why didn't you ever throw a pass to my son's boy?" Charlie's grandson had played on the two high school state championship teams Fenberg had quarterbacked way back when.

Fenberg considered the question.

"Your grandson ran like the deer. His feet and heart were of the wind. But his hands,"—Fenberg raised his fists heavily

—"his hands were cast of iron. Sadly, he could not catch a pass to save the entire Alliklik nation."

"Yeah. I guess so," said the old Indian resignedly. He swung back on the lower bunk and clasped his hands behind his head. "Maybe you should have used him on the end-around."

Fenberg didn't say anything.

"It is the time of the *Mandrango*," said the old Indian solemnly.

"Sounds Tahitian."

"I can't help that."

"May I have a spelling?"

"Like it sounds."

Fenberg rapidly scribbled notes. This would be the sidebar to tomorrow's lead story.

"*Mandrango* is the white men's 'devil.' Translated, it means, 'bottomless pit.'" The word also had a second meaning in the Alliklik tongue, which, out of courtesy to the widower Fenberg, the old Indian would not mention. "The *Mandrango* has a great hunger, and is formed of all foul things and evil thoughts from beneath the surface of the earth."

"Sounds like Mrs. Villareal," said Fenberg, recalling Tuberski's former common-law mother-in-law.

"Yes. She was a very homely woman and contrary to live with," agreed Charlie Two Eagles, staring at the exposed springs in the upper bunk mattress. "I hear she poisoned your brother, the big one, a few years back."

"Not fatally, but enough to make her point."

"Your brother has a spiritual quality to him. Many of my tribe go to him for guidance."

"I'm probably too close. I never noticed. I always thought it was laziness."

"There's nothing wrong with resting," said Charlie, matter-of-factly. He was in jail on a vagrancy charge. "The *Mandrango* comes from out of the earth once every hundred years to mate with a woman. A special woman. Legend says that until he finds his bride, he will kill on the nights of the full moon. Once, twice, maybe more, until his bloodlust is filled."

"Which, being a bottomless pit, could be never?"

"Yes."

"Or until he mates with this special woman?"

"Yes."

Fenberg caught the discrepancy of "once every hundred years," and let it pass. Charlie was a spry eighty-seven, so he couldn't have been alive during this myth's alleged reign of terror. Simple math. But Fenberg also knew that much Indian folklore was metaphorical, sometimes even psychological in nature.

"Do you have a description of this character?"

"Yes. It is a great creature. Covered with the hair of a buffalo, with the fangs of a lion. It sees in the dark and can smell particular things, like fear, at a great distance. It can see your heart beating. It is a head and a half taller than the tallest man. Strong and tireless. No shelter can deny it, but for some reason, he cannot escape his own home. I hear they're real smart, but I've never seen one, thank you very much."

"Sounds like quite an attraction. If you caught one, you'd be in the chips."

"Yes. But it would eat you," said the Indian stoically.

"You said something the other day about it happening before, after the war . . . ?" Fenberg flipped over a page on the pad and scratched his back against the bars. In the next cell over, the hatchet-faced Red Dog Rassmussen stared, fascinated by the editor's unprotected kidneys.

"There was a wedding in my tribe, a young man and a young woman," Charlie Two Eagles Soaring recalled. "He was the son of a pretty good trapper and a guide and took to modern ways outside the tribe. He left to build a cabin at the foot of the face of the cliffs, you know, over by Webster's Leap. It was safe from the cold wind and high enough to stay dry in the worst of the spring runoff. It was a good cabin, I remember, but it's not around anymore. Some of the elders warned him not to leave the safety of the village, as the time of the *Mandrango* was coming near. He would be under no protection if he did.

"Well, he didn't listen. It wouldn't rain. His crops were dust. No animals visited his traps, and none of the white hunters who came to Basin Valley back then would use him as a guide. His wife went hungry, and so did he. This young man got himself a regular job in town, helping out at the livery stable, which he mistakenly believed was a blessing. I told you, didn't I, that he took to then-modern things?"

"Yes."

"Because of this, his ears and heart were closed. For several days, he would leave the cabin in the early morning. Bright, clear mornings. But there was no breeze at all. No birds singing. No squirrels chattering. At the village, I remember the women chanting and surrounding our houses with rocks, in a circle, you know, while the men smoked and talked. The young man thought nothing of this. He went to town to do his work. This was the day he was paid, so he didn't go home right away. He went to the saloon and spent a portion of his money on liquor. He was laughing and feeling quite carefree when, I'm told, the smile froze on his face and his blood turned to ice water. His eyes went wide, and he ran from the saloon, screaming the name of his bride. He ran all the way home, too, a good distance. But it was a bright night. The moon was full, and he made the trip in short time because he was greatly frightened."

Fenberg had stopped writing.

"He called for his bride as he ran through the thin woods and across the meadow in front of his home. But she did not answer. The door, a strong door, had been torn off its hinges and thrown out into the yard like it was some child's plaything. I myself saw the door later. It had great scratch marks from huge talons." Charlie Two Eagles rolled over on his side and raised head on hand to face Fenberg. "The young Indian found blood, his wife's blood, here and there around the cabin, as she had been chased inside. But this was not the only sign of her.

"The *Mandrango* had carried her off. She was a brave woman because she pulled great tufts of hair from the beast.

This young Indian, he found these tufts and held them in his hands and wept. He heard a faint voice, in anguish and grief, call his name from a great distance away. It was his wife. And then, the young man heard a great scream from a faraway mountaintop. It was a godless scream, telling the woods and the Alliklik people of the *Mandrango*'s triumph and mocking the foolish young man."

"Did they ever find any trace of the woman?"

"No."

"What happened to the guy?"

"He was as the walking dead. None of our people were allowed to speak to him or look him directly in the eye, or they too would become walking dead. He went searching up in the back hills for her. He died of a broken heart not too long after that. Two years later, I think."

"And they never found any trace of his wife?"

"My father said the Hairman savagely took the woman, entered her, and made her heavy with his child. His child walks the shadows. He is here for his time."

"Jesus."

"Hardly."

"I just meant, it's a hell of a story."

"It's the woods," said the Indian, nodding toward the forest that lurked on the other side of the jail wall. "There are many things out there that the white man knows nothing about."

"Yeah. Well."

Trees, bushes, dirt. Lots of it. What could Fenberg say?

"I've got lots to do." Fenberg stood and stretched. "Still got half my Christmas shopping to do and gotta get this into a typewriter," he said, holding up the notepad. "Buy you a beer when you get out?"

"I'd like that," said the Indian with the long, white braids.

In the next cell, Red Dog Rassmussen languidly watched the editor of *The Basin Valley Bugle*, measuring Fenberg. Fenberg calmly stared back. Red Dog looked away. Red Dog was the Indian who shot Henry Darich. Red didn't particularly care for reporters. He had even said so.

"I heard you got some new competition in town, Fenberg,"

said Charlie. "Some A-type personality who puts out like he's real holy."

They were distracted by the heavy jangling of keys.

Fenberg shrugged as the guard unlocked the cell.

"Heard he's opening a newspaper right across the street from you."

"Yup."

"What was his name again?"

"Behan."

Charlie held onto the bars and considered for a moment. "Fenberg, I have heard of wealthy, bizarre cults, populated mostly by you white people, that have taken over small towns. But I've never heard of a Baptist doing something like that."

"He's nondenominational," said the deputy. "The Baptists are just letting him use their chapel until he gets his own church built. Me and the missus are going to hear him preach Christmas."

Charlie looked at Fenberg and shrugged.

"Something else troubles me," said Two Eagles.

"Yes?"

"Why would a man worth many millions of dollars, with many better things to do with his time, start a church and newspaper in a burg like Basin Valley?"

Fenberg half-smiled, half-smirked. "Said he liked the air." The guard and Fenberg were halfway down the cold cement corridor when Michael turned around.

"When you getting out?"

"Christmas Eve."

"What'd they get you for this time?" Fenberg asked, smiling.

Behind Fenberg's smile, deep in the eyes, Charlie Two Eagles Soaring saw the haunting. He tucked his hands in his pockets. "I got a bad attitude," said the Indian.

Fenberg nodded understandingly and held up a hand good-bye.

* * * * *

Outside, on the jailhouse steps, Fenberg took a deep breath. "Why *would* someone worth twenty-eight million want to start another newspaper out in the middle of nowhere? You got any ideas, honey?" Fenberg thoughtfully touched his shirt pocket, reassured for the moment in feeling the photograph's familiar outline. There was an invigorating snap to the cold air, which carried the aroma of burning wood and living pine. The small community of Basin Valley, with all its fireplaces contentedly puffing, was peacefully framed by the silent and endless ranges of the snowcapped High Sierras. There was a melancholy to Michael Fenberg that matched the brooding skies of the great Pacific Northwest. He was tall, about six-two, and rather imposing. He had an engaging, mischievous mouth that halfway turned somewhere between a smile and a smirk, and his eyes were sparkling gray, almost silver against his tan face. But when he wasn't breaking hearts, or joking with the boys, the wrinkles from all the smiles would sag, and something would swell and rise in Fenberg's chest, always to be forced down with a sigh. Michael shook his head and patted the picture of his wife and baby.

A long day stretched ahead.

He had a million things to do, the most important of which was to find a replacement for Henry Darich.

ELAINE MITIKITSKI

"I seem to be home again," said Elaine. "With my boxes and my parents. The universal symbol of the recently divorced woman," she noted. "Boxes, I meant. Not parents."

Elaine Mitikitski bore a striking resemblance to an estranged Snow White. Leggy. Still hometown good-looking with that effortless, perfect posture, but now, somehow, different.

"How does that make you feel?" asked the therapist.

"Home. Two parents, one little brother. Nicely framed photos of non-divorced sisters. Meals warm and on time. It lacks adventure."

"You're blocking. How does it make you feel?"

Elaine wiggled and wrapped her arms around herself. She avoided looking at the small, bony woman with the shock of severely short hair. Elaine stared blankly at the floor.

"Like running away and ending it all both at the same time? I don't know." She did. "I start each day crying. Sometimes I can't stop. I guess I'm one of those bright, capable women they write about who marries ill-advisedly, and I guess I have dreams. Bad ones. Actually, it's just the same one bad dream that reoccurs nightly." Elaine Mitikitski had long, wavy raven-black hair, light blue eyes, rosy cheeks, full lips—which wasn't to say she was saccharine or anything. She had enough of a contrary nature to be attractive to men, albeit peculiar ones. The office where she sat was dark and woody, the overstuffed sofa secure, womblike.

"And the days have their swings," Elaine went on. "Sometimes I feel quite together, untangled, forgiving. Other times, exhausted. And still other times, angry. So very, very angry." She crossed her legs. "Sometimes, and I guess I shouldn't be saying this, but I'd really like to punch my ex-husband in the nose." Elaine made a fist. "Just sort of haul back and . . ."

"They're boys, you know," her therapist interrupted.

"What?" Elaine shook her head, distracted and pulled out from the deep place she had been. She blinked as her analyst exhaled a cloud of cigarette smoke toward her.

"Men. They're boys. I hate them." The birdlike psychologist wore all black and chain-smoked harsh brown Sherman's.

Mitikitski turned her head to the side. "Well. They do have their bad moments, I'm sure. But I imagine they also have their feelings and insecurities, their doubts and pains, just like—"

"Oh, don't you say it." She inhaled a hissing puff. "You know, of course, that I'm presently going through my own separation?"

"Well, yes. . . ."

"My own primal, gut-wrenching, painful, terrorizing, anti-life-enhancing separation?"

Mitikitski knew. That's mostly what they had talked about the last three sessions.

"They call themselves men; I don't know why." Drag on the cigarette. Exhale. "Pompous, insignificant, autocratic, self-centered sons of bitches, the lot of them."

Elaine considered adding *phooey*, but didn't.

"The best years of my life. For what?" The therapist wanted to know. Elaine adjusted a shoulder pad and smiled with neutrality. While the thin woman in black explored those best years, Elaine nodded politely from time to time, pretending to listen, but soon drifted. She stared at the thriving vine that slithered through the beige blinds.

There was a time when Elaine Mitikitski'd had a real streak of the dickens to her. But she married poorly. Three times. Elaine wanted babies, but couldn't have them, and the doctors said it was her fault. Unlucky in love, an old maid aunt once categorized her.

Statistically late in life to be giving up her virginity, Elaine finally did so at the tender age of twenty-one to the unspectacular Louis Tinker. "Tinky," Louis's friends called him, and Elaine found out why on her wedding night at the Holiday Inn in Fresno. Louis was a bed-wetter. He had a bladder the size of a thimble, and he was a bed-wetter. After having his way with Mitikitski, Louis fell asleep and went tinky on her leg.

"It's a vile act. Dump the little cheese-weenie. I told you not to marry him in the first place," advised her sister, Kamali Molly Mitikitski.

But Elaine was basically a forgiving soul and blamed the champagne. She made a mental note to curb her husband's intake at the next social gathering. But the condition was chronic, and, worse, premeditated. Eighteen damp and fitful nights passed until finally, one evening, Mitikitski vaulted to a sitting position and strangled it out of Louis that yes, he actually liked wetting the bed. Ha. Ha-ha. You made me say it, and I'm glad I did.

Later that night she wrote:

> *Dear Louis,*
>   *I know we've only been married three weeks, but it strikes me we're growing in different directions. Please find it in your heart to forgive. It's not a question of good and bad, right or wrong. No one's to blame. I'm sorry. Please forgive.*
>
> > *Warmest regards,*
> > *Elaine Mitikitski*
>
> *PS Bed-wetter.*

Elaine dragged her belongings and half the wedding loot (still in boxes) and meekly moved home, averting the narrow stares of her father, who still owed over three thousand dollars on the wedding.

Mitikitski didn't date for a year. The guilt of the annulled marriage and the wedding bill ate at Elaine, and she found Jesus. She also found Bobby Maldanado, a born-again biker who likewise found Jesus. Elaine and Bobby were married not quite a year, during which time they misplaced Jesus, and each other.

Elaine moved back home.

A full three years passed without Elaine marrying anyone.

Mitikitski was twenty-five and in journalism grad school when she entered her Mormonette period. She started wearing a little more makeup, invested in designer body underwear, and relinquished any passion, surface or subliminal, to throw rocks at sea gulls. She became engaged to the rarest of men: a Mormon gone bad. "That Rocky Mountain Jew," as Elaine's father once called him.

With his chiseled, ski-instructor good looks, large, toothy smile, and abundance of wavy blond hair, Norman the Mormon was easily the handsomest and most exciting of any of Mitikitski's beaus. Elaine soon discovered what many women on the talk show circuit knew to be gospel: that handsome/rotten guys make exciting lovers—but they don't hang around for long. After a spinningly quick two months, Elaine and Norman the Mormon were married.

The writing on the wall again appeared, and shortly thereafter, Elaine said, "Oh dear."

Fearing she would suffer some supernatural curse for being married and divorced three times before the age of twenty-six, Mitikitski hung in gamely. Basically, Elaine was a shoulder-rubber. A card-sender. A swell-dinner-by-candlelight, shall-we-walk-by-something-scenic? atmospheric type of person. Norman the Mormon wasn't. And while Mitikitski planned various save-the-marriage diversions—gourmet home-cooked meals, Swedish massage, getting interested in boxing, helping him pick out his cigars and other thankless sell-your-personal-self-worth-for-a-plug-nickel ploys—Norman was being quite uncooperative. In fact, during the six months they were married, Elaine found this to be true about Norman, that he:

1) refused to get a job;

2) made sure that Elaine did;
3) stole money out of her purse
    ("It's not stealing when you're married.");
4) attempted to mount Elaine's close personal friends; and
5) was boring over coffee, or, in fact, was boring over
    everything.

To be fair, such were the things that made many a poor marriage. But Norman the Mormon took bad behavior to extremes. Because Elaine couldn't have children, he slapped her and called her an old fruit. He followed that up by using her car to hold up a convenience store. Elaine had to borrow money to bail him out. Without a thank-you, Norman strode past Elaine at the jail. On his arm was his girlfriend, five months pregnant.

A week later, Elaine was sued for divorce and alimony.

Men.

Phooey indeed.

Elaine attempted a halfhearted suicide in a cheap hotel. Her father took her home, and oddly, what hurt most was that he hadn't hugged her or said that everything was going to be okay.

* * * * *

A cigarette dangled from the corner of the therapist's mouth. "God, I don't know," said Mitikitski's analyst. "There's just something wrong with life."

"All I ever wanted was to be a reporter and have kids with someone taller than me, someone with a sense of humor who liked to hug," said Elaine.

The psychologist said lots of luck.

. . . and maybe wide shoulders and kind eyes, while I'm asking. Elaine sat dreamy-eyed for a moment. She opened her mouth. An egg timer went off. Her therapist said she thought Elaine had made good progress this session and asked for a check for eighty-five dollars.

* * * * *

Elaine was quiet through dinner, spending most of her time shoveling little piles of peas and rice from one side of the plate to the other. The family ate in silence. Lavonne Mitikitski worried about her daughter. She wanted to ask directly about the nightmares, and the sneezing, but didn't.

"How did the session go today, baby?" she asked.

"My therapist hates men," said Elaine, not looking up.

"Well. Hm-m-m-m." Lavonne waited a polite moment. "And you?"

"I don't particularly care for three of them."

Her father stopped chewing, calculating which three to whom she had been referring. Secure she meant husbands, her father continued eating.

"I noticed you got some mail today, honey. Anything important?" her mother asked.

A little over a month ago, Elaine had shipped a hundred resumes to newspapers around the country. It had been a bone of contention between Mitikitski and her parents. Her father didn't want her on the road in her present mental condition.

"Nope. Just polite form letters. 'We'll notify you if there's a death on the staff.' Same old . . ." said Elaine, not finishing the sentence. The phone rang, and her brother rocketed into the living room to answer it. He yelled that the call was for Elaine.

"Maybe it's a date," Elaine said wryly, tossing her napkin onto the table. Her mother smiled weakly.

"Hello?" said Elaine.

"Hello," said the falsetto voice. "May I please speak with a Miss Elaine Mitikitski?"

"Speaking." Elaine held the receiver a foot from her ear. The caller's voice was high-pitched and grating.

"Oh! Am I ever so delighted to have caught you, my dear. My son was supposed to call you. My son is editor, and I'm so proud of him."

"Excuse me. You're yelling in the receiver," said Elaine. "Would you mind not speaking so loudly, please? You're hurting my ears."

"I wasn't yelling," said the Mickey Mouse voice, sounding a little hurt. Elaine thought the voice belonged to a woman. An older woman. "I was just calling to tell you the good news. You know, old people sometimes have to talk loud."

"Excuse me. Who is this?"

"Mrs. Fenberg. Nice Mrs. Fenberg."

So? thought Mitikitski.

"Mrs. Dale Crawford Fenberg? I'm the owner and publisher of *The Basin Valley Bugle*, a small newspaper in Basin Valley, California. . . ."

"Yes."

". . . and I just called to say we hired you."

"Hired me?" Elaine stood on her tiptoes. God, a job, she thought. Her mind raced through a stack of resumes and envelopes, trying to place the paper.

"Don't mock," said Falsetto.

"I wasn't mocking, ma'am. I'm sorry, but you said you hired me. For what position?"

"Missionary. Ha-ha. Just a little newspaper joke. Your salary will be a whole thousand-dollars-a-week. . . ."

"Give me the phone," said a voice in the background.

"No!" cried the little voice with indignation. "I wanted to tell her the good news. You never let me . . . !"

"Give . . . me . . . the phone. Please."

It was a man's voice. Elaine strained to hear. She heard scuffling in the background and heard the woman yell that her arm was broken. Elaine heard crying.

"We're having a small problem on this end," said the new voice. "Can I call you back in a few minutes?" Elaine heard more scuffling, and the line went dead.

"Yeah. Sure." Elaine looked puzzled. She shrugged, hung up, and turned to face her concerned and sweatered parents. "Strange," she said, shrugging again.

True to his promise, Michael Fenberg called a few minutes later to apologize and assure Elaine that no one's arm was broken.

"That was Clifford," said Fenberg. "He's my baby brother, and he's going through this stage. He imitates women. He saw *Psycho* the other night on cable, and the little stinker has been slinking around the house in a shawl and squeaky voice ever since."

Elaine's parents sneaked upstairs to eavesdrop on the extension.

"Yeah. I know how little brothers are at that age," said Elaine, looking at the freckled face opposite. Her brother was eight. She shooed him away. "To tell you the truth, I did suspect something was up when he offered me a job for a thousand dollars a week."

"Well, wait a second. I really did call to offer you a job," said Fenberg. "It's nothing in the fifty-thousand-a-year category, but it is a bona fide criminal reporter's position, or should I say, crime reporter's position?"

Fenberg didn't tell her she was the fifteenth person to whom he had offered the job. From her resume, she was lacking in work experience, and he distrusted hiring a straight "A" student. He would have preferred someone with a slight drinking or emotional problem, about four years older and lacking ambition. The bright ones, the college all-stars, had a tendency to stay at *The Bugle* for three months, using the paper as a springboard to a better job.

"Think you'd be interested?"

Elaine, of course, wanted to know a little about Basin Valley and the job. Fenberg lied about both. Henry Darich had made an obscenely and insultingly paltry salary for an American-dream-track college-educated individual: two-hundred-fifty dollars a week. Figuring he could save a bundle on a young, inexperienced female, Fenberg offered Mitikitski one-forty. Mitikitski tapped the phone on the banister and asked Fenberg if he was calling from McDonald's in Bolivia, where such a wage would be considered a staggering fortune. Fenberg chuckled nervously.

"I, uh, have no snappy comeback," said Fenberg.

Soon, the conversation ended. Elaine waited five seconds before setting down the receiver.

"You can hang up the phone now, Mom and Dad," she said.

* * * * *

In two hours, the call was forgotten. Elaine was in bed, cotton swabs between her toes. She wore a loose, gray flannel nightshirt and judiciously dabbed fire-engine-red polish on her toenails. The television was on, and Elaine flipped through magazines, added many important things to do to her things-to-do list, then flipped over on her stomach to read one of the five novels she had started. Anything to procrastinate sleep. Anything to keep the dream from returning.

But the dream always did.

Pacific Northwest in locale, thematically it was a cross between "Charlie's Angels" and Betty Boop.

Elaine had the recurring nightmare of wiggling in a fashionable yet skimpy leather-and-feather Indian suit, bound at a stake. Surrounding her were ex-boyfriends and ex-husbands, cavorting about in shaggy fur coats and wearing these horrible, tusked masks. Or were they? Elaine couldn't tell. She remembered bad breath. They'd all writhe and circle sinisterly around, caressing her bare thighs with cold, fat, wiggly snakes, and she'd say oh no, and they'd say oh yes, and you didn't have to be Freud to figure that one out.

Some man, older (a father figure?), would appear as high priest. He had a thick beard and bushy eyebrows. He'd lead the charge, tearing into Mitikitski's prized boxes, which were richly filled with the crystal and electrical convenience booty from three failed marriages. And there the animal men would be, shredding through Tupperware and smashing her Cuisinarts. Elaine would make one of her famous wisecracks, and the monsters would freeze. Like gargoyles now, they slowly turned their crouched attention toward Elaine. Whatever followed was censored, buried deep within her psyche. It had something to do with sex, which even under the best of circumstances Elaine Mitikitski avoided.

It made her sneeze.

* * * * *

It drizzled the next morning in Los Angeles. The air was cool. Elaine's long black hair was frizzy from the moisture. She was bundled in a yellow rain slicker and drove with the window open past the neatly trimmed estates along Sunset Boulevard. Mitikitski's routine had been pretty much the same the last couple of months since returning home. She taught dance at a local studio four hours a day, then bicycled over to her father's insurance company to answer phones until her night job. Sometimes, she visited girlfriends or her fashion-plate sister, Kamali Molly. Except for Molly, all her friends were bright, married, and had at least one child by now. Mitikitski would waste a few hours holding children, drinking gallons of herb tea, and listening to plans to remodel and garden, anecdotes about babies, and the problems their husbands were having at work. Elaine listened more than talked. Yes, she had resumes out. No. Nothing promising. No. She wasn't dating anyone. Her friends wouldn't press.

But today, Mitikitski had borrowed the family station wagon to visit the university and do a little snooping. She had always been a favorite in the journalism department and still had free run of the UCLA halls. Elaine commandeered a desk. Thumbing through the authoritative *Straile's Guide to Rural California Newspapers* and a casual conversation with an old professor unearthed that *The Basin Valley Bugle* was indeed an excellent little newspaper with a bizarre history. It was 128 years old. Numerous national and state awards for merit. It was delivered free of charge, whether you wanted it or not. The front page still ran the old-fashioned eight-column set and really hadn't changed much in over fifteen thousand issues. *The Bugle* ran a balanced menu of stories about sports, society highlights, traffic accidents, murders, births and weddings, maniacs (when they were available), fires, politics, and an interchangeable tired photo of the captains of local industry shaking hands and grinning inanely while hunched over some new ground-breaking ceremony celebrating the cementing of some portion of Basin Valley which had not previously been cemented. There were lots of barroom brawl stories (many featuring some character named

John Tuberski), blurbs on who looked nice at the prom, updates on recent heart attacks, baby and puppy pictures, and the annual feature on how the senior citizen mobile home park had once again been demolished by flash flood (the park was built in the wash). As for the community itself, Basin Valley was isolated, hot in summer, freezing in winter, and leaned toward brinksmanship both publicly and domestically. It had the highest homicide rate of any small county in the United States of America.

"I'm not really sure where it is," said her former instructor.

"It says here it's in California," answered Elaine.

"That's not what you'd call California-California. It's a whole different world up there." The professor asked Elaine if she had seen this morning's paper. No. He showed her a small, one-inch wire story buried on page 24:

REPORTER SHOT AT HIS DESK

(WPI) BASIN VALLEY, CALIF.—Henry Darich, an editor for a mountainesque community newspaper, *The Basin Valley Bugle*, was shot in the chest yesterday morning while sitting at his desk.

The 29-year-old Darich was listed in stable condition.

Mitikitski smiled. "Well, that little stinker," she said, referring to Michael Fenberg.

* * * * *

"Hi, there. It's me again," said Fenberg, calling right after dinner.

Elaine cupped her hand over the receiver and yelled that she had it. "Me who?"

"Mike Fenberg of *The Bugle* newspaper—I called you yesterday? Hi. How's the world treating you? How are you doing?" he asked, a little too warmly. What a perfectly awful day. After wasting a whole morning at school (Angry Joe and Clifford had perpetrated yet another unspeakable atrocity) Fenberg had rushed back to the paper to work on the largest issue of the year. He then begged another twenty potential reporters to work for him. None were interested.

"Oh, fine. Fine. I'm pretty good," said Mitikitski. She had had an offer that day from a San Francisco daily. Unfortunately, it was as a secretary. "It's been my week. The *Chronicle* offered me a job, nothing much to start, but with lots of room for advancement. How's Clifford?"

"The San Francisco *Chronicle?*" Fenberg made a face. "That paper's been a rag for decades. You wouldn't want to work there. Clifford's fine. He stabbed the shower curtain this morning with a plastic fork dipped in ketchup and nearly scared Tuberski to death."

"Who's Tuberski?"

"John Tuberski. He's my brother."

"Oh, I see," said Elaine. "Half brother." No. Fenberg clarified that John was his one hundred percent brother. Same father, same mother.

"Then why does he have a different last name?"

Fenberg sighed heavily, then dutifully recited his standard answer. "He changed his name years ago for career purposes, although neither at that time nor presently does he have a career. I think it was sort of a parental rebellion thing that stuck. Mitikitski, I'm offering you a great experience, bucolic splendor, the tranquility of the snowcapped high desert-slash-timber country in December, and a whopping one hundred seventy-five dollars a week, plus expenses."

"Don't worry about Clifford," said Mitikitski, fiddling with a nail that was about to chip. Mitikitski felt up. She had visited with Kamali Molly today, and that always made her feel better than analysis. "I think all kids go through some sort of weird stage as they're growing up. You didn't tell me the other reporter had been shot," said Elaine. She smiled and leaned against the banister.

"Oh. You heard, huh?"

"Uh-huh," said Elaine. "One-seventy-five is not enough. What happened to him?"

Fenberg sat on the edge of his desk and multiplied a figure on the steno pad. He wondered if Elaine was fat. She had a nice voice. Deep, with a hint of mischief. The ones with deep, mischievous voices were always fat. "Oh, you wouldn't believe me. It's no big deal, anyway."

"Try me."

"Indians."

"I beg your pardon?"

"Indians. Henry, the reporter, was shot by Indians. Actually, it was only one Indian."

"You're right. I don't believe you."

"How about one-ninety-five?"

"A week? The *Chronicle* offered me three-eighty. To start," said Elaine.

Fenberg winced, then lied. "That's one-seventy-five more than what the old reporter was getting. Besides, cost of living up here is less. We trap our own food."

Mitikitski was enjoying the conversation, probably because she had no intention whatsoever of working for Fenberg or *The Bugle*, wherever it was. And, this *was* the safety of long distance. It felt good to smile. "One-ninety-five is not enough. So come on now. Tell me, really. What happened to your reporter?"

"Henry was shot by an Indian. Honest," said Fenberg, raising his hand in Scout's honor. He rummaged through a desk drawer, pulled out a framed picture of his deceased wife, and tossed it off to the side. Underneath was an open case of cookies. And Mitikitski's application. Judging from the copies of her work, she was good, very good. But two-fifty a week was as high as he'd go. Fenberg half-smiled, half-smirked. He'd nail her on overtime.

"You want to hear what happened to Henry?" Fenberg asked. He stood and paced, rehashing as if reading a fairy tale from a police blotter. "It began just yesterday, Mitikitski, when the gentleman of whom we spoke, Henry Darich, was the general assignments editor at this newspaper. He sat at that desk," pointed Fenberg.

"In last Thursday's edition of our paper, Mitikitski, we ran a story about a very bad person named Mr. Red Dog Rassmussen. Mr. Rassmussen is a partial Indian. He was pulled over for drunk driving, and who should be his passenger?"

"I've a feeling this is someone I don't know," said Elaine.

"None other than one Miss Betty Beecroft."

"Doesn't ring a bell."

"Miss Beecroft, likewise being drunk, was also naked."

"As in stark raving?"

"Not even underwear."

"Woo," said Elaine.

"My God!" blurted out Elaine's mother. Lavonne had snuck upstairs to listen on the extension.

"Who's that?" asked Fenberg.

"My mother," said Elaine. "My parents sometimes eavesdrop on my private conversations. Some parents are like that."

"Oh," said Fenberg. "Hello, Mrs. Mitikitski."

Click.

"Let's see, where was I?" asked Fenberg. "Okay. Worse yet, as you may have noted from the dissimilarity of last names, Miss Betty was not Red Dog's wife. When Red Dog's real wife, one Mrs. Jane Dark Crow Rassmussen, a one hundred percent Alliklik and a very vile-tempered lady to boot, read or had read to her this little episode in the paper . . . well, Mitikitski, you can certainly understand how miffed she was. How about two-ten a week?"

"Warmer. So then what happened to the reporter?" Elaine, phone cradled in ear, slid down the wall and sat cross-legged on the floor. She put a throw pillow on her lap and hugged it.

"I'm getting to that. Mr. Red Dog, the bruised laughing-stock of Chromium, the Indian reservation about thirty miles from here, came into town to scalp a certain smarty-pants white man newspaper reporter whose byline, unfortunately, was sitting above that story. Red Dog went into the Do Drop Inn first, to work up his courage. The drinking process put him in a foul mood, and he stabbed a couple of patrons with an eleven-inch hunting knife."

Mitikitski's brow furrowed, and she scratched under her brassiere strap. She was glad her mother had hung up. "Geez."

"Slit them open like canoes, Red Dog did. Then he came into this very office, and he shot old Henry right in the chest, *Ka-tow! Ka-tow!*" Fenberg shouted, pretending to shoot an imaginary reporter.

Mitikitski flinched.

"Shot him right at your desk, should you, of course, take the job. If you were here, I'd show you the bullet holes in the wall. Poor Henry. He broke his nose on the edge of the desk when he fell. He's lucky. A few more inches down and to the right, he would have been history, but I guess, on the other hand, a few more inches over the other way and Red Dog would have missed him altogether. Two-hundred-fifty dollars is my absolute, final offer."

"You're putting me on, aren't you?"

Fenberg shook his head no and fingered through the rumpled pack of Oreos. "No. Look. It was a random occurrence. How many people were shot by Indians last year? Maybe a hundred. More people get struck by lightning. So what do you think of two-fifty a week? You're not scared, are you?"

"I think concerned is more appropriate." She sneezed.

"Godzilla."

"Thank you." She reached up to the hall table for a Kleenex and also grabbed a notepad and pen. "If I take this job, which I'm not saying I would, I'd be making a commitment to move to Basin Valley." Mitikitski rubbed the goose bumps on her arms.

"And you'd love it here. Recreation, culture, freeway-close to everywhere. Entertainment, culture . . ." said Fenberg, gesturing. "There's a standard fifty dollar bonus for any reporter who can sneak the phrase, 'It was a dark and stormy night' into the lead of any story. I didn't tell you about the business editor's end of the job, did I?"

"I'm almost afraid to ask. What happened to him?"

"He died," said Fenberg. "Had a heart attack when Red Dog Rassmussen shot Henry. Bad ticker, I guess, though I'm not surprised. He was eighty-four."

"I'm sorry. . . ."

"No need. He wasn't a very good business editor."

Elaine looked at the receiver. "So what you're telling me is that I'd be handling *both* jobs?"

"Mitikitski . . ." chided Fenberg, "don't make it sound so dismal. The guy who handled business made it his life's work to stretch the phrase, 'low prices, friendly service,' into a forty-eight-hour week. Business only comes out on Sundays, anyway, and I'd help you along until you're comfortable."

Mitikitski had an idea. She figured she had nothing to lose by asking.

"Let me get this straight," said Elaine. "You are minus the services of two reporters, right? Well, Mr. Fenberg, I don't want to seem mercenary or anything, but two-hundred-fifty dollars is just not enough for handling two full-time positions. I think I could do a real good job for your paper, Mr. Fenberg." Mitikitski was blushing. She could feel her heart beating. "But for two jobs, I'll need four hundred. A week."

It was Fenberg's turn to tap the phone on the edge of the desk. "I'm sorry. You know, we must have a bad connection, because I could have sworn you said four-hundred-dollars a week."

"Plus a week's pay to help with moving expenses."

Fenberg laughed out loud. "Did you want me to throw in a microwave oven?"

"Thank you, no. I have three already."

The multitude-of-appliances reference went over Fenberg's head, and he said, "Look, I'm not asking you to turn around the General Motors Corporation or star in a miniseries, Mitikitski. I'm asking if you'd like to be a reporter at a glamorous, albeit itty-bitty, newspaper."

"No, you're asking me to be *two* reporters at a glamorous, albeit itty-bitty, newspaper."

Fenberg took a deep breath and let it out slowly. Four hundred a week? Hell, he thought. He rubbed the back of his neck. He made a pained face and paced with the receiver cradled on his shoulder. Hell again. He was already feeling the pinch of that new newspaper, and it hadn't even printed an issue yet. And I'm not going to keep on killing myself with those nineteen-hour days. Fenberg thumped the photo in his shirt pocket of Tracy and the baby. "Mitikitski, I've known you all of ten minutes total, and I don't like you already. You've got the job. And the moving expenses, providing you give me your word as a gentleman that you'll stay at least three months. And there's another stipulation." Fenberg paced back. "You have to start work in seventy-two hours. That's like, three days."

Elaine Mitikitski's stomach tightened. "I do?"

"Yes. You do. A deal then, you little bandit, you?"

The nightmares, Pacific Northwest in locale.

"Well? Hello? Mitikitski?"

Later, it seemed the last minute of their conversation took place under water. Elaine didn't remember saying yes, but she must have, and at first she was frightened. Really, she had never been away from home before. Well, she had, but it was always with some bozo husband, and even then her room was always within running distance. Still sitting cross-legged, the phone on the pillow and the pillow on her lap, Elaine Mitikitski wondered what in the hell she had done. Some people are impulse shoppers.

I am an impulse reporter.

Then she smiled. It wouldn't be so bad. Yes. It would be an adventure. A challenge. A clean slate. A chance to shop for a woodsy yet highly fashionable winter wardrobe and the opportunity to once-and-for-all swear off peculiar men in an environment of fresh air, where no one knows I'm 0-for-3.

*　*　*　*　*

Nine thirty at night.

It had been two hours since Fenberg had spoken with Mitikitski. Another end of a long day. Michael switched off the lights and locked up the rustic offices of *The Basin Valley Bugle*. It was a cold evening, even for December, the sky clear, crisp, beautiful, and a moon so full and swollen it seemed five times its normal size.

THE NIGHT OF THE FIRST MURDERS

To Victor Duffield, who was vacationing from Iowa, California seemed garish. The sort of place where people wear dark glasses, hug to excess, and have suntans on their heinies. It seemed odd that any place in the celebrated Golden State could be so dark and desolate. Maybe it was just the woods at night.

Duffield, his wife, and two children were on their second week of vacation and had just spent the last few days on a whirlwind tour of the big amusement parks. Next on the agenda was a bullet train view of national monuments. Victor unrealistically figured he could make Mt. Shasta by noon tomorrow. He and his family had just finished a late dinner in Basin Valley and were inching their pachydermic motor home north, climbing ever higher, in and out of the mountain switchbacks, searching for a spot to pull over and spend the night.

Duffield felt lonely. No reason. Behind the wheel of the huge motor home, he looked back to check on the wife and kids. His son was still plugged into the Walkman, oblivious and bouncing his head to some silent drumbeat and screaming guitar. His wife managed a tired smile. Bored, but okay. His little girl was still wearing the Donald Duck hat with the orange plastic bill. Duffield smiled and felt better. He was probably just homesick. They would make camp, and although it was cold out, they would build a roaring fire for at least a few minutes' enjoyment.

"What was that?" Victor yelped.

Duffield eased to a stop, then cautiously backed up. "Whatdya think?"

His family was far from impressed. It was another dirt road, not unlike the many they had pulled off on before to spend a night. His daughter had wanted to stay in a motel.

"Well, it's going to be home for tonight," announced Duffield. With the help of a bright and early timber moon to light the tree-lined logging road, Victor docked the camper a hundred yards off the highway. The family unpacked. Victor sent his son, a lanky twenty-year-old, for firewood. "Make sure the damn wood isn't green this time!" Victor shouted to the boy, who didn't give any sign of hearing him. Too damn old to be wearing those earplugs, he thought, watching the boy disappear into the underbrush.

The Duffield family had all the modern comforts in the mega-camper—portable generator, TV, video games, kitchen, and bathroom. Victor had even packed his scoped Enfield 9mm rifle, just in case. They would sleep in the camper, but first, they'd make a fire, have coffee and dessert, and just watch the flames. Except tonight, there was no fire. The Duffields' son never came back.

"Damn kid is out there baying at the moon, listening to that music," complained the father.

"It's his vacation, too," reminded Mrs. Duffield, tucking her hair under a red bandana. "He's probably just stretching his legs. Or maybe he saw a raccoon or something."

A half hour passed. Victor Duffield clicked six rounds into the Enfield and went to look for the boy. He found him, a few yards from the camp, dead, mutilated, and partially devoured.

*   *   *   *   *

Eugenia Duffield and her daughter had been instructed to stay inside the camper. Mrs. Duffield was just locking the doors when she heard her husband scream in surprise and anguish. She knew.

"Victor . . ."

Mrs. Duffield heard her husband scream again, but this time, the cry was different. Terror. Three shots fired. More screams and a hideous, animal snarling. The screams stopped, and for a few moments the only noise Mrs. Duffield heard was her daughter softly crying and the crunching sound of something eating her husband.

She sat on the floor, in the back of the camper, holding the girl. All the lights were on.

The door.

It swung open. She hadn't locked it, and a gust of wind slammed it loudly against the aluminum siding. The snarling stopped.

"Be quiet," whispered Mrs. Duffield. "Be very quiet. I'm going up to the front and turn off the lights and close the door. I'll be right back."

The little girl let out a shriek, begging her mother not to leave.

"It's okay. I'll be right back. I'm going to get us out of this." The Iowa housewife smoothed her daughter's hair. Mrs. Duffield stood and quickly tiptoed across the narrow center aisle and turned out the lights. It took a second for her eyes to accustom to the dark. As an afterthought, she fumbled through a drawer, searching for a weapon—a small paring knife was all she could find. Mrs. Duffield inched toward the yawning doorway, darkness on the other side. She stood to the left, not wanting to reach her hand into the cold night to pull the door shut. She thought of her daughter.

Close the door.

Mrs. Duffield was short, about five-foot-one. Leaning out, she couldn't reach the handle.

You'll have to go outside and close the door.

She hung on tightly to the side of the door frame, as if it were home base and safe. Three long steps to the ground. Grab the door handle.

She could *smell* something. Sweat. Animal sweat. Like a

horse after a long run. One step. Two steps. Top step. She
was back up, her foot inside the camper when she heard an
angry, delighted snarl and the sensation of something large
and powerful galloping at her. The pain started at the top of
her shoulder and went to the base of her spine. She stumbled
forward from the blow, crashing into the formica coffee table.
The pain was searing, and she felt a dampness spreading on
the back of her blouse. Funny, she thought. It should hurt
more than this, and my little girl should be crying. Mrs.
Duffield felt lightheaded when she fell next to her daughter.
The door was open.

The beast outside savored the anguish of mother and
child. It inhaled the sobs they tried to hide. It felt the invisible quivering from the hopeless knots in their throats, vibrating across the cold air. His was the tribe of ten thousand
centuries. The band of evil, the Dark Brotherhood that ruled
the human plane of good and evil. For six hours, it circled
their family motor home, sometimes inquisitively scratching
the aluminum siding, sometimes viciously rocking the recre-
ational vehicle to the point of tipping it over. Two hours
before dawn, the torture ended. The *Mandrango* of Basin
Valley threw two bodies outside and ransacked the camper,
searching.

Nope.

No bride in here.

Not yet.

4

THERE'S MONEY IN MANIACS

The moon was impartial. It smiled benevolently on the darkness below, casting its light on the just and unjust, refracting its moonbeams into Fenberg's room.

Fenberg slept alone tonight. No date. No cat curled up on the end of the bed. No Clifford sleepily shuffling in because he was lonely or thirsty. Fenberg slept with his mouth open, facing the silent forest outside, oblivious in deep slumber. He didn't see the huge silhouette glide past the picture window.

Fenberg dreamed.

And although most of his dreams were unpleasant, they were the only chance he had to be with his wife and child.

The Tracy and Baby Fenberg Show.

Tonight, Fenberg was driving by the ocean. He piloted an old, sensible convertible, happily expectant, not a care in the world. A beautiful blonde, wearing a long, fluttering scarf and a smile of invitation, laughed and waved as her round sedan roared by in the opposite direction. So close. Fenberg felt he could reach out and touch her face. A wave crashed over the hood of his car, and he was mired in salt water, sand, and foam. He tried turning, but the power steering unit or something had jammed, and he could barely control the car. It took all his strength to crank a U-turn and give chase to the retreating blonde. What was she driving? He couldn't remember. And then, all of a sudden, he was in a late-model hardtop.

Sluggish. No pep. Gritting his teeth, no matter how hard he stood on the gas pedal, the car only moronically plodded. Tracy effortlessly glided away. The baby peeked through the rear window, smiling, waving an infant's good-bye, and soon they were out of sight around a bend in the distance.

The huge figure outside impatiently wrestled with the window. It was locked. The shadowy form, elongated to extreme angles by the moonlight, moved alongside the house, crushing azaleas in the planter. It tried Clifford's window next.

The Tracy and Baby Fenberg Show was different every night. Fenberg watched helplessly as the pair fell off bridges, off cliffs, off skyscrapers. They would be swept away by a thunderously loud tidal wave, or would founder at sea, surrounded by the purposeful meandering of shark fins. Bears carried them out of camps. Indians shot them with arrows. The government carted them off for tax fraud. It was a hell of a way to sleep, if you could call it that, and every morning Fenberg would wake with bags under his eyes, the back of his neck a tight knot, more exhausted at morning's light than when he went to bed.

The back door was unlocked.

Fenberg slept with lots of pillows. The patented Fenberg pillow fort. He wrapped one leg around a pillow and another protected his back. Thank God he was through dreaming for the night so he could finally get some rest.

There was an odor in the house, foreign, pungent.

Subconsciously, Fenberg sensed something stealthily drift past the dresser, past the framed pictures of wife and child. His mind's distant outpost bleeped distress, but Fenberg was exhausted and unable to see something immense towering over him, blocking out all light, staring.

Fenberg's neck was exposed. The bed creaked from a great weight.

The eyes bore through the dark, as if to illuminate the room on sheer will. A jagged smile creased the visitor's face. Two huge hands slowly propelled forward. They stopped an inch from Fenberg's throat.

"Ah heck," said the intruder, the hands drooping. "Who am

I kidding? He'll kill me." The intruder sighed. "Michael? Buddy?"

Fenberg groaned and turned his back on the visitor, who was now gently shaking him.

"Mike? Come on, Michael. . . ."

Fenberg didn't budge. A light went on.

"Michael," he whispered. "It's me, your dead wife. I've come back to visit you. Wake up, honey. . . ." Fenberg smiled and smacked his lips together in nubile satisfaction.

The stranger delicately moistened his index finger with saliva and gingerly inserted it into the editor's ear. Fenberg screamed and vaulted to a sitting position.

The visitor sat on the edge of Fenberg's mattress, hands patiently folded in his lap, waiting for Fenberg's convulsions to stop. Finally:

"I've been out in the woods all night. Walking. One of those dark nights of the soul, I guess."

Fenberg's breath came in hacking stabs, then stabilized to heavy breathing. Holding up his hand as a visor, Fenberg shielded his eyes from the blinding overhead light and squinted, trying to place the face.

It was his brother, John Tuberski.

Formerly Norwood Z. Fenberg, John Tuberski had the same laughing gray eyes, curly hair, and lumberjack good looks as did all the Fenberg boys, but there the family resemblance stopped. As if his DNA had been frapped in some whimsical genetic cross-wiring, Tuberski bore a haunting resemblance to both Cary Grant and Popeye's nemesis, Bluto. John stood a few inches shy of seven feet tall, weighed a trim 291 pounds, and had a head too small for his body. He served as president of the local chapter of the Phoebe Cates Fan Club, where part of his official duties, and his only known act of unprovoked bullying, was to make the Magono-gonovitch brothers, the second and third toughest persons in Basin Valley, or perhaps anywhere, write lengthy fan letters to the angelic, albeit fire-down-below, Hollywood star. Tuberski kept a large mason jar filled with the butts of frosted animal crackers. Only the butts. He never got cold or paid income taxes, but, showing little prejudice, he rarely paid other debts, either. When anything struck Tuberski as terribly funny, he'd reverberate the halls with a bass, graveyard laugh, although he preferred his patented inane grin and a simple, abbreviated, ". . . 'kay."

"After much soul-searching, I've been brought to a very important conclusion," said Tuberski.

"Dear Jesus," said Fenberg. He weaved narcotically and clutched at his heart.

"There's money in maniacs," pronounced Fenberg's sibling. He swung around into a prone position, weight on one elbow and eye-level next to his brother.

"What."

"You have these little bags under your eyes," Tuberski pointed out. "I was just saying. There's money in maniacs."

Fenberg blinked and continued to unintentionally salute his younger brother. Heavily, Fenberg's head angled a degree past John to the heavy oak nightstand in the corner. As if scanning it with X-ray vision, Fenberg searched for a weapon, something, a revolver, then dimly remembered. Because of Clifford and Angry Joe, they never kept guns or explosives in the house. The digital clock clicked to 3:00 A.M., exactly.

"What do you want?" asked Fenberg.

"I wanted to talk to you about going on a safari."

"You're not allowed in my room," said Fenberg.

"I felt it was important."

"What happened to your shirt?"

Tuberski did most of the housework and once beat up an entire motorcycle gang. He glanced down at his normally impeccably-pressed white T-shirt. Blood and unrecognizable foreign substances were splattered boldly across. It was stretched and torn, and there were scratch marks from desperate fingernails on his biceps.

"I guess I was roughhousing," Tuberski said. "Would you like some tea?"

Fenberg was still sitting up. "Go away."

" 'kay," said Tuberski. But instead of leaving, he fluffed a pillow and stuffed it under his arm.

"Get off my bed," said Fenberg. "Get out of my room. Please. I hate you."

Tuberski had been rehearsing all evening. He made eye contact and paused for effect.

"In a world that has no more secrets, where every town and hamlet is freeway-close to everywhere and children's stories are televised and not read by bedside, I find it comforting to believe that out there," Tuberski said, gesturing broadly past Fenberg to the forest beyond, "somewhere beyond the dark shadow that borders civilization, lives a reclusive giant."

"You dick," said Fenberg, trying to dry a floating eardrum on his pajama-clad shoulder.

"It's not only here." Tuberski shook his small head. "In isolated towns and forgotten specks on the map whose names veritably ache with a faraway loneliness—the Three Sisters Wilderness, the Yolla Bolly, Devil Bear Gorge—are people, Michael, who will tell you of a giant creature, not man, not ape, whose howls reverberate at night, shrill and high-pitched, like a mortally wounded banshee. They will use their hands to measure footprints seventeen inches long with a stride of eight feet, and they'll point to hidden valleys where no birds sing and no animals go and the quiet makes the hair on the back of your neck tingle. It's the last American legend, Mikey, and I propose we catch it." Tuberski clenched his fist.

"You've come to borrow money, haven't you?" asked Fenberg.

"No." Tuberski unclenched his fist.

"How much?"

"Twelve thousand dollars."

"For a safari?"

"Precisely."

"Coincidentally the total amount in our joint savings account."

"Not so coincidentally."

Fenberg gingerly rubbed his face and stubble. The little digital clock clicked to 3:04 as Fenberg shook his head sadly. "What is happening tomorrow—Christ, this morning—in just a few, short hours, John?"

"Do I have to say it?"

"Yes."

Tuberski bobbed his head and looked away. "You're being protested, Michael," he said reluctantly.

"By?"

"A Baptist, Mike."

"*Just* a Baptist, John?"

"The Saddam Hussein of Baptists, a man who, for unknown reasons, has sworn to bury you. The Ayatollah of hostile takeovers. Mike, I can have the money back in three weeks," pointed out Tuberski. "And more."

"Would you care to tell me—what happens in twenty-eight days?" asked Fenberg.

"The final balloon payment is due on the ranch," answered Tuberski. Bored, he collapsed into the down pillow, face first.

"And how much is this final balloon payment on a ranch that was built by the sweat of the brow off our dearly departed parents and which is currently the only shelter over the heads of our two despicable brothers?"

"Fifteen thousand dollars, Mike," said a muffled voice.

"Which is three thousand dollars *more* than what we have in the bank. Am I correct in my math?"

"Yes."

"And you want to withdraw all of our savings, lose a perfectly good 175-acre ranch, and put two children out in the street in the middle of winter to finance a—what?"

"Safari," said the muffled voice from the pillow.

"And that concludes our program for this evening. Harvard Debate Team, 52—Warsaw Community Tech, 0." Fenberg submerged under the covers.

Maybe someday Tuberski would work up the courage to tell his brother that he had never particularly cared for Michael's huffy tone of voice in discussions such as these. Tuberski lifted his head and might have responded, but Fenberg rose one last time and pointed a violent hand, shaped arthritically, at his younger brother. Fenberg went on to say that he would be struck blind and impotent before he would lend any money to a person such as Tuberski, who had a worse debt problem than Fenberg's beloved United States of America, and furthermore, if Tuberski ever again woke Fenberg at three in the morning, Fenberg would beat Tuberski like a redheaded stepchild, set him on fire, and choke him with both his hands, and everyone in town would throw Fenberg a parade because everybody in town hated Tuberski.

Knowing this last part to be true, Tuberski's smile wilted.

Tuberski engulfed a breath, ready to present his case to the lump under the blanket, but reconsidered. He gingerly tucked in the corners of the comforter around Fenberg.

Oh, well.

No sense in tempting fate and let sleeping dogs lie and all that.

Tuberski reflectively chewed on the inside of his cheek, wondering how he could persuade Fenberg to part with twelve grand. Absentmindedly, he rubbed his brother's back, but soon the fingers were distracted into an energetic drumming on Fenberg's shoulder blades.

"Don't do that," said Fenberg.

"Sorry."

Tuberski was well read, and, among the Indians who knew such things, it was rumored that he was supposed to be the Earth's next great spiritual light, a responsibility he understandably avoided like the plague. That Tuberski was fascinated by monsters, or even maniacs, was not so much the issue. That he had latched onto this idea of selling his soul for yet another ill-advised venture was.

Tuberski's eyes narrowed with zeal and vision. "Maniacs may be the next great, untapped market," he said, staring off at some distant horizon. Outside, an owl hooted, and the trees sidestepped slowly in the wind, waving icy shadows gently back and forth across the room where all the Fenberg boys had been born.

Tuberski stretched and said " 'kay." He considered that what was needed here was a nice cup of hot tea.

* * * * *

Tuberski didn't start out wanting to be a spiritual light. It's a hell of a lot of work. He didn't particularly care about discovering the one fundamental thing wrong with life. His goals were simple: paint, roughhouse, and be a venture capitalist.

In part, this was Fenberg's fault.

It used to be the tables were turned. It used to be, when they were younger, Fenberg who lured Tuberski into scams without number. It started with a worm farm in elementary school, when it had been easy for Michael to charm lunch money out of the oversized palm of his then butch-headed and good-natured brother. There were grand themes here, albeit on a child's level. Worms died. Lemonade stands were lashed by freak summer storms. Childhood life savings were wiped out in plummeting blueberry futures. All these Amos 'n Andy treks toward effortless and instantaneous wealth left the boys broke and maybe a little round-shouldered, but never undaunted. Until Tracy died, and Fenberg lost interest in masterminding the big score. He passed the family entrepreneurial baton to his brother, who gladly accepted. Tuberski had even less luck, but on a much larger scale.

After the *Iraqi Joke Book* fiasco, Tuberski talked Fenberg into putting up the money to market a plastic *Time* Magazine cover that would fit snugly over standard bathroom mirrors.

"So that every time you look at yourself shaving, your face is on the cover of *Time* Magazine," Tuberski had explained, beaming to his no-good barfly pals.

Time sued Tuberski.

The latest project had been the Doggie Intelligence Test. For the better part of a year, the Fenberg brother with the different last name sent away for obscure canine periodicals and animal behavior books. He designed the cover: a dog in college robes and mortar board, thoughtfully pondering a question. He constructed a simple, twenty-question format and then tested a significant cross section of Basin Valley's dog population. The test worked smashingly, Tuberski pronounced. Dogs *do* have IQ's. Some were smarter than others. Tuberski calculated that with roughly 160 million dog owners in the United States alone, at three dollars a pop (or pup, as Fenberg had wisecracked) they were looking at nearly a half-billion dollars in revenue before taxes.

"Less twenty percent for expenses and the possibility that some pet owners might not actually buy the book," Tuberski pointed out.

The test did net a little over four million. Unfortunately, this sum went to an Austin, Texas, woman who had independently marketed an amazingly similar doggie IQ exam a scant three weeks before Tuberski went to press.

This crushed Tuberski.

He begrudgingly went back to his daily routine of housework and keeping up the ranch, doing odd jobs in town, and terrorizing cowboys, lumberjacks, and the Magonogonovitch brothers. He returned, halfheartedly, to his search for the one fundamental thing that was wrong with life. And, of course, he painted.

His last work, left unfinished, was a soft pastel of Jesus, the Buddha, Lao-Tse, and Babe Ruth, all in Hawaiian shirts. They were leaning against a '58 Cadillac convertible.

"Why Babe Ruth?" Fenberg had asked one day. Hands on knees, he inspected the canvas.

" 'Cause the Babe could hit the hell out of the ball, Mike," Tuberski had answered, brush anchored between his teeth.

As an artist, Tuberski was indeed blessed, although some unknown torment had kept him away from the canvas these past two months.

He heard voices.

And he owed fifty-seven thousand dollars.

*　*　*　*　*

Fenberg cuddled deeper into his pillows and slept for what seemed hours. In reality, it had only been ten minutes. The bed creaked. Tuberski gingerly lifted his brother by the armpits and propped him against the headboard into a sitting position. Fenberg groaned weakly in protest as John slid a pair of aviator sunglasses over his brother's eyes and turned on the blinding overhead light.

"Here, buddy. I made you a nice cup of tea," Tuberski said, trying to mold the fingers of the sleeping Fenberg around the stem. "Careful. It's hot. Say 'kay."

" 'Kay," said Fenberg, not opening his eyes. His head tilted.

John, before he was John, and Mike, who had always been Mike, used to sleep together as little kids. Fenberg used to draw an imaginary line down the middle of the bed and with appropriate sound effects, lower the Colgate Invisible Protective Shield to bisect the mattress. The purpose, or so Fenberg claimed at the time, was to cut off, with surgical precision, any part of Tuberski's anatomy that happened to stray across the force field. But Tuberski was thirty-one now and no longer fell for the ploy.

Tuberski sat on the bed next to his brother and wiggled to get comfortable. He balanced a tray with his own mug of tea and a sandwich that housed most of the week's lunch meat. At 3:25 Tuberski wiggled some more, ate, and made several things perfectly clear to Fenberg, the salient points being:

1) Why his normally clean and accurately-pressed white T-shirt was splashed with blood;

2) That it was good Fenberg was hearing Tuberski's version first, elsewise, Fenberg might be prejudiced by outside, emotional opinions from the victims and victims' families;

3) That indeed, there *was* money to be made in maniacs;

4) In reference to the above, a detailed explanation of how Fenberg could get in on the ground floor of what could be this century's great fortune;

5) How a loan of ". . . approximately twelve thousand dollars," coincidentally the amount in their joint savings account, would be just the ticket Tuberski needed to get the ball rolling;

6) That the profits from said venture (Tuberski lowered his voice on this part) would more than cover the fifty-seven thousand dollars in expenses he had already accrued;

7) And that, swear to God, hand in air, Tuberski would have the money back in the bank, and more, before the final balloon payment was due on their dearly deceased parents'

ranch next month.

It had been a hell of a day for Fenberg. All of them were. At first, Fenberg mumbled a few perfunctory mm-hmmms, but dozed more than listened, and not once did he ask for a clarification. By 4:15 A.M., the lights were out, the tea and sandwiches gone, but Tuberski was still talking, his eyes sparkling in the dark. The lips moved rapidly, showing two rows of perfectly straight little Chiclet teeth, and the soft, resonant baritone voice droned Fenberg deeper and deeper into dreamland. Millions. Billions. How Tracy had loved Tuberski. They would drink tea and gossip for hours during the day. Tracy was an art major, and it seemed she had more in common with John than her husband Mike. Tuberski would hold both babies, his mother's and his sister-in-law's. He'd bounce them on his lap or carry them around the house, one in each hand, like soft, round, little pink suitcases.

Tuberski seemed to take their deaths so much harder than Fenberg, Fenberg who held all things together. Tuberski got drunk, stinking, belligerently drunk, every night for the first few months. And when he wouldn't be arrested, he'd stumble into his room in the dark hours. Fenberg could hear the muffled, gut-wrenching sobs and bit his own lip hard so he wouldn't join in. The ache. Fenberg never cried, although he publicly professed it to be good therapy.

He hugged his pillow with a smug smile of satisfaction. It was nearly time again for The Tracy and Baby Fenberg Show. This time, she was in tights (she had a great set of legs, that girl), balancing on the high wire with the baby wrapped in a small blanket. Fenberg watched from the stands and wanted to say something to her, but she was too far away.

5

M. J. BEHAN

It was a bright morning at the Fenberg ranch. The cold air froze the sky bluer and highlighted, with a technicolor pop, the granite mountains that erupted vertically from behind the house. But such issues as maniacs being a good investment and the protest of *The Bugle* had to be placed on a back burner due to yet another breakfast episode in which Angry Joe used his mysterious power to make Clifford turn red.

Actually, it wasn't so mysterious. Angry Joe would say, "turn red," and Clifford would oblige.

Clifford was six, a pale, freckle-faced little boy with a round, cheese face. On cue, the youngest Fenberg would hold his breath and clench his fists, initiating the violent vibration stage. Then he'd change color. From his natural alabaster white, his face would darken to actual flesh tone, then change to pink, then change to salmon, red, crimson, magenta, and on down the color scale to deep purple. Usually, these exhibitions ended with Clifford getting dizzy and gasping at the last minute for a big gulp of air. He'd stagger around, recover his balance, then look up at the big, grinning male faces, and he'd grin sheepishly, pleased at the attention. Only this morning Clifford took it beyond the envelope and vibrated to a sickly blackish blue. He might have permanently turned into a Greek olive had he not fainted.

Tuberski and Angry Joe were at the counter, eating breakfast and reading. They ignored Clifford, who was sprawled unconscious on the floor a few feet away.

Steno pad in hand, Fenberg ambled to the counter. Preoccupied, he was pouring water for tea when he happened to look down. That's when he discovered the baby he'd raised, pathetically spread-eagled across the Congoleum.

"Goddamn it!" Fenberg screamed, reaching the boy in three long strides. He asked just what in the holy hell had happened. Tuberski and Angry Joe crunched cereal and shrugged. Clifford had been holding his breath again and was faking. "Goddamn it, I can't find a pulse!" Michael set the boy's head down and opened the cupboard under the sink. He unscrewed the top to the ammonia cleaner.

"What are you going to do?" Angry Joe asked, spoon poised in midair. Joe was built like a young Kirk Douglas. Gritted teeth, dimpled chin, prizefighter body, significant inner rage, the whole marianna. He sported a parrot hairdo, an earring, Ralph Lauren pleat-front slacks, and a black T-shirt which featured the fuhrer in skintight leather pants, fashionably shredded blouse, and burning electric guitar. The shirt advertised: ADOLF HITLER, 1939-1945—THE EUROPEAN TOUR.

"Just give him a whiff of this to bring him around," blurted Fenberg, holding Cliffie's head.

"Can I do that?" asked Joe.

"No!"

Cliff made an awful face at the smell and came around quickly. He was dazed and cried. He said he didn't like fainting. It took an hour out of Fenberg's morning, holding and rocking his brother, gently reassuring him that he hadn't died and come back as a different little boy. ("Thank you, John, for your stories on reincarnation.")

The justice of Solomon was meted. Blows were exchanged. Fenberg, as usual, had little trouble taking the thirteen-year-old in the first round. The Hitler shirt was confiscated, and Joe, who already owed more confined servitude than Charles Manson, was strapped with extra manly ranch hours. Weeds, weeds, oh God, not the weeds.

Fenberg choked Tuberski, adding painful monkey punches to the bicep for good measure. Tuberski was the toughest person in Basin Valley, or perhaps anywhere, but he solemnly acknowledged his brother Michael was the alpha-dominant male when push came to shove.

Fenberg sighed. He looked out at the frost on the kitchen window and the bright blue morning outside. Gently, he rocked his brother.

"Come on. I've got to get to the paper," said Michael. "I'm being protested."

"I'm dead," said Clifford, suspended in air, arms dangling.

* * * * *

A blast of wind bowled through town. The oversized red plastic bells and holly that crisscrossed Main Street's telephone poles clattered and hissed and furiously yanked at their moorings. Shoppers and the curious, with red noses and cheeks, were bundled up for winter. They clutched packages and goose-stepped against the gusts, marching toward *The Bugle*.

Fenberg's eyes narrowed. He peeked through the venetian blinds. Car doors slammed. Eight more Bible thumpers climbed out of a beige Chevy wagon. Michael recognized them. Locals. Four women, one man, three children. Five Bible thumpers and three Bible thumperettes and no Mr. Behan.

Fenberg turned his neck awkwardly, trying to read one of the signs. BEWARE, BUGLE! JUDGMENT DAY IS COMING! was the only placard he could make out.

Michael had met M. J. Behan once before, briefly. It was a quick handshake affair at a Chamber mixer. Behan had a clammy grip, like squeezing cold gravy in a rubber glove. He said he admired Fenberg's paper and style, but wasn't Fenberg interested in printing the truth? Sure. What's truth? That Jesus died for your sins. Then why do I still have them? Fenberg asked. M. J. Behan smiled. It was polished and ingratiating. Come on, Michael. Isn't some part of you religious? Behan shook his head, the smile turning to a poor-lost-lamb sadness.

He knew quite a lot about Michael Fenberg. He said that despite the death of Fenberg's wife, Fenberg's escapades still had to be considered adultery, and the poor child must be turning over in her cold grave with grief. The bemused light went out of Fenberg's eyes, and they stopped shaking hands.

Fenberg looked with irritation at the clock. His photographer was late. Again. And so was the new reporter. Elaine What'sheriski. Outside, the murmur of the crowd rose to pre-lynching level. Something was going on. Fenberg opened the blinds all the way to get a better look. Down the street, three storefronts away, a car docked next to the curb. Martin James Behan could have pulled into town on the back of a brontosaurus and caused less furor. He climbed slowly out of a new black Corniche that featured the license plate: FEAR GOD. He was greeted by Basin Valley's three Protestant ministers and a throng of Sunday regulars. But while he shook hands, something made him turn directly toward the window. His dark gaze parted the crowd and met Fenberg's.

Question: Why would a wealthy man, with no experience in newspaper publishing, suddenly get the whim to start a paper out in the middle of nowhere? The query had been posed by several of Basin Valley's captains of commerce.

"Fresh air," Behan had confessed. "I'm tired of the city, the traffic, the smut, the crime, eighteen-hour days, and warnings from my doctors to slow down. I wanted a clean place, a nice Christian place to raise my family." The Chamber of Commerce moguls had all nodded their heads eagerly at this sage observation. "And, my new friends, there are values here, in this community, that a man can really sink his teeth into."

Fenberg snorted. Fresh air indeed.

* * * * *

The air was, indeed, fresh, and Basin Valley was pleasant enough, small town charm and all. But it was a bit of an enigma.

It wasn't quite desert. And it wasn't quite forest.

It was in the middle. Sort of high desert, low forest.

Basin Valley proper, the county seat, rested on a windswept
plateau, sixty-eight hundred feet above sea level. Hovering
over this small community of nineteen thousand souls was
the rugged Sierra rain forest, an area more vast in size than
the state of Maine, largely unexplored, and, in some spots,
mapped only by air.

And below, where Bean Breath Brown lived, was the
desert.

Like Newton Minnow's television set, this brown, sandy
region that straddled the California-Nevada border was a vast
wasteland. Without the slightest provocation and in an
unholy frenzy, megalomaniac dust storms periodically rolled
down from nearby mountain ranges, intent upon leveling the
few vertical landmarks. This bottomworld of Basin County
boasted a climate like the moon's—barren, too hot in the
daytime, and freezing at night. The people who lived here
were a crusty lot, cast from the same mold as the nomadic
Arab or Eskimo—resourceful enough to live in a mean, miserable environment and too dumb to get out. But for all their
environmental tenacity, they considered Bean Breath Brown,
one of the area's many village idiots, a genuine local phe-
nomenon. In a land dotted with bleached skulls and overheated cars, tall trees and Arctic blizzards, where all points of
interest were twenty miles away from all other points of interest, Bean Breath Brown's sole means of transportation was a
green Stingray bicycle.

"Mnugida."

Pedal.

"Mnugida."

Pedal.

"Mnugida."

Raymond (his Christian name) Brown was twenty-nine
years old but looked a hellish sixteen. He stood five-feet-four
and weighed about one hundred ten pounds, most of which
was leg muscle. Even as a baby, Bean's teeth had been bad,
terrible, yellow teeth which matched the scraggly blond hair
jutting out at wild angles from beneath his Genuine GM Parts
cap. Looking past the pitted, horned-rimmed glasses, there

was a faraway, wild look in the right eye. The left was rather passive in comparison, and it was a source of consternation to both Fenberg and Tuberski that Bean Breath Brown looked a lot like their late, dearly departed mother.

"Mnugida."

Pedal.

Bean and Mrs. Fenberg, however, weren't related. Raymond held a position of great responsibility in the community. Bean was the half-deaf, all-mute sports editor and head photographer of *The Basin Valley Bugle*, and he was bicycling into town to cover his first-ever protest.

* * * * *

Fenberg ended up snapping his own photographs.

As he left the office, camera in hand, he noted that it wasn't much of a protest. No riot police squirting unruly crowds with a water cannon. No overturned cars, engulfed in flames. No vicious attack dogs snapping at the unprotected ankles of elderly Baptist women. No Bible study teenagers with angry, contorted faces hurling Molotov cocktails at *The Bugle* window from the middle of the street. Just two dozen people smugly yet politely wearing an oval into the sidewalk, handing out pamphlets and carrying placards. Another fifty or so rubbernecked on the perimeter.

Fenberg switched lenses. He used the longer, 135mm to condense the crowd and close in on a mug shot of Behan. The motor cranked off five quick shots.

Through the viewfinder, Martin James Behan looked like a well-dressed but aging Soviet homicide detective who never got enough sleep. Though he appeared ill, Behan radiated charisma, power, control. He probably wasn't aware of his automatic and humorless politician's smile. The meat-and-potatoes face was framed by an abundance of thick, black hair, gray at the temples. Behan's brutish, fireplug body was out of place in the expensive clothes, but the most unusual portion of M. J. Behan's anatomy was his head, a nearly perfect cube.

He headed for Fenberg. Behan limped, pronouncedly. The crowd bisected.

Fenberg felt the blood pounding in his heart. The camera around his neck felt like a toy, and he was self-conscious.

Step-limp.

Fenberg's pulse quickened.

"Hello, Michael," Behan said, offering an outstretched hand.

"Nice day for a sit-in," said Fenberg, counting to five before shaking. Neither man squeezed. Behan's gaze bore into Fenberg's, running a quick inventory.

"You don't like me, do you, Michael?" he asked. As a boy, Behan had tried hard to make people dislike him. Growing up in the East, he used to tie up the smaller kids in the neighborhood and read them Scripture, mostly Old Testament, mostly the scary parts. Years later, he had the luxury of owning his own children and now, right across the street from *The Bugle*, his own newspaper.

"I don't know you," said Fenberg. He wanted to wipe his hand on the side of his pants.

"You're dodging the question," said Behan, his smile broadening. "See? I'm a newspaperman, too."

"Let's just let it stand that I don't know you. But I am curious."

"About what?"

"Why would a man of your apparent means move his fortune and family to a little out-of-the-way resort and logging town just to start a small newspaper?" Fenberg glanced at the *American Gothic* family lined up like quail. The wife looked gaunt and terrified. She wore dark glasses and designer Nancy Reagan clothes. The children were queued stepladder fashion by height. They caught Fenberg's stare and looked away, except the daughter. She was maybe thirteen, maybe twenty-eight, with long, curly, hot-red hair and matching lipstick on a pouting mouth. Darla Behan looked out of place, and Fenberg could tell from her attitude that she and Angry Joe could have a nice time together as black clouds over the sea.

"I wanted to settle down," said Behan. He was doing just

that. In less than a month, he had started construction on a tract house the size of a canning plant on the outskirts of town. He had made a six-figure donation for the construction of a nondenominational church and had tithed heavily to Basin Valley's three existing ones. "I wanted a safe, comfortable home for my family, in an environment that is conducive to their emotional and religious growth." The daughter looked away, as if the remark had been made for her benefit.

"Hard to swallow," said Fenberg. He towered over the middle-aged man, yet felt smaller.

Behan laughed, then coughed. His wife quickly held his elbow. "You speak your mind, don't you?"

Fenberg looked coldly at him. "I'm just a guy covering an intriguing story. A multimillionaire moves here. Rather suddenly. He opens a second newspaper in a one-newspaper town. Rather suddenly."

"Maybe soon it will be a one-newspaper town again," said Behan. "Rather suddenly."

Fenberg had indulged in a little investigative reporting.

The easy parts were these: Martin James Behan made his initial fortune running a chain of quickie print shops in Orange County, then diversified into real estate, investments, electronics, and heavily into those laser-operated price scanners every grocery store in the country now seemed to have. He was a behind-the-scenes mucky-muck of a conservative charismatic religious group, and he had his own bank.

"I'm a hard man, plain and simple. I work hard. I have a hard religion. And this religion teaches me to be an instrument for God. What better way to spread the word of God than in a newspaper? You don't, Michael. I will." Behan smiled at the picketers. They were marching slower now. Fenberg realized everyone was staring at them. Waiting for someone to throw the first punch?

"Why here?"

Behan shrugged and skipped back a step, regaining the balance on that good right leg. "Look around," he said simply. "It's beautiful here. That's one reason. Another is that I'm an expert in printing and real estate and investment. I really know little about the newspaper business."

Fenberg nodded slightly with understanding. It had been a recent trend, in the last ten years, for outside companies and individuals to invest in small papers. They were a good investment if run correctly, and with centralization—buying bulk supplies, group bookkeeping, chain discounts—someone with money could put together a syndicate and turn a tidy profit.

Behan chuckled affably. "Maybe it's just a roll of the dice or your bad luck. I'm not here strictly on a black-line basis. The organization I represent, a vast community of churches, has singled out this area, Michael. Frankly, your paper has been targeted as one of this state's more blatant abusers of our Christian way of life."

Targeted?

"You have run stories on sex. . . ."

Fenberg shook his head. *The Bugle* was far from a libertine publication, and while he wasn't *against* running stories about sex, he couldn't remember publishing any recently.

"Your paper parades an endless column of debauchery in front of its readers, covering everything from barroom brawls to murders."

"Don't forget maniacs," Michael pointed out. The picketers had stopped pacing. The crowd circled closer.

"And that's another thing. You print irresponsible stories, which may even be fabricated, I'm told, about some maniac lurking in people's back yards. You are actually doing the work of the devil when you do this, do you know that?"

"There's one wandering around town," said Fenberg. "People have seen him. I don't condone maniacs. I only write about them."

"I understand you have a brother."

"Three."

"One, I understand, is quite a large fellow, with antisocial tendencies and a prison record."

"No," corrected Fenberg, standing up straight. "He's never been in prison. He's been arrested a few times, for matters of grave inconsequence. It's on record."

"He does fit the police description of this man or thing?"

Fenberg's mouth opened, a little. He knew where Behan was going. Fenberg had heard the argument before, that it was his brother, dressed up in some sort of monster suit, scaring the bejesus out of everyone. Tuberski *was* the sort to do it, too, a lot of people grumbled. Fenberg would give them that.

"I can't see what purpose it serves to print these irresponsible rumors about hairy maniacs or to send your own community into a furor with sordid sensationalism. Unless, of course, you're interested in scaring little old ladies and small children."

The protesters mumbled approval.

Scaring old ladies and children, boo.

Fenberg looked past Behan. He had grown up with these people. From their looks, they weren't sitting on his side of the bleachers. Behan's daughter shrugged apologetically, then began filing her nails.

"I've said it before; I'll say it again," Behan raised his voice. There was a curious singsong quality to it, like a TV gospel preacher's. Behan's wife looked worried. "Your newspaper is sacrilege. It's what's wrong with America, and I swear to you, by all my faith and power, that I will—"

"He gave a dog a heart attack," interrupted Fenberg.

"I beg your pardon?"

"The maniac," said Fenberg. "He evidently snuck up on a guard dog at the auto salvage yard and gave it a heart attack."

Behan looked off for a moment. The crowd moved in a step. "Maybe he was an old dog, and he just died of natural causes."

"No," said Fenberg. "He was a puppy."

"I thought you said he was a guard dog."

"He was a guard puppy," said Fenberg. He smiled and blinked twice. Even some of Behan's protesters chuckled.

"We'll see, Mr. Fenberg, who'll have the last laugh here," whispered Behan calmly. He lightly held on to Fenberg's coat and leaned forward, as if he were a coach trying discreetly to bawl out a player on national TV. "You're small potatoes, one very small backwoods businessman, and how long do you think you're going to last against me? A year? Maybe two or three? You're mortgaged up to the hilt. Me? I can afford to run in the red for a thousand years. You make fun of me? I'm going to bury you, Mr. Fenberg," he whispered. Behan straightened. He let go of Fenberg's coat and gave Michael his best Sunday smile. It had an aggravating insincerity to it, as if a police artist had made a composite grin from the lips of Jimmy Carter, Dan Quayle, and James Watt. Fenberg wanted to wipe it off his face with a garden tool.

"If you'll excuse me, I'm being impolite in ignoring my gracious hosts and neighbors," Behan said. He herded his family together and limped back to chat with a pastor. Behan turned and smiled, waving warmly, as if he were boarding a plane overseas. "Good luck to you then, Michael."

The crowd oohed adoringly.

Dickhead, thought Fenberg, making a duck face.

Before Behan, Fenberg had been comfortable. Certainly not happy, certainly not rich, but comfortable. The paper brought in a personal salary of thirty-two thousand dollars with many hidden benefits: free pens, free Constant Comment tea, paper on which to scribble for Clifford and Tuberski. Fenberg leased his pride and joy, his truck, through the paper, and it should be pointed out that this was a special factory-order, Darth Vader-black, four-wheel-drive, four-door, chrome-and-custom, no ordinary Earth pickup, thank you very much. Still, after taxes, there wasn't much left when you had to raise two children and the artistic next spiritual-light-of-the-world. There were bills, clothes, food, medical and dental bills, and, coming next month, that final balloon payment on the ranch their parents had built. It'd be tight, Fenberg had originally figured, but he'd make it.

Until M. J. Behan came.

Fenberg watched Behan. He was perfect. Maybe a little sick, but perfect. The pastors, the parishioners, even some of the old suspicious townies who hadn't darkened a church hallway in half a century were eating out of M. J. Behan's palm.

What was slowly sinking in for Fenberg was that Behan could make good on his boast. He could run Fenberg out of business. He had the money. He could afford to run his new *Basin Valley Clarion* in the red for a thousand years. But why? Why was not germane.

Fenberg could find another job, but it wouldn't be in Basin Valley. There were a lot of trees around, but jobs that paid thirty grand certainly did not hang from them. He and the boys would have to move—somewhere—and it was starting to gall Fenberg that someone could move into town and just close the doors to a perfectly good 128-year-old institution like *The Bugle*.

Fenberg turned to walk back inside and bumped into a very wide, clean white T-shirt.

"Hello, buddy."

"Yeah, hi, how are ya."

"Buddy, you look a little upset," said Tuberski. He stood nonchalantly, hands in pockets. A toothpick dangled from his mouth.

"Awful."

"I hear your pain," said Tuberski. "Listen. I know this may not be the best time in the world. But then again, Mikey, maybe it is. I would like to talk with you regarding a banking maneuver that will allow you to buy out yon blockhead Baptist and have enough remaining to purchase at least three of the eight continents."

"There are only seven, and that's counting Antarctica."

"We'll have enough left over to dredge for Atlantis."

Fenberg smiled at the setup. He sighed. "It's nice to know one can still laugh at times like these."

Tuberski put his arm around his older brother. "Hey. We'll be all right. Especially when you've heard what I've done this morning, started the ball rolling that will ensure our safe and secure economic future. I . . ." Tuberski spotted something across the crowd. He smiled broadly. "Heh, heh, heh. Hello, Betty. Who's the babe?"

A chick is what Tuberski called a woman.

A babe is what Tuberski called an especially attractive woman, or, in this case, Darla, Martin James Behan's teenage daughter.

She was leaning against the Rolls, one round hip out, jeans tight, wearing a coyote fur jacket with that red hair flowing over it. She was staring at Tuberski from behind her sunglasses, and when John grinned and waved a little too-da-loo wave, she stifled a giggle and turned away.

"Say 'kay," said Tuberski, with a very wide smile.

"Oh, please, no," hushed Fenberg.

"Under those clothes she is naked," Tuberski declared, not taking his eyes off the Lolita.

"Please!" pleaded Fenberg. If he could have added moisture to his eyes, he would have. "She's Behan's daughter."

"She's just about my size," said Tuberski.

Darla looked at John, smiled demurely, then looked away.

Fenberg groaned. "Oh geez, *please*. Don't start anything, not here."

Tuberski took the toothpick out of his mouth and told Fenberg to hold it. He excused his way effortlessly through the crowd, ambling toward the teen angel. She wasn't exactly blushing. Tuberski smiled and leaned against the car, and must have said something funny because Darla put her hand to her mouth and laughed. Fenberg peripherally saw someone else moving in—her father. Fenberg said shit and pushed his way through the throng.

"You won't be doing any of that here," said Behan, wrapping a bony hand around his daughter's doll-like arm. He forcefully guided her in a small arc, putting himself between her and Tuberski. "And you, I know who you are. You keep away from my daughter!"

"Will you let go of my arm?" Darla asked, embarrassed at the scene her father was making.

"Get away from my car." Behan turned toward Tuberski. John stood up straight, towering over everyone. He took a baby step back.

"I said, get away from my car."

Tuberski took another baby step back.

"Will you please let go of my arm? You're hurting me," Darla said, forcefully trying to control her voice. Fenberg stood close by, in case of accidents.

"You embarrassed me before, and you embarrass yourself, acting like a common tramp in public," Behan said, shaking her once so she would pay attention. "Do you want me to tell these good people what you did? Do you?" The good people were mildly stunned by Behan's outburst. "You have an opportunity to turn over a new leaf here—"

"Let—go—of—my—arm. . . ."

Behan jerked her again. Tuberski glowered. "I don't ever want to find another scene like the one I found before. There will be no more entertaining dark-skinned boys in your room, will there? There will be no more entertaining of boys, period, will there? We've learned that lesson."

Darla stared helplessly at the sidewalk, trying not to look at anyone. Tears of rage welled.

"Now get in the car and wait," Behan said, pushing her toward the door. The protest signs were all lowered now. "Move along, young lady."

Darla meekly allowed herself to be guided to the car door. When Behan let go to reach for the handle, she turned and faced him. "I despise you," she said. "You're a weak, cruel, hateful man and a fraud, and I know all about you and I hate you," she said. Tears, but no emotion in the voice. The mother watched, paralyzed. Darla walked past the open door and jerked her arm away from her father when he tried to grab her again. Tuberski waited a long fifteen-count before casually striding in the opposite direction, and Fenberg knew that his brother would hurry around the block and cut through an alley to catch up with her.

Behan turned. He seemed oblivious to the other people. He looked at Fenberg with bland disinterest. Something in the eyes—Fenberg could see there was some link, some subtle recognition of a common bond. It gave Fenberg the willies. Behan and the rest of his family drove off, and the crowd begrudgingly dispersed. A flash went off, and Fenberg squinted. Bean Breath Brown rubbed his nose on his sleeve, grinned, and pointed to the sickly flat on his front bicycle tire.

Fenberg shook his head and gave up on the morning. "Rats."

6

NAKED CAME THE SASQUATCH

"Balls," said Elaine Mitikitski, disgustedly throwing a rag at the radiator. She was six hours late already.

The 1971 Chevy Vega hissed back and gurgled. A cloud of dirty steam, thick and pungent, billowed into the cold mountain air.

Mitikitski angrily paced in front of the car, hands on hips, not taking her eyes off the engine block. "Goddamn it anyway," she said, picking up a rock and measuring the Vega. Discretion lobbied a last minute reprieve for the lemon, and Elaine rifled a sidearm shot at a weathered road sign instead:

WELCOME TO BASIN VALLEY, CALIFORNIA
Home of the Mighty Cougars
State Champs in Football & Basketball
19————

Someone had scratched out the dates and written ". . . in Better Years" in their stead.

"Cougars, rah," said Mitikitski, halfheartedly.

She missed her father. Him, oddly enough, of all people. He had been up before dawn with her, securing tarps and cargo ropes as only fathers knew how to do. He had given her a there-there hug and some awkward wisdom from the *Reader's Digest*.

Elaine always thought Mr. Mitikitski didn't like her.

She couldn't see through his eyes his newsreel of memories of a serious little girl in an ill-fitting grass skirt, wiggling, sort of, in cadence to the music, her skinny little arms waving an obscure sign language that no real Tahitian could decipher. She didn't know he loved the way she laughed—like a baby, with her whole body. Or that after every divorce it broke his heart the way she cried. Or that he appreciated her never missing his birthday or Father's Day, and although he had bailed her out with thousands, how proud he was of her paying back every cent. She couldn't see his fondness of recalling her as a preteen doing the twist with great concentration in front of a cheap, plastic 45-rpm record player, or looking out the window to spot a scrawny, toothless second-grader wrestling a neighborhood boy to the ground and kissing him while he screamed. A portent of future relationships.

Mr. Mitikitski's last advice to Elaine was to count to fifteen before marrying anyone. He winced, imperceptibly, when the car door slammed. Elaine's father had the premonition that he would never see his favorite daughter again.

Two days of tugging a U-Haul trailer through small towns over roller coaster roads and listening to low-powered country-western stations had not dampened the adventure of leaving home for the first time. Well, for the first time without, spit, a man. It had been a long trip, uneventful except for the damned Vega overheating every fifty miles.

Mitikitski picked up another rock.

Then she heard the sirens.

Faint, at first, they grew in pitch and desperation. It was late afternoon when the speeding caravan roared by, aimed in the opposite direction. A pair of low-slung California Highway Patrol cruisers, all three of Basin County's forest green sheriff's cars, and two ambulances.

"Got any water?" Mitikitski asked quietly to the retreating fleet.

Probably an accident, she thought. Elaine planted herself on a smooth boulder, her back to the dark wall of woods. Hugging her legs, she bounced her chin on her knees. Late or not, there was nothing to do but wait until the car cooled. It was the dead of winter, and the air was cutting at the eight-thousand-foot elevation. The sun would be setting soon, the moon coming up.

Mitikitski perked. A noise?

Elaine was wearing shorts, and her legs were red from the cold. No, no noise. Just imagination. She vigorously massaged the tops of her thighs and walked around, then stopped again to listen.

"Nah," she said to herself and continued pacing. But what if? Elaine pulled a pair of binoculars out of a bag and climbed to a higher vantage point. With the spyglasses, she could see maybe three miles behind her on the windy road.

Sometimes, Elaine's husbands followed her.

Mitikitski was a looker. She had that wavy raven hair that hung in loose curls down to her waist. She was willowy, with long Wilma Flintstone legs, and had an ivory complexion with rosy cheeks and soft blue eyes. With a face and smile that carried an automatic pardon for any crime, Mitikitski sported an unpredictable mix of charm and contrary nature that attracted men.

Sadly, Elaine Mitikitski only attracted peculiar men.

And she wished she didn't.

As if scanning the horizon for enemy planes, Elaine swept the binoculars up and down the highway, looking for a familiar car or face behind the wheel.

Peculiar men.

No sign of them, but then, you could never tell.

Elaine took a deep breath through her nose. The air had a bite to it but was invigorating. For the first time in a year, Elaine felt pretty good about herself. On her own. No more therapy. No more living at home.

"Goddamn it! I feel healthy-thank-you-very-much!" she yelled. Her echo bounced off the hills, then faded. Mitikitski smiled. She hadn't noticed the birds. They'd stopped chirping, and the forest had fallen silent.

Elaine raised the binoculars, taking in some of the spectacular scenery. She spotted something, and it wasn't a car. It was a stream, down an embankment maybe a quarter mile away. A stream. Water. Water for the radiator.

Elaine tossed a few pebbles into the brush, then rubbed her arms. Goose bumps. She trotted back to the Vega to trade the sweater for a warmer ski jacket and find a large container to carry back the water.

Yellow fingernails parted the bushes behind her. Eyes, bloodshot, measured Elaine's retreating figure.

The brush was thick. The cold was making her nose run, and Elaine had thought the little stream was closer to the road. It wasn't. Elaine was kneeling by the brook, patiently scooping water, when she heard a branch snap and noticed the silence.

She thought of her trip. The gawking gas station attendants who all looked typecast for *Deliverance*, the grinning and gesturing truck drivers, both motel clerks. They all looked at Mitikitski knowingly. "There goes a girl who's 0-for-3 and all by herself."

Elaine shook her head and mumbled. "Come on, get a grip." Mitikitski sighed a self-chastisement and went back to scooping water.

About forty yards away, maybe less, there was a rustling in the bushes. Elaine stood up quickly.

"Hello?"

No sound.

"Anybody there?" Elaine strained to hear an answer. A husband? Elaine had taken elaborate measures to sneak out of town. "Norman . . . Louis . . . if that's you out there, I swear I'll kill you. Come on. You're scaring me."

Silence.

Mitikitski quickly screwed the lid on her container and headed back for the car. Although afternoon, it seemed very dark under the shade of the dense forest, and this wasn't the way she had come.

Elaine heard a grunt and stared at the bushes. For a full minute, she stood frozen, staring wide-eyed at the darkening woods. Then she saw, and she ran in panic. Someone, or something, very large, very powerful, was loping after her.

Elaine Mitikitski zigzagged through the dense underbrush. She had a crazy thought about all the old movies where the woman is being chased in the woods—and how they always find a way to awkwardly trip and sprain an ankle. Elaine didn't want to fall. Branches were crashing behind her, and she could smell a nauseating, musky, animal odor. Mitikitski scrambled up a steep embankment leading to the road.

"Damnit!" she screamed as she slipped down a few feet in the loose gravel. A large, calloused hand grabbed her ankle. Mitikitski screamed and kicked free.

It was a twenty-five-yard dead sprint to the car. Gasping, Mitikitski rolled up the windows and locked the doors.

"Shit!"

The hood was still up. No water in the radiator. And the moon was rising.

Elaine Mitikitski sat in the stalled car, trying to catch her breath. The windows were fogging. She clutched her stomach and rocked quickly back and forth.

Although Elaine didn't realize it at the time, she had spent a few days her sophomore year reading about her pursuer in a required anthropology class. He was a celebrity in an offhanded sort of way, having made the cover of every supermarket slash-and-flash tabloid at one time or another. He was also the mysterious protagonist in several of those cheap, gee-whiz documentaries of a speculative and 16mm variety.

Elaine checked her ankle for bruises, not knowing she had been chased by an Abominable Snowman.

Keep it together. Don't panic, Elaine told herself. You're going to have to put some water in that radiator before it gets dark.

Not the regular, lumbering, reclusive Abominable Snowman, but a beast of a different tune.

"The road," Elaine said out loud. Maybe she could flag down a car. But I'm going to have to step outside to do that, she thought.

It had something to do with the genes. The creature had more than his fair share of mischief chromosomes, and, had Tuberski been able to administer a Bigfoot IQ Test, the thing would have scored off the scale. Standing in an eight-foot gully on his tiptoes, the creature peeked over the edge, reflectively watching Elaine's head move through the blurry, steamed windows. He was overweight and short according to North American Sasquatch male weight and height tables. Except for the leathery face, he was completely covered with shaggy fur. He clicked his molars together. He liked the sound. It was also an unconscious habit he picked up while thinking. He was the first of his kind to think—good in the respect that he could now solve problems. Bad in the respect that now that he could think, he was plagued with boredom. And when plagued with boredom, he was driven to fits of mischief. Like chasing Elaine Mitikitski and pulling on her ankle.

The Bigfoot sniffed his hand, picking up Elaine's perfumed scent and filing it to memory. He raised his eyebrows appreciatively. He liked her, but then he liked a lot of things. He had no tail, prehensile or otherwise, hated dogs, and liked to go to the movies. The drive-in, actually. He had just seen *Ghost* and was feeling sort of romantic and maybe a little lonely.

He whined, a soft, whimpering whine.

I'm just going to have to open the door and flag down a car, Elaine Mitikitski reasoned.

And she did.

She opened the door to her 1971 Vega. She had one shapely leg out when a large hand reached for the handle.

7

ELAINE MEETS MIKE, AND . . .
THE NIGHT OF THE SECOND MURDER

"Didja wanna buy an ad there, honey?" the receptionist asked, spitting the husk of a sunflower seed into a Styrofoam cup full of wet, discarded shells. A big-boned woman, she balanced a tall, beehive coiffure on a sad hound dog's face and wore a low-cut blouse over a push-up brassiere. Her name was Malulu, Malulu Jean.

"I . . . uh . . . No thank you," said Mitikitski, almost staggering. "I've come to see Mr. Fenberg."

"He's busy."

"He's expecting me. . . ." Elaine's pocketbook seemed to weigh a ton. She was drained. And bruised. And dirty. And although the purse was heavy, she didn't think about setting it on the long oak bar that separated her from the receptionist.

"Could you tell him Elaine Mitikitski is here?"

Malulu brightened. "You're not Polish, are you?" she asked, spitting another shell into her collection.

Please, thought Elaine. "Dad is. My mother is Dutch-Spanish."

Malulu's brow furrowed at the odd combination. "I'll bet you hear a lot of Polish jokes." A grin creased her face, and she leaned forward. "Know any?"

"No."

"Come on, please?" Malulu pleaded, tilting her head sideways.

Elaine took deep a breath through the nose. Calm. Be calm. She spoke with a polite deliberateness, like someone trying to explain something to a non-English-speaking tourist. "I came to see Mr. Fenberg. If you'd just—"

"Say! I got it. You wouldn't be an old girlfriend or somethin', wouldja?" Malulu interrupted.

"I'm no one's girlfriend, old or otherwise. I'm the new reporter. Please, Miss, I . . ." Elaine stopped in midsentence, momentarily mesmerized by a large, lounging Florentine nude Tuberski had painted. On the other wall was a huge mural of the great Alliklik uprising of 1854, featuring explosions, people getting scalped, and general Bosch-type mayhem. This had been Tuberski's angry period. Dozens of awards, plaques, and photos framed a moose head over a stone fireplace. Otherwise, the office looked like a hunting lodge. Elaine held on tightly to the bar. "I . . . I . . . My car overheated, and I was chased by something, and the trailer has all my things in it." Elaine gestured weakly toward the window.

"You look kind of dirty for a reporter," Malulu suspiciously noted. "Of course, we've got this sports editor who looks like he sleeps in the driveway under the truck. Here, have a Handi Wipe." She tossed the plastic box of wet-napkins on the counter. "Didja know Mikey's a widower?"

"No, I didn't." Elaine vacantly wiped her hands, not noticing the scrapes on the palms and knuckles. She dabbed her face, smudging more than cleaning. "Who's Mikey?"

Mikey was what people around town called Fenberg, Malulu reported, along with his salary and a brief history of Michael being a womanizer. "Makes a girl wish she weren't married." Malulu took a casual glance at Mitikitski's left hand. It was suspiciously void of a wedding band. Malulu asked where Elaine would be spending the night and confided that it better not be at Mikey's ranch because Mikey had more moves than a bowl full of Jell-O.

Elaine drooped. Dizzy now, she had a blurry, vague vision of herself, alone in a cheap motel, standing over a dirty tub with no hot water.

"Doughnut?"

Elaine stared at the Alliklik massacre, shook her head no. "Organic." She considered fainting. Attention-getting. To the point. Mitikitski thought she'd go with the feeling, just let it happen and swoon, but was interrupted by a scream from the next room.

"I hope you get cancer and die!" yelled a voice, tiny and outraged. It belonged to a boy.

"Goddamn it, put the scissors *down*!" boomed a second voice, older, wiser. The women heard the sound effects: a light slap, an *ow*, and scissors clattering across the floor. "Do you have any idea the phone calls I've been getting all day? Mothers in hysterics and yelling words like 'revenge' and 'lynching'? You two are in trouble from hell to breakfast, and if you *ever* pull such a depraved—"

"You butt pirate, I hate you!" yelled the six-year-old.

Fenberg spoke calmly, and the boys sensed the calm before the storm. He gave them a choice. "Bend over or die."

"Why don't *you* bend over, you queer pillow-biter?" taunted Angry Joe.

"The ankles. Grab them."

"Queer," said Joe.

"Penissaurus," said Clifford.

Mitikitski's faint was momentarily postponed. She thought she recognized Fenberg's voice from over the phone.

"Sometimes it's kinda like a zoo around here," said Malulu Jean. She got up from the wooden swivel chair stuffed with four pillows and shuffled to the doorway where she could better eavesdrop.

"The talking's over. If I said this was going to hurt me more than you I'd be lying."

"Not with the belt buckle!" pleaded Clifford.

"Don't be theatrical," said Fenberg. "I've never hit you with the buckle."

"You have! And you liked it!"

"Shut up and take it like a man," snapped Angry Joe.

Mitikitski waited for the explosive *thwops* that never came.

"I've never hit you and I won't start now. Grounded, for

two weeks, the both of you," announced Fenberg. Malulu made a sour face, disappointed at the leniency. "And, boys, so help me, if you ever pull another stunt like that I will amend my policy of enlightened child-rearing, and I swear I'll beat you two like rented mules."

Mitikitski looked at an Indian about to scalp a helpless miner in Tuberski's epic oil, then at Malulu standing by the door with the Styrofoam cup of sunflower seed shells.

"I can do two weeks standing on my head, you asshole!" answered the littlest voice.

There was the loud *thwop* of a belt hitting a desk, and a child screamed, "My spine! My spine! You paralyzed me!"

"Go on. Beat it," said Fenberg. Malulu scrambled back to her chair. "Get out of here and get rid of that stupid wig."

The door opened. Elaine was standing in the narrow walkway between the bar and the wall. Cliffie and Joe Fenberg walked out of the office, through the waist-high swinging door, past the disapproving eye of Malulu Jean MacClean. They were staring at their shoes and trying not to giggle. Joseph, the muscular one with the parrot haircut, honked Elaine's breast and ran out the door. Shocked, Elaine covered her chest while Cliff stealthily walked past. He measured the cowering Mitikitski. He was wearing a shawl, granny glasses, and a woman's gray wig. He pulled a white plastic spoon from his wrap.

"You must stay sometime at my motel, dearie," said Clifford in his best Norman Bates voice. He tucked the spoon back into his belt, aloofly following his brother outside. Mitikitski still had her arms crossed like bandoleros across her breasts.

"Those are the youngest Fenberg brothers," said Malulu Jean, "Joe and Clifford, pissants the two of them."

Michael Fenberg ran out of his office, slipping his Western belt with the big silver buckle through the loops. As he headed after the boys, he brushed by Elaine, knocking her against the wall.

"Hey!" Fenberg stuck his head out the door and yelled. "I want you both home for dinner by seven!"

"Ass . . . *hole*!" yelled a distant small voice.

"I hate them," Fenberg mumbled to himself. "From a deep and special place." He walked back to the front office, past the bar, brushing next to Mitikitski again. "Who's she?" he asked Malulu, gesturing toward Elaine.

"New reporter."

"She's late."

"I told her."

"I hate them," said Fenberg, taking a deep breath and trying to pull himself together. "I really do. Why is she covering herself up like that?"

Mitikitski self-consciously dropped her arms, then offered Fenberg a hand. "I'm Elaine Mitikitski," she said.

Fenberg's mouth opened. It was a few seconds before he realized he'd been holding his breath and that Elaine's hand was hovering in midair, waiting for a shake.

Oh, my God.

Her jacket and blouse were torn and caked with mud. Her shins were scraped and dirty, and there were goose bumps on her thighs. Michael couldn't tell without staring and being obvious, but he thought her knees might be knocking together. She had smeared mascara, a large swath of dirt on her forehead, and a twig with a few cracked leaves was still sticking in her sweaty, matted hair. Next to Tracy, she was the most beautiful woman Fenberg had ever seen.

He shook her hand, mesmerized by her eyes.

"You're kind of late," said Fenberg. So it happened.

"I'm sorry," she said, forcing a smile.

"You're a little dirtier than I expected." This is the one.

"Someone was chasing me."

Fenberg looked down at Elaine's pretty but scuffed knees and winced. "Did you come all the way on foot? You made very good time," he said, gently. "Come on." Fenberg still held Elaine's hand and guided her past the swinging half-door that separated the public area from the front office. He made it a point to give Malulu a long, severe stare, and she begrudgingly looked away. Fenberg led Elaine into his office and closed the door. He sprinted back out a second later and grabbed the Handi Wipes from the bar, warning Malulu Jean,

". . . not one word. Thank you."

"Looks like you've taken a nasty spill," he said, gingerly sponging the dirt away from the scrape on one of her shins. Fenberg knew. *He knew*.

"I'm sorry, real sorry, but I think I'm going to have to cry," said Mitikitski.

"Tears soften."

"I think I'm going to have to cry a lot."

And Mitikitski did. She wrapped her arms around Fenberg and bawled like a baby. Fenberg rubbed her shoulders and told her softly to cry as much as she wanted, but don't forget to breathe through the nose. She fitted so perfectly in his arms. So this is the one, he thought. This is the girl who's going to take Tracy's place and break my heart in twelve places.

Mitikitski had no idea, of course, although she liked the hugs. She thought she was just going to be a reporter and felt she hadn't really made a very good first impression.

* * * * *

They sat opposite each other at dinner, and Elaine noticed there was something about her new employer, though she couldn't place what it was.

Something haunted Fenberg. There was pain behind his eyes, an invisible hand that warned her to keep a polite distance.

There was a much-nurtured loneliness there. No relationship worked. On purpose. No woman born of same could ever hope to compete with the blonde specter that Fenberg carried warm in his shirt pocket.

Not that Fenberg had been a saint after Tracy "entered her transition," as Tuberski put it. Fenberg dated just about every eligible woman between the ages of seventeen and thirty-five and a few who weren't exactly eligible.

There had been Roulette Rozinitti, the nineteen-year-old checker at the A&P with the tiny waist and bosoms that, from an engineering standpoint, were impossible on a frame her size.

"Tits so big, giant herds of bison could thunder across one, taking a week to pass." Tuberski waved a large palm across an invisible autumn plain. Tuberski always described Fenberg's love life publicly to The Trails regulars on Saturday nights, much to the embarrassment of Fenberg, who always sat in the same corner booth, nursing a beer and trying to ignore him. Tuberski would always look to see if Fenberg was paying attention. "On one, it would be a sunshiny day of summer. On the other, it would be the darkest day of winter, with an angry front moving in from the Alaskas." To augment his dissertation, Tuberski would adopt a squinting eye and Long John Silver voice affectation. It was just sex, as far as Fenberg was concerned, and there was no chemistry between him and Rozinitti. Too much a coward to brush her off in person, Fenberg called it quits over the phone and stammered that, uh, they could still be friends. Roulette called Fenberg a rat.

There had been Faedeane, too, the greasy spoon waitress from the truck stop who snapped gum and shouted instructions, shouted instructions *loudly*, while they mated.

"Over there! Over there! That's it! Yes! *Ye-esss*! Go for it!" she'd yell. And that was during afterglow.

Fenberg didn't like people who said "Go for it." Even more, he didn't like being cheered on during sex, thank you very much. Lean to the left, lean to the right, stand up, sit down, fight-fight-fight. Faedeane had very long legs and always smelled of french fries. Fenberg had never seen her in the daylight.

Nancy, the girl in pasteup, was suicidal. She was round-shouldered, wore her long brown hair parted down the middle, wore black dance outfits, and looked like a satanic Tinkerbell. Tuberski would make it a point to slap her on the back and ask, "How's it going, Smiley?"

After a hard day of uncovering grisly finds and covering highway carnage, the last question Fenberg wanted to hear was, "What does it all mean, Mike?"

"What does what all mean?" Fenberg always responded, question for question.

No amount of good cheer made her crack a smile, nor could Tuberski's answer, "Life has no meaning. To ask that is to ask, 'What is the meaning of a rose?'" To which Fenberg would later ask, "What is the meaning of a rose, John?" To which Tuberski would say, "Life, like a rose, has no meaning. It is to be lived, and lived well. Say 'kay."

Humor is demeaning, Smiley told Fenberg. Terrorists, chauvinists (one of whom she considered Fenberg to be), assholes (one of whom she considered Tuberski to be), nuclear accidents, Republicans, unfulfilling work, war, starvation—they were all Smiley's cup of tea. She always made it a point to show Fenberg where her previous husbands had abused her. "Here, see," she said in a monotone voice, pointing to her rib cage. "This is where Carl, my second husband, shot me one night 'cause I came home late. He cut me here, too," she said, lifting up a leg. "That—that's just appendix. Don't look at that." Fenberg didn't. He always looked off toward the wall, wincing.

The price one pays for sex.

Fenberg had had a brief affair with a local captain-of-industry's wife, three long, lousy years ago, and she was still pinching him in the jeans publicly. The woman in question was Mrs. Fia White, aka One-Night White, as Tuberski, the giver of unwanted nicknames, dubbed her. She was Basin Valley's only cruel and unusual swinger.

"Mike . . . I want you to use me; I want you to abuse me," Mrs. One-Night White would plead, dressed only in this ridiculous-looking lingerie that made her look like the Marquis de Sade's maid. She licked her lips and undulated up, down, and sideways, doing everything but the hokeypokey around Fenberg, who stood at attention like a cavalry officer tied to a stake by Indians.

"Say nasty things to me, Mike!" she whispered in husky desperation. "Dirty—so dirty, talk dirty to me. Talk dirty!" Fia shrieked as she clawed Fenberg's back with long red fingernails, making Fenberg wonder whether he should continue or excuse himself for a minute to put on a few sweaters. But it was close to that moment that all guys like, and Fenberg's mind was not in gear for snappy one-liners or sexual insults. The best he could come up with was, "How do you like it like *this*?" The "this" being accentuated by a pelvic thrust.

"Let me get this straight. 'How do you like it like *this*'?" repeated Tuberski when Fenberg told him later. Men *do* talk. "How do you like it like *this*?" Tuberski cried. He collapsed on the floor and rolled around in a convulsive ball, repeating Fenberg's classic line, "How do you like it like *this*?" He looked at Fenberg's stoic face, and it made him laugh even harder. He tearfully pointed up at Fenberg. "What a jerk!" he said.

"I'm sorry I told you," said Fenberg, trying to muster some dignity.

* * * * *

"How do you like it like *this*?" the waiter asked, setting a steak down in front of Fenberg and giving him a knowing smile. Fenberg glowered. At least the waiter didn't bump the table with a pelvic thrust. Add to the price of sex, the cost of living in a small town.

"It's fine. It's just absolutely, perfectly fine," said Fenberg, staring daggers at the waiter. "Just set it down, there, fine."

The waiter stood at attention and clasped his hands together. "And is the lady certain that all she'll be having is salad and warm bread?"

"Oh, this is just perfect, thank you," said Elaine.

"I'll be checking back," said the waiter, making sure Fenberg saw his mincing look.

Fenberg had whisked Mitikitski away to Basin Valley's finest restaurant, Bill & Emma's Mostly Fish, which also served steak and prime rib. Bill & Emma's also served tropical drinks and a better class of people than the Zoo Bar, Fenberg and Tuberski's favorite watering hole.

"I'm starved," said Elaine.

"I'd hate to see what you eat when you're dieting," said Fenberg. She seemed to have bounced back remarkably, Fenberg noted. Changing clothes and washing up at Malulu's place, just two blocks away from the paper, had helped.

They talked over dinner. Elaine liked vegetables, whole grains, and the rare fish or chicken. Fenberg leaned toward caffeine, red meat, and non-easily digestible carbohydrates. She apologized for making such an entrance and said she did call three times that day to say she was having car trouble. Fenberg made a mental note to talk with Malulu, who was supposed to be his secretary but refused to take messages. Fenberg, the skilled interviewer, carefully and gently pulled the details of the car overheating on Vista Ridge, her search for water, and the mysterious encounter in the woods.

"You know what scared me the most?" Elaine asked.

"Meeting Malulu."

"Second. No. When that highway patrolman tapped on my car window," said Mitikitski. "Now *that* scared me. I must have startled him, too, the way I screamed. He said he saw me running to the Vega."

"Did the patrolman see what was chasing you?"

"Nope," she said, then gestured with her dinner roll. "Have you noticed we've been talking about this person as a 'what?' "

Fenberg didn't want to scare her with maniac stories. Elaine seemed to be doing rather well, but he predicted the delayed trauma would soon hit, and she'd have another long cry, followed by a good sleep.

"But you know what?" Elaine went on. "It didn't seem like a man, and what's even stranger, now that I think about it, is that I wasn't *that* frightened. I mean, I was, but when I thought about it later, I had this sensation of whoever was chasing me was more of a prankster than anything. That he wasn't going to hurt me. As if he were a big child, and it was just a game." Tag, you're it. "Am I making sense?"

"Absolutely not," said Fenberg, smiling, a little too open too early. Elaine smiled and looked back down at her salad. He had curly eyelashes, she noticed.

"He said—the patrolman, that is—that he was on his way to a big accident or something down the road. I remember, because when the car stalled, every cop in the world whizzed by."

Fenberg's brow furrowed inquisitively. He should have heard over the police radio, or someone should have called. Someone probably did call, and Malulu forgot to tell him. Again. He'd check later.

"You know what else? The policeman didn't seem very eager to go into the brush to see for himself that someone was chasing me. I feel like I'm talking a million miles an hour, and I want you to know I normally don't run off at the mouth."

Fenberg shrugged it off. One of those hard-on-herself people. Who wasn't? "I don't find you at all run-off. I think we ought to start with you getting some rest for a few days."

"I thought you were short-staffed. . . ."

"I am," said Fenberg, rolling a steak tidbit inside the baked potato with sour cream and butter. "But a day or two or three won't matter much in the scheme of the universe. Malulu handles the classifieds and can help you find a place to stay. You can bunk at the ranch in the meantime."

"The ranch?"

"That's where I live. About four miles out of town. There's plenty of space. You can stay in my parents' room."

"Where will your parents sleep?" Elaine asked.

Fenberg resisted the temptation to say the North Pole. He shrugged and told Elaine they had disappeared in a plane crash over the Arctic several years ago, no, condolences no longer needed, but thank you anyway.

"There's an empty king-size bed, private bath, fireplace." Fenberg cleared his throat. "I sound like a real estate agent. At any rate, it's roomy, and you're certainly . . ."

His sentence dangled. Fenberg stared blankly into space.

His brothers.

Basically, they were good kids, hearts of gold and all, but stringent counter-terrorism precautions would have to be taken with Mitikitski under the same roof.

". . . um . . . welcome."

Mitikitski smiled neutrally. Welcome indeed. She vaguely remembered Malulu mentioning ". . . more moves than a bowl full of Jell-O" and pictured a fiendish Fenberg lurking on the outside of the bedroom door, gingerly trying the doorknob.

* * * * *

Neither realized they hadn't looked at one another through dinner. The few times Mitikitski had glanced directly at Fenberg, she blushed. Please, she thought. Gray eyes? Shy, unnerving, undressing, humorous gray eyes? Isn't this a little early? The cheekbones were high, five o'clock shadow, tan face, lips. . . . She sneezed twice and stopped that right there. He wore a blue denim snap-button shirt and unless that was padding, he had very broad shoulders. Forty-six long, Kamali Molly, the retail monster, would have pegged him.

Fenberg admirably forced away any mental wanderings and, to his credit, didn't blurt out anything stupid. She was so pretty though. Athletic, he guessed. Would probably like the horses. There was a lot of strength to this girl, the way she'd handled the afternoon. And mischief. And something about her Fenberg fiercely wanted to protect. Everyone had stared at her when they walked into the restaurant. The men sheepishly grinned and whispered to one another. The women were antagonistic.

Fenberg opened the glass front door to *The Bugle*, letting Elaine enter first. Long legs. He wondered, prematurely, if she liked kids and then chastised himself. "We are not responsible for our thoughts," Tuberski had always said, "only our actions."

"I do have an assignment for you," said Fenberg, leading Mitikitski past the old oak saloon countertop. "I could use three pages, no more, of your impressions on being chased by this . . . I don't know, what do you want to call him, a maniac?"

"Sure."

"It'll be a nice way to introduce you to the community. Have to get your picture taken. We'll . . ." Fenberg snapped his fingers. "Malulu Jean, did a call come in this afternoon about a major accident or something the Highway Patrol was on?" Fenberg turned back to Mitikitski. "Make it first-person. Animation. I want the reader to taste, touch, smell, and feel what happened to you out there. And, while you're at it, make it factual."

"Yeah. We had a couple of calls, but you were busy with Frick 'n Frack, and you said you didn't want to be disturbed. . . ." With her purple fingernails, Malulu picked up a small stack of messages, including the three that warned that Mitikitski would be late.

"Deadline is two o'clock tomorrow, if I'm not rushing you," Fenberg said to Elaine.

"Said they found four bodies," said Malulu, having trouble reading her own writing, "then they called back and said they found the *parts* to four bodies." Malulu slid a large, cheap purse over her shoulder. It was her late day, ten to eight. Hands on hips, Fenberg spun.

"*Who* found bodies?"

"Said they found this big motor home parked off the logging road on Parkinson's turnout, you know the one?"

"Yes." Fenberg nodded impatiently.

"Said they found four bodies. Man, woman, two kids. They had been buried, sort of. Evidently, they died, and some animals got at them or something, maybe coyotes."

Mitikitski crossed her arms, pressing them against her stomach.

"That's all I know," said Malulu. "I'm going home. Got kids to feed myself."

Fenberg paced. He was at the beginning of his standard for-God's-sakes-alive-riot-act-what-makes-a-good-secretary speech which Malulu, thick piece of cake that she was, always ignored. The phone rang. Malulu glanced at the large wall clock and made it known by her slow shuffling and long face that she was doing a saintlike deed by answering it.

Fenberg's secretary lethargically picked up the receiver, said her perfunctory uh-huhs, and it was Elaine who picked it up first: the subtle, minute changes of facial muscle that by moving just a thousandth of an inch can convey mirth or terror. Malulu's face registered tragedy.

Fenberg sat on the edge of a desk, his hands on his hips. He had read her reaction, too. He immediately felt the distortion of time, the light-headed sensation of being swept back five years when they had called about his wife and child.

"Oh, Mike, I'm so sorry . . ." Malulu said. She shook her head, helpless. "There's been some sort of accident at your place. It has to be an accident, or a mistake. . . ."

She held the receiver out for Fenberg.

"It's the sheriff," she said. "He's at your ranch. He said that Mr. Behan's daughter has been cut to ribbons, dead, and that your brother did it. He said John's the one"—she swallowed—"who killed that family. He said John even confessed to all the maniac business that's been happening around town."

Fenberg stared through Malulu. All he could think about was that this was the night Tuberski was watching the boys.

8

MEANWHILE, BACK AT THE RANCH . . .

The question of John Tuberski's enigmatic nature was a favored topic around Basin Valley. Here was a man who talked to houseplants, who had mastered the art of creating a snug-yet-undebilitating diaper, yet here also was a man capable of great acts of violence without remorse.

Case in point. The See 'Em Dead Zoo Bar & Grill Massacre.

Fenberg and Tuberski weren't into hunting, quite the opposite. But they considered the Zoo Bar a fitting place to rest their contrary natures. Horses, Studebaker pickup trucks, and motorcycles often associated with unwashed, bearded white supremacy types could often be seen in the parking lot. Nestled conveniently between the Orion Wilderness Area and Basin Valley proper, the Zoo Bar earned its moniker because of the curious collection of taxidermy inside. Nothing new had been added since 1936, but by then, the proprietors had already managed to have on display every mammal indigenous to North America that was over six inches tall. Bears, wolverines, goats, weasels, rabbits, and such were all perched about, frozen in ferocious demeanor. Because things tended to get real Western here, it wasn't the sort of place a man took his family.

It was here in the parking lot one night where Fenberg, Bean Breath Brown and Tuberski were accosted by three frowzy bikers and three equally frowzy bikettes. Unkind

remarks were exchanged. The Fenberg party easily won the
verbal exchange, tallying big points with references to IQ's,
heredity, and fatness (the center biker was about the size of
Orson Welles). The bikers would have been content to leave
it at that, salvaging some team pride with a few "oh-yeahs?"
But the bikettes grew yangy and one suggested to Tuberski
in particular that if he were such a big man, why didn't he
prove it?

Tuberski said, " 'kay," and placed his foot on the tubby
biker's front tire. He grabbed the gooseneck handlebars and
bent them straight up into the air. He smiled widely at his
accomplishment.

Not stopping to put two-and-two together, that someone
who could bend stainless steel in his bare hands could also
quite possibly hurt you, the three bikers launched themselves
onto Tuberski in certain fury.

Tuberski pummeled them.

He was basking in the retelling, fabricating here and there,
when, a half hour later, the back door to the Zoo Bar opened
and a half-dozen members of the Aryan Motorcycle Club
sauntered in like the beginning of a bad video.

Then the front door opened, and the rest of the "Club"
entered. Their leader, Mason Vaturi, ambled over to the
brothers' table. Mason was a sociopath. Big scars, tattoos,
unpleasant outlook on life. He had recently been paroled
from San Quentin, where he'd delegated torture and murder
for the white prison gang there. He addressed Tuberski.

"You busted up our pals," Mason said, turning his head
awkwardly to the side, like Marlon Brando searching for a
line. "You busted up our pals, and now you're gonna pay."

"Ah, cut it out," said Tuberski. He smiled and winked at
Fenberg. Fenberg was pale.

A braless, greasy woman in fringed knee-high moccasins
yanked the pay phone off the wall with a crowbar.

The president of the Aryans was six-foot-six and weighed
about two-forty. He watched Tuberski, like a missile out of a
silo, rise and tower above him. Tuberski bent, shoving his
face close to Mason's.

"You're weak," Tuberski informed him.

The biker pulled a knife, slicing Tuberski across the shoulder. Tuberski dodged another lunge by grabbing Mason's wrist and lifting him off the ground. With the other hand, Tuberski made a fist. He punched the leader of the Aryans in the chest, collapsing both lungs.

Tuberski seemed to inhale all the air in the bar. He looked around at the other gang members. "Lock the doors," he ordered, still holding their dazed and gasping leader dangling off the ground. "I am in my element."

It was a barroom fight of Homeric proportions.

Fenberg broke his wrist and suffered two black eyes. Tuberski was treated for minor stab wounds and was quickly released. He offered, as an alibi, that all thirty-one members of the hospitalized Aryan Motorcycle Club had sustained their injuries by accidentally and simultaneously tripping. Lots of furniture was destroyed, and many feelings were hurt at the See 'Em Dead Zoo Bar & Grill Massacre that night.

*　　*　　*　　*　　*

They sped in silence, along the dark, windy forest road. Fenberg's black four-door pickup bounced a yard aboveground on giant Kelly-Springfield tires, digesting the blacktop beneath it. They were eight miles from the ranch.

Fenberg drove with the heat on and the window open. Cold air flooded the cabin, blowing Mitikitski's hair back. She looked over at Fenberg, hand draped over the wheel, staring intently ahead. She wanted to offer condolences and somehow tactfully suggest to Michael not to drive so recklessly on these treacherous, ice-slick roads. Neither gesture seemed appropriate. Elaine put her head back, tired, but exhilarated by fear and the mysterious smells of the winter forest.

"So how did you get into newspapers?" Fenberg asked. A car whooshed by in the opposite direction, momentarily bathing the cab in a breeze of headlights. Mitikitski could see the cold perspiration on his forehead. "I'd like to level with you. I'm trying like the dickens not to think about what happened at the ranch. My brother John said if there ever were an anthropomorphic devil, it'd be the human mind, knowing all our fears and secrets, keeping us hurt and crazy with a lot of whispered lies and should-haves. Good today, bad tomorrow. My brother is truly an amazing fellow, and I begrudgingly admit more often than not he's right. So, I'm not going to think. If you could join me in some banal conversation, I'd dearly appreciate it."

Okay.

She was glad he broke the silence. "Would you mind repeating the question?"

"Newspapers. How'd you get into them?"

"Sixth grade editor of the *TeePee Times*. On to junior high for an illustrious career as a columnist and editor. Same thing in high school and college. I watched a lot of Mary Tyler Moore. Things sort of fell into place. Are you all right?"

Seven miles.

"Yes. Ask me a question."

"Uh . . . how'd you get into newspapers?" When they had spoken over the phone long-distance, Elaine had a feeling she might have trouble with Fenberg. Maybe that's why she came.

"Is that wind too much on you?" Fenberg asked.

"No."

"Good. Okay. That's a good question, Mitikitski." Fenberg let out a heavy sigh. "Spencer Tracy and Clark Gable. I used to watch those old movies where they'd talk fast and do anything to get a story. Plus having your mother and father own the local paper didn't hurt." Five miles.

Another car roared by. Fenberg had a nice profile, Elaine noted. Strong jaw, honest face. He wore a blue denim work shirt buttoned all the way to the top. "I haven't counted the years, but it's been in the family since 1906. My parents bought it from my mother's uncle. My brother used to work with me, did you know that?"

"No. I didn't."

The truck passed a sprawling scrub oak with Halloween features.

"Very talented fellow. Great columnist. He sees things differently than you or I." Or maybe anyone. "Did these great political cartoons. I'm prejudiced, but I think he had the talent to work for a big metro. But we Fenbergs, we like the woods. Besides. He gave it up." They were only a few minutes away.

"For?"

"His art."

"What sort of art does he do?" asked Elaine, instinctively reaching for the dashboard as the tires skidded around a bend.

"He sculpts. And paints. It's aggravatingly effortless, and he could be a major talent, except he's given up that too, lately. We're just about there."

"Why?"

"Because we've been speeding."

Elaine smiled. "No. Why did he give up his art?"

"He hears voices."

"Voices?"

Fenberg turned his head and looked long at Mitikitski. She had his coat wrapped around her. "Yeah. Like Joan of Arc."

Mitikitski nodded her head, feigning understanding, as if she were back in therapy.

"Is he one of those temperamental artists?" Elaine wished she could have taken that one back.

Fenberg laughed sardonically. "I guess we'll find that out real soon."

Fenberg hung a hard right under a weathered timber archway that proclaimed, "Scared O' Bears Ranch." A beat-up tin mailbox bore the name "FENBERG" on top and "(Tuberski)" in smaller letters underneath. Fenberg's pickup plowed a furrow of dust on the dirt road as he and Elaine Mitikitski bounced toward the lights of the ranch.

"They're here in force," said Elaine. She had never been to a murder. Her closest brush with the world of crime was covering a break-in at her college bookstore and bailing husband number three out of the pokey. Three sheriff's cars, a paramedic truck, an ambulance, and a couple of Highway Patrol cruisers were parked at odd angles in the Fenbergs' front yard, flooding the hills around the elongated ranch house in the eerie glow of their flashing red and yellow lights.

A deputy stopped Fenberg at the gate.

"It looks pretty bad, Mike." Fenberg knew him—Raphael Cruz. He was young, likeable. Not the hardnose his boss, the sheriff, was. "They haven't touched the body of the girl yet. Waiting for a doctor to get here and make the coroner's report."

"Is my brother all right?"

"He's not here. . . ."

"What about the boys? They didn't tell me a damn thing over the phone."

"They're not here, either, Michael."

Fenberg didn't know whether to be relieved or not.

"There's not a sign of Tuberski. You know the way he is. Your cousin thinks he must have taken off into the hills."

Cousin? thought Mitikitski.

A few drops of rain sprinkled on the windshield, and the deputy looked heavenward. Just what they needed. Rain.

"What on earth's been going on here, Raphy?" Fenberg asked.

"I took the call myself," said the baby-faced Hispanic deputy. He gestured toward the house. "Tuberski called the station forty minutes ago. He seemed, I don't know, like in shock or something. Real quiet, you know? He said that that new guy . . ."

"Behan."

"Yeah. His daughter was dead on the front lawn, and that we better come out. And he hung up. We were only five minutes away, over at Wheeler Ridge. You know, the camper full of tourists?"

"I just found out about that one myself," said Fenberg.

"Something real weird going on here, Mike," the deputy said. He looked at Mitikitski. "That family, looks like some sort of animal got at them. And the same thing with this girl. Which doesn't make sense. She's only been dead a short while. Coyotes wouldn't have time to do this much damage.

Would have had to have been a bigger animal."

"What makes you say that?" asked Fenberg.

"Part of her is missing."

"Which part?"

"Well. Lots of parts. Sheriff thinks she's been, uh, eaten. Uh, sorry, ma'am." He tipped his hat toward Elaine.

Elaine smiled with uncertainty.

"Elaine Mitikitski. She's going to be working for us. Taking Henry Darich's place," said Fenberg, looking ahead at the civil servants combing his front yard.

"Nice to know you." Cruz nodded. "Uh . . ." The deputy stared at the ground, kicking loose a rock with the point of his boot.

"Uh, what?" asked Fenberg.

"Well, so far, this isn't the worst part."

"Oh."

"Your cousin thinks this may be the work of a cannibal."

"I see."

"And your brother, uh, sort of left this confession note."

"Oh, he did, did he."

Fenberg made a tired face and draped his hand over the steering wheel. Cannibal? He looked at Mitikitski, who had the same shocked expression.

"The sheriff is going to organize a search party for him," said Cruz. "He's none too happy about your brother, Mike. I suggest you better get over there."

"Thanks." Fenberg eased the pickup behind a sheriff's unit and killed the ignition. "You want to wait in the truck?"

"I think I'll be fine." Elaine handed Fenberg his jacket. "I want to help."

"Look," said Fenberg, mustering what sincerity he could under the circumstances. "You've had a pretty tough day, and this isn't going to be the easiest part of it. You might not like what you see over there." He thought for a second. "Hell. *I* might not like what I see over there." Angry Joe and Clifford. Where were they?

"Okay then. This is what we'll do." They climbed out of the Ford F-350. Fenberg assigned Mitikitski to go into the house and start making calls. Try to locate the boys. And when she ran out of numbers . . .

A car turned off the highway, lightly honking its horn twice. It was a Dodge station wagon driven by a generic housewife. Deputy Cruz pointed her to Fenberg. Elaine squinted past the glare of the wagon's high beams, and then she thanked God. In the back seat were Angry Joe and Clifford. In the front sat the woman's son.

Fenberg jogged over to the car.

"God, for once I'm happy you two didn't listen to me," said Fenberg, bending over and looking inside.

"They're not supposed to be over to our house. My husband said. Not after what happened the last time." The woman had a beggy voice. It was early evening, and she was still in her bathrobe. "Hey, what's going on here?"

The woman filled up most of the front seat. She bobbed and weaved, gawking past Fenberg. In the back, Clifford dug his fingernails into Angry Joe's leg, gritting his teeth and slowly increasing the pressure. With a lightning-fast open palm, Joe popped him in the forehead, and Clifford pretended to be knocked out. The woman thought the police were looking for the two younger boys. Fenberg told the woman they had found an Indian burial ground on the property. She didn't buy that. Then he told her there had been an industrial spill. She didn't buy that either. And then he told her the truth, asking if she could just let the boys stay over at her house for the night. The large lady said thanks for the money, and it more than covered all the damages from the boys' last visit, but her husband had really laid down the law. Fenberg was beginning to lose his patience. He asked if they could at least sleep in the car or could she take them to Malulu's or the YMCA in San Francisco or the goddamn Motel 6 in Elvira, New York, just please take them someplace where they wouldn't have to stare at a corpse. At that, Clifford tried to climb out the window to get a closer view. Fenberg pushed him back in by the head. Some maternal instinct finally stirred, and the mother agreed to drop them off at Malulu Jean's.

Fenberg gave Joe a reassuring nod, which Joe ignored. Clifford made an obscene face and wiggled lewdly as they drove off.

Two brothers down, one to go.

"I just never, ever liked that woman," Fenberg said to Miti-kitski.

Fenberg and Elaine walked in cadence. The crunch of the gravel driveway under Fenberg's feet reminded him of being a kid, chasing his larger Baby Huey brother around the front yard. They were probably the only brother combination in the world that never fought. Fenberg handed Elaine his Olympus.

"So you want me to just take pictures?" Elaine asked, wondering how to work the camera. "Is there anything else I can do?"

"Do what our regular head photographer does. Maintain a low profile. Do not get in the way. Smile nicely, nod, and pretend you don't speak English."

"I could interview the first person on the scene. I could look for clues." She ran a couple of steps to catch up with Fenberg.

Fenberg nodded and put his hand up in the air. Yeah. Fine. That'd be nice. "I'll be over here talking to my cousin," said Fenberg. Elaine wondered if there was anyone in town he wasn't related to. She watched him walk away and shrugged. She pulled her hair back, expertly forming a ponytail and tying it off with a rubber band from her pocket before heading off in the opposite direction to look for clues.

Fenberg's cousin was squatting next to the girl's covered body.

"Bubba," Fenberg said, nodding a terse greeting. He bent down next to the sheriff, but Bubba Fenberg didn't answer. He was staring at the lifeless form under the turquoise tarpaulin. Bubba took all crime in Basin Valley personally, homicide especially. It gave him an opportunity to sulk. "Any sign of my brother?"

Bubba turned full-face toward the editor. The sheriff wasn't a handsome man. He had a no-nonsense face and was built like a big chimp—huge chest cavity, short legs, powerful arms.

"You know, I should have put a few more two-and-twos together," the sheriff said.

Fenberg resisted the obvious math joke.

"We've got literally a hundred witnesses saying they've seen a giant wandering around, causing mischief. I look around town. How many mischief-making giants do we have in a community this size?" He didn't wait for Fenberg to answer "One."

Fenberg couldn't take his eyes off the blue plastic tarp and the lifeless mound underneath. Tracy. The baby. It was Tuberski who wouldn't let him look under the blanket at the hospital.

Fenberg shook his head quickly. "John's had his moments of breaking up a bar or wrestling with some lumbermen, but he isn't a killer. You know him as well as I do."

"Maybe he snapped. People do." Except for the badge and the thick leather gunbelt, Bubba could have been mistaken for a washing machine repairman.

"Not John."

"Knees are going to sleep," Bubba groaned, standing. Fenberg joined him. They both looked at the body. "I've been thinking. I've got a theory. It seems to me Norwood might have had a drug problem." As family, Bubba had never accepted John changing his name. "This looks like the work of maybe someone who was snorting that angel dust, what do you call it, that TSP."

"I think you mean PCP." corrected Fenberg. "TSP is an industrial cleaner."

"Oh. Well, hell. Whatever they call it technically. We've had a couple of arrests this year, and I'm telling you, it makes people do crazy things. We nailed some long-hair hippie last week who hadn't got the message the sixties were over. It took three of us to wrestle him to the ground. Shit. He probably didn't weigh one hundred fifty, wet. I thought he was going to break the handcuffs. Imagine what the stuff would do to a guy the size of Norwood."

That's not his name, thought Fenberg.

"Except John hates drugs," Fenberg said. He glanced away. Elaine was bending over, staring at something on the ground, maybe fifty yards away. "He doesn't even drink hard liquor. I live in the same house and see him sometimes more than I care to. Don't you think I'd be aware if he were taking drugs?" A gust of wind ripped through the open porch, and the old wooden beams creaked.

"Maybe you don't know him as well as you think," said Bubba, pulling up his belt around a big stomach. "I'll tell you what I know. This child wasn't just beaten, she was mangled, mangled badly."

"Gotten in touch with the parents yet?"

"Can't reach the father. Mother's on the way. Looks more like a traffic accident than any murder I've ever seen. Go ahead. Take a look for yourself."

"I'd rather not," said Fenberg.

"I think you should." Bubba squatted back down, lifting the cover off the girl. Fenberg winced. The soft body was now cold and stiff, the colors ugly. There were gaping wounds—bite marks on her arms, back, and legs. Her dress was ripped to shreds in the back and pulled up, exposing a mangled spinal column. She had evidently been caught from behind, dragged, and beaten. And bitten. Fenberg shivered. No. This was not right. Cover her up. Leave her her dignity. Bubba looked up. Fenberg had seen more than he wanted. The sheriff draped the tarp back over the body and stood.

"It looks like an animal did it," said Fenberg.

"An animal, huh?" Bubba jerked his head. A deputy ran into the house.

"I don't know. Perhaps some animal in a circus escaped. . . ."

"Last I remember, we don't have a circus in Basin Valley."

"Maybe one was passing through, a cage got jostled from a train."

"I'll check," said Bubba. "I'm a reasonable man. But I doubt it."

A little whirlwind of dust kicked up, bringing in a few of the advance-guard raindrops. The men turned their backs to the wind.

"Have you checked into the angle that this might be a cult killing? You know, a Charles Manson type of thing?"

"I haven't checked into much of anything," said Bubba, rubbing his beefy fingers over his salt-and-pepper flattop. "We just got here ourselves. We spent the better part of sundown and on with that family of campers from Iowa. Grisly. Same MO, too. They were torn to pieces. Happened at least forty-eight hours ago. Crows and ki-yotes got after the remains. You know, your brother was seen in the company of this girl for several hours earlier in the day."

Fenberg wasn't surprised. Tuberski liked younger women. The deputy came out of the house. He handed Bubba a large Baggie. Inside the plastic bag was a piece of paper.

"We found it inside, tucked into the typewriter," said the deputy. "It looks like a note for Mike," he said apologetically.

Bubba held it up, trying to balance it between the light from the house and the high-beams from a patrol car. He couldn't read it, but hell, he'd read it already. He handed it to Fenberg.

Dear Mikey,

   I'm truly sorry for what I've done, but I know in the end you'll understand.

   Explain it to the boys as best you can. I have a feeling in a few years we'll all be sitting around with the grandkids, having a good laugh at this one. And also, sincerely, dear brother, thanks for your support and go-ahead in this matter.

                                                      Adios,
                                                      Johnny

   PS As you can probably surmise, I won't be coming home. Please feel free to use my part of the grocery money to hire a part-time Contra housekeeper and don't overwater the houseplants.

"What the hell . . . ?" said Fenberg, turning the letter to make sure he was reading correctly.

If there was some joke that he and Tuberski would be laughing over in years to come, it certainly was flying over Fenberg's head.

Bubba didn't feel victorious about the confession. He placed a calloused hand on his cousin's shoulder. "You want to share with me the meaning of the part that says, 'thanks for the go-ahead'?"

"I have no idea," said Fenberg. Yes. It was Tuberski's signature.

"Didn't think you would. Think though. We're going to have to talk," said Bubba.

Fenberg nodded.

"He's probably up in the hills right now, I'd guess," said Michael's cousin, hitching up his belt again and staring off at the dark, silent guardians that surrounded Basin Valley on all sides. Tuberski loved the outdoors. Frequently, he'd disappear into the mountains for days. "I got a call into neighboring counties for some additional help. The Highway Patrol is here, but I think we're going to need more men anyway. I'm going to get a mounted search going. We'll probably ride out on horseback to look for him, but hell, that's just for appearance' sake. We won't find Tuberski in the dark."

"Nor would you want to," added the deputy.

Fenberg looked at the faces of the deputy, the paramedics, the state police. They looked away from Fenberg. Brother of a cannibal.

The sheriff reached into a squad car and pulled out the long chord to the two-way. "Six-Henry to station. Mary Jo, this is Bubba."

"Go ahead, Bub," a woman's voice scratched through the static. It was hard to bounce signals with all the rough terrain surrounding Basin Valley.

"Mary Jo, I'm still at Mikey's. I want you to give a call around and ask the Volunteer Mountain Rescue if they could meet out here within the hour."

"How many of them?"

"All of 'em, Mary. Tell them to be prepared for an all-nighter, cold and wet. We'll use Mikey's ranch as command central. . . . Do you mind?" he asked the editor.

The editor shook his head no.

"They can park the horse trailers up here, and ask Cecil to bring an extra horse for me and line up some food and hot coffee."

"You got it."

"Call the Magonogonovitch brothers, if you can find them."

There was silence on the other end.

"Did I copy you right, Sheriff?"

"That's a ten-four. Call the Magonogonovitch brothers. We might be getting a little storm, and we'll need all the help we can get, tracking at night and all."

"I don't exactly think they'll want to, Bubba. . . ." said Mary Jo with uncertainty.

"Tell them we're hunting Tuberski. They'll be here. We meet in one hour. Ten-four, over." He tossed the mike onto the front seat.

"I'm real sorry, Cousin," said Bubba, putting a chunky hand on Fenberg's shoulder. "I wish you'd come along. You're a good horseman, and you know the terrain. I'd feel better."

Bubba barked orders, and men moved rapidly around the front of the house. The commotion stopped when they heard a muffled yell.

"Someone needs help!" yelled a state trooper.

"Mr. Fenberg! Hey, Mr. Fenberg!"

It was Elaine Mitikitski.

"I've got a clue!"

"What the hell . . . ?" Bubba looked to Fenberg.

"New reporter."

"I found something!" she yelled.

"Sounds like she's in back of the house," said Fenberg.

A half-dozen men in heavy boots trotted around the house, to the back orchard. It was winter, the trees bare. Mitikitski was standing, bent at the waist, staring at something on the ground. The only light came from a dim forty-watt bug bulb over the stalls. Three horses looked on with curiosity, the warm breath from their nostrils huffing skyward. "Careful," she warned. "Don't stomp all over the area." She pointed to a pathway where the men could walk. Bubba, Fenberg, and four deputies tiptoed single-file to where she was standing.

"My God!" said one of the deputies, shining his flashlight on the ground. "Will you look at the size of that thing!"

It was the track of an unshod foot, nineteen inches long, seven inches wide at the ball, and five inches wide at the heel. A perfect print. A perfectly huge print.

"That Tuberski must have the biggest feet in the world," said another deputy. Crickets chirped in the woods nearby, and, as the mountain air froze rapidly, a light ground fog vaporized into air.

"I don't think so," said Fenberg.

There were four more prints, at eight-foot intervals, leading toward an adobe ruin. Whoever made them had climbed over the wall. Or stepped over it.

"What do you mean, you 'don't think so'?" asked the sheriff angrily.

"John wears a size sixteen boot," said Fenberg. "That's big, sure, but this print is longer than that and easily twice as wide. Geez, Bubba. Take a look for yourself."

Elaine stared at Fenberg, then at the sheriff, trying to find a family resemblance. There wasn't any. "May I interject something?" she asked.

"Who's she?"

"Elaine Mitikitski, the new reporter for *The Bugle*," said Fenberg.

Elaine smiled and blushed.

"Pleased to meet ya," said Bubba, jerking his head.

Elaine excused herself and guided Fenberg next to the print. "Not only is this print larger, but let me show you something. Mr. Fenberg, how much do you weigh?

Fenberg sucked in his stomach. "One-eighty-seven." Everyone looked at him blankly. "Two-O-eight." I hope you're happy.

"Okay," said Elaine. "Could you please just make a footprint right next to this one?"

Fenberg did.

"You see," said Elaine, "the print here is about two inches deep. Mr. Fenberg, who weighs around two hundred pounds, makes a footprint that is only a half-inch deep."

"So you're trying to tell me that whoever made this print weighed four times what Mikey does?"

"Yes," said Elaine. "About eight hundred pounds."

They heard the scream, and it was close, an eerie, high-pitched wail, lonely and terrifying, that rode with the cold winds down the canyon and made the hair on the back of the men's necks bristle.

"Sweet baby Jesus in the manger," whispered Deputy Cruz.

"What the hell was that?" asked Bubba.

Mitikitski found herself holding on to Fenberg's arm. The group of men looked at one another in silence. Flashlights darted against the curtain of dark forest, and Mitikitski expected a beam to catch some demonic eyes glaring red back at them. Ears strained to hear that pained, primeval scream again. Although the men in the group were well armed and bunched together, each felt alone and vulnerable.

"Let's move away from the woods. Let's go back to the house," said Fenberg. Everyone thought it was a good idea. As they walked, looking behind them all the way, Michael bent over to whisper in Elaine's ear. "This may be a shot in the dark, no pun intended, but when you get a chance, I'd like you to dig up what you can on the North American Abominable Snowman."

Elaine stopped. Michael stopped.

"The North American Abominable Snowman?" she repeated.

Fenberg smiled. "Mitikitski. This isn't Jack in the Box. Or the Grand Canyon. You don't have to repeat everything I say." He nodded his head and walked on.

"Sorry." Elaine stood alone. She looked back over her shoulder to the woods. The firs whistled and creaked in the wind, waving gently in front of the maniac's moon. From the thick branch of a distant tree, the great beast crouched, watching her. Mitikitski ran to catch up with the men.

9

ALL THE FINE YOUNG BIGFOOTS
or
ELAINE MITIKITSKI'S HISTORICAL ARGUMENT
FOR THE EXISTENCE OF NOT ONE,
BUT SEVERAL GIANT, HAIRY MONSTERS

The tired horse with the old furniture blanket draped over him tapped a hoof wearily on the sidewalk, snorting once and looking again through the window. Past Santa and his reindeer, drawn on *The Bugle* window by Tuberski and Clifford, the gelding could see Fenberg lying on the old green leather sofa. Mike was still wearing his full-length yellow rain slicker. A plastic-covered Stetson sheltered his eyes. It was ten miles closer to town than the ranch, and Fenberg had just ridden straight in to work from the manhunt. Odell Foley, the man who ran the local feed store, would be by in a few minutes to brush and feed Fenberg's tired mount, but of course the horse didn't know that. All he could see was Fenberg, asleep by the fireplace.

Actually, Fenberg wasn't quite asleep. He was trying to manufacture a pleasant dream about his wife and kid and at the same time, consciously figure out why things always went wrong. They had had this conversation before, he and his brother. Why do innocent babies die? Why do assholes who lie, cheat, and steal often make it to the top without any apparent punishment for their deeds? Why can't I ever stop thinking about my wife? Fenberg's eyes had patiently waited for an answer. Something tangible. Not hope or faith or belief. I don't want to be fooled or settle for a wish-you-well in the hereafter. I need a method. "Geez, buddy. Don't know," Tuberski had said. But Tuberski was working on it. There was some fundamental unit, one fundamentally monstrous thing common to all men, that was wrong with life. Of this Tuberski was certain.

Erupting vertically above the cozy hamlet of Basin Valley was the great Sierra rain forest, an area vaster in size than the state of Maine, largely unexplored, and in some spots, mapped only by air. Sheets of freezing rain wiped out any footprints, but still they had hunted John Tuberski with men, dogs, and horses. Except for Fenberg's cousin and the Magonogonovitch brothers, everyone in the forty-five-man posse secretly hoped they wouldn't bump into Tuberski in the dark. Only the hounds were uniformly eager.

The dogs were tireless. Sniffing low to the ground, they effortlessly glided across the scent Tuberski had left. At the base of the Timberlane, an alpine meadow about fifteen miles from the ranch, the dogs went no farther. They had picked up a new spore. All evening, through fog and rain, the dogs had galloped, chests out, eagerly snarling and yipping with gained confidence. Then they came upon the new scent and stopped. They whined and cowered. Sorry, fellas, excuse our disgustingly squirmish behavior, but this is as far as we go on what you're paying us. No amount of swearing or beating from their masters would make the hounds cross that grassy meadow.

A few minutes later, the posse had heard that ungodly scream again. A few of the men were thrown from their horses. It wasn't a cougar, one of the Magonogonovitch brothers clarified, although the howl was high-pitched and grating. It was long. And unhuman.

It had seemed surrealistic to Fenberg. The forest lit to extreme angles from the full moon peeking through the rain clouds. The long shadows of trees lashing back and forth in that insane wind. You could smell the fear. By dawn, the storm broke. They had not found Tuberski. A new shift would take over, with fresh men and horses. They would add helicopters to the search, and infrared body-heat-seeking devices. Later in the morning, they would call in the FBI.

In his dreams, Fenberg rode under a hangman's oak. Something large and furry fell from a branch, clutching at his throat. Fenberg sat up and coughed, throwing off the blanket. He swallowed air and looked wide-eyed around the room. There was Santa, still on the window, and the morning sun was pouring in.

"Howdy," said Mitikitski.

Fenberg took a deep breath and collapsed back on the couch.

"You look like you were ridden hard and put away wet, so I brought you a blanket," explained Elaine Mitikitski. Fenberg adjusted his hat and snuggled back down under the thick wool Pendleton. "Good morning, Mr. Fenberg."

Mr. Fenberg grunted.

Elaine placed a hot cup of tea on the hearth next to him. She leaned over and examined Fenberg closely, remarking that he was a little dirtier than she had expected.

Fenberg looked dully at her, then at the Constant Comment.

"That's not oat tea or anything, is it?" he asked suspiciously. "I've heard you're one of those organics."

"Loaded to the brim with caffeine," said Elaine, "which should deplete what remaining B vitamins you have in your body. No offense, Mr. Fenberg, but you look terrible."

"You're a sweet-talking dame, Mitikitski," said Fenberg, uncreaking his legs and sitting up. He took a big swig, then held the hot mug against his sinuses. He watched Mitikitski rummage through a pile of books.

Elaine smiled. She was wearing a high-fashion version of the official newspaper reporter's suit on this, her first day of work—Levi's, yellow-and-black plaid designer blouse, new running shoes, gray corduroy sports coat. With shoulder pads. Her nose and cheeks were still pink from the morning cold, and she looked disgustingly healthy. When she turned away from Fenberg, his eyes darted, trying to catch the silhouette of her breasts, estimating size and shape. It was habit. Fenberg had a wandering eye. And hand. And other things, if a woman let him get momentum. "From the looks of things, I take it there is no news yet on your brother," she asked, skimming through one of her volumes.

"Nope." Fenberg looked down at his expensive Tony Lama packer boots. They were caked with mud. So was he. He needed a shower. "I've got to go pick up the boys at Malulu's and take them to school," he said, standing.

"Oh, you don't have to," said Elaine. "Already taken care of."

"You already picked them up?" Fenberg asked.

Mitikitski turned around, but didn't look at Fenberg. She stared at the ceiling, trying to find a way to explain.

Angry Joe Fenberg and Clifford never made it all the way back to town the night before. After Fenberg had left with the posse, murder or not, bad environment for impressionable young boys or not, the fat housewife had crashed the police barricades to return Fenberg brothers number three and four.

"The little one—he . . . he . . . he . . . !" was all the corpulent babysitter could hysterically babble.

Mitikitski had bent down to look inside the car. The woman's frumpy bathrobe was torn, and her Annette Funicello was mussed. There was peanut butter smeared on her neck and ears.

"You really shouldn't dress that way," Elaine had suggested, deadpan. "It only excites them."

The woman shoved the boys out of the car, then brodied her station wagon out the front gate. Elaine put her arm around Clifford. He didn't resist. "Is anything sacred with you two?" she wanted to know.

"We like to watch," said Clifford.

"So they stayed at the ranch last night?" asked Fenberg. "With you? Alone? All night? In the same house?"

Mitikitski shrugged. "Yeah."

"Huh."

She didn't tell Fenberg that in the middle of the night, Clifford got scared and climbed in bed with Elaine. She rubbed the freckle-faced terror's back, as one is supposed to do with scared little boys. Clifford liked Elaine. She was soft. There was a pleasant give to her not present when John or Mike consoled him after a traumatic scrape, contusion, or run-in with Angry Joe. In the dark, Angry Joe had eavesdropped in the hallway outside Elaine's room, lonely, but too proud to go in.

Fenberg took off the rain slicker but left the hat on. He wandered around the office, sipping tea, turning on the UPI machine, waving to Odell through the window as the old-timer cared for his horse. Fenberg and Elaine chatted, about last night, the day ahead. She didn't want to probe, or ask something indelicate her first day, but Fenberg didn't seem overly concerned about the safety of his other brother, the one with the different last name. She rifled through pages. Has it dawned on you, Mitikitski, that maybe he's not overly concerned about his brother, who might be a cannibal, because he could be hiding him or may have been in cahoots with him from the very beginning? Hmmm, Elaine?

"Something bothering you, Mitikitski?" Fenberg asked.

"No." She shook her head.

Fenberg warmed his backside by the fireplace.

"Yes." She looked to Fenberg for encouragement, got none, but went on anyway. "Maybe it's me. I'm new. I've been blamed for being too sensitive. . . ."

"The measure of being alive is one's sensitivity, Mitikitski."

"Then why don't you seem more troubled about your brother's disappearance and possible involvement in a series of murders?"

Fenberg put his hand on his hip. You don't waste much time, do you? he thought. He sifted possibilities. Well, 1) I put up a good front. 2) I don't think I could stand another loss, thank you very much. 3) Maybe it's none of your beeswax.

But instead, Fenberg said, "What Tarzan is to Africa, John is to our particular section of North American flora. I've never known anyone, white or red, who adapts so well to such unforgiving country. He can live for a month in the woods and not get his T-shirt dirty, and no, Mitikitski, to answer your deepest, darkest fears, I'm not involved with his disappearance or the murders, and yes, Mitikitski, I believe the guy is innocent." Knock on wood.

Elaine wanted to crawl in a hole.

"Forget it. They're honest concerns," said Fenberg. "Where did you get all the books?"

"I didn't mean . . . I didn't want to come across . . ."

Fenberg shooed her off with a hand. Nonsense. "The books?"

"Okay. Don't you remember last night? You wanted me to dig up some background information on the Sasquatch. Here it is."

Fenberg wanted to brush his teeth. He made a quick count of the books from across the room, then glanced at the clock. A few minutes shy of eight. "Where did you get all that information at this hour of the morning? The library doesn't open for another two hours, and all they have anyway is a couple of dog-eared copies of *The Western Horseman*."

"They're mine," said Elaine, with a hint of smugness. "I'm sort of a follower of the Bigfoot. That's why those tracks intrigued me last night. . . ." She stopped. The tracks last night. Besides being the size of a compact dinosaur, there was something strange about them. Something didn't match.

"Earth to Mitikitski . . ." called Fenberg.

Elaine shook her head. "Sorry. Daydreaming. Anyway. I took this anthropology class from this professor who used to go on these summer expeditions looking for the Bigfoot. He was supposed to be one of the nation's foremost experts on the creature, though, I have to admit, all he ever brought back were slides of trees." Elaine neglected to mention they had dated.

"Is that so?" Fenberg rummaged around the office, looking for something to eat. He remembered Henry Darich's desk and snapped his fingers. "Do you still keep in touch with the guy?"

"God, no."

"Mitikitski!" Fenberg grinned. "Do I detect a note of bitterness in your voice?"

"It showed, huh?"

"That's okay. Bitterness gives you dimension. Character. And I thought you were just another pretty face. Oh, boy!"

said Fenberg, pulling out an unopened package of Nabisco Assortment cookies. "Treats. Well, listen. Let's not take turns delving into each other's personal tragedies the first day on the job. Why don't you brief me on what you have?"

Elaine thought that somehow she should be offended, but she wasn't. Fenberg settled back into a slouch on the sofa, rattling the cellophane wrapper. What a strange thing to say, she thought. It wasn't rude. His tone wasn't nasty. Oh, stop analyzing, Elaine, she chastised herself.

"Well," Elaine said, picking up a folder of notes but not reading from them, "from what I recall, there is a mountain of evidence to support the existence of not one, but a race of manlike creatures living in the uncharted regions of the United States. Even the world. Depending on where you come from, these creatures are known by many names—Bigfoot, Ragman, Yeti, plain old Abominable Snowman, although that's passé, Omah."

Fenberg munched on cookies and took in Elaine's figure, looking away whenever Elaine looked at him.

"I've read these creatures are incredibly strong, maybe as strong as ten men. Case in point." Mitikitski opened the file. "In July of 1936, an old Indian medicine man named Frank Don testified he had seen a Bigfoot strangle a full-grown grizzly with its bare hands."

"It'd take a big set of mitts," said Fenberg.

"I beg your pardon?"

Fenberg held up his hands. "Mitts."

"Oh. Uh, yes. Well. The Bigfoot's principal domain is the Pacific Northwest, but as I said, it's been seen in just about every spot on the globe. In the last two hundred years, there have been countless reported sightings and dozens of documented encounters. Tape recordings have been made of the thing's voice, and there are a few fuzzy photos and a 16mm movie of the Sasquatch. The famous Patterson film."

"The one with Arnold Schwarzenegger and Audrey Hepburn?"

Mitikitski cleared her throat. She stood with one hand on her hip and read through the notes. "Essentially though, there's little hard evidence to support the existence of such a race of creatures."

"What do you mean?"

"It's just with all these bits and pieces of information, adding up to thousands of articles of evidence. No one has ever actually stumbled upon a dead one in the woods. Although some speculate that this race of hairy hominids could be an offshoot of an ancient species, *giganpethicus*, supposedly extinct for tens of thousands of years. Point being that they, like say, Cro-Magnon, buried their dead. The scientific community generally pooh-poohs—"

"They what?"

"Stop interrupting. They . . . the scientific community cannot buy the notion that something weighing between three and nine hundred pounds, completely covered with fur, standing six to ten feet tall, and walking upright like a man could exist so close to civilization in this day and age without being captured." Mitikitski looked down at Fenberg. She thought he would be overwhelmed by her research. He wasn't.

"The professor I used to know," she said, "the one who was one of the top experts on Bigfoot in the world?"

"It was the nation a few minutes ago," said Fenberg. "Your boyfriend, right?"

"He even theorizes that in some respects, these creatures are smarter than we are."

"That doesn't say much for our newspaper staff."

Elaine took a deep breath. "I was speaking in general." Fenberg stood to pour more tea. He offered Elaine some. "Please," she said, producing her own herbal blend from her purse. She sniffed for impurities and took a sip. "Some three hundred years ago, the padres left records in several California missions that told of seeing huge, hairy demons, or of finding giant footprints close to their graveyards. Many North American Indians even worshiped huge, no-necked, bullet-headed gods."

"Sounds like my wife," said Fenberg, sitting on the ledge by the window and looking out. He glanced heavenward.

"Just kidding, dear."

Elaine ignored the interruption, but made a mental note to ask Malulu about the late Mrs. Fenberg. "Not much was written about these creatures until the California Gold Rush. Here's something interesting." She pulled out a photostatic copy. "In 1892 when Teddy Roosevelt was going through his cowboy stage, he wrote a book called *The Wilderness Hunter*. It was about two mountain men who were out in the backcountry checking their traps."

Fenberg opened his mouth, and Elaine held up a hand.

"When they returned to camp, all their gear had been ransacked, and there were these giant footprints all over the place. Human in shape. So, they went off by themselves to look for whatever made these footprints, one following the tracks, one circling around. After a few hours, one of the hunters returned to the rendezvous point, and there he found his partner. Every bone in his body was broken. His jugular was ripped open."

Fenberg sat at the window, staring down the street. It had gotten to him last night, when the mother had arrived, forcing her way past the deputies to see what remained of her daughter. Linda Behan was a pale, scrubbed woman who wore sunglasses at all hours, and Fenberg smelled the unmistakable odor of alcohol seeping from her pores. What little Fenberg had seen of her gave the impression of a woman who was always terrified and drank to forget about it.

"And then there was this other case in Oroville," said Elaine, reading and pacing. "A guard was found at the entrance to a mine. Just like the hunter. Just like Darla Behan, every bone in his body was broken."

The final straw. That's what Mrs. Behan had said, standing dumbstruck over the covered body. Fenberg wondered what she had meant. Linda Behan had shaken her head, over and over, repeating, no, not this way. She wouldn't be consoled, wouldn't accept an arm or blanket. Fenberg understood. The final straw, Mrs. Behan had said, suddenly straightening and apologizing for making a scene. She said she wanted to drive around for a while, sort things out, find a way to explain it to her husband. Fenberg looked across the street. M. J. Behan would be opening his newspaper in a few days.

"You know what I can't figure out," wondered Elaine. "Let's just say, for argument's sake, there is a giant manlike undiscovered species, and that for whatever reason, one of these creatures goes bananas and starts killing people. He's hiding in the foothills and sees Darla walking up to the ranch, catches her, and kills her. It obviously happened in the front yard. I would think she would have screamed. I would. I think." This time, Elaine didn't say anything. But then, she added to herself, if I were a subhuman species gone bananas, I wouldn't walk into the house and forge a confession note on a typewriter.

"Maybe she didn't scream," said Fenberg. "Maybe whatever she saw left her petrified with fear."

"She wasn't too petrified to pull out a hunk of the thing's hair," said Elaine, wondering what color Tuberski's hair was.

Fenberg was listening. He was thinking of Charlie the Indian, the story about the bride pulling the hair out of the creature. The bride of the beast. "Scream or not, where the hell was John?" asked Fenberg, standing, suddenly a little agitated. "Why did he run off? And what the hell is the story about that stupid note he left? Forged by someone else? And why hasn't anyone ever been able to capture one of these creatures?"

"They did." Elaine shuffled through another pile of notes and books. "Here. One of the more famous incidents. July 3, 1884, in Yale, British Columbia. Crewmen stopped their train when they saw a hairy creature apparently asleep on the tracks. I guess what had happened was he fell off a ledge and knocked himself unconscious."

"I've done that a few times myself," said Fenberg, rubbing the back of his neck." In a few days, Tuberski's head will be poking around that corner wearing that impish grin, Fenberg thought. I'll be mad, but there'll be an explanation.

"After a few years, they lost track of the little fella," said Elaine. "He probably died in some sideshow."

"So why would a larger version of this thing visit my ranch

and do a Cuisinart on my competition's oldest daughter?" asked Fenberg. "Huh? Have you an answer for that one?" He moved over to a swivel chair and carefully put his feet up on the desk.

Mitikitski shrugged. A reason? Perhaps, sex?

She sneezed.

There were actually two precedents for a Yeti forcing his attentions on women of the human kind. There was, of course, Charlie Two Eagles Soaring Johnson's folktale, and a story originating in British Columbia that supposedly took place in the 1870's. A Bigfoot evidently carried off another Indian woman and kept her in a cave for nearly a year. According to the Canadian Royal Mounted Police records, the woman finally escaped and returned to her village—several months pregnant. Versions of what happened to the bastard child differed. Some said the baby was stillborn or died shortly after birth. Others said the child-creature was raised by Indians, away from the eyes of the white man, and later escaped to join its own kind.

Elaine shivered. Suffering through the sexual act, which Elaine suspected was undignified anyway, with a smelly, nine hundred pound, well, never mind. She didn't want to think about it.

"So. Do you have a boyfriend?" Fenberg asked.

Mitikitski flinched. "Respectfully intended, what's it to you?"

Fenberg sat with hands behind head, leaning back in the chair. "Just nosy."

Mitikitski nodded understandingly. She walked over to the silver-framed picture of his dead wife Tracy and picked it up. She walked back and placed the eight-by-ten frame on Fenberg's desk and adjusted it a quarter-inch. It faced Fenberg like a crucifix, and he half-smiled, half-smirked.

"That's pretty funny, Mitikitski," he said.

10

FENBERG ASKS MITIKITSKI ON A DATE

Fenberg paced in front of Elaine Mitikitski's apartment door, debating a question of ethics. It was cold. Was it ethical to ask a staff member on a date when she had only been on the payroll for three days, and was it considered appropriate to ask her on a date the morning of a funeral?

"This is not like me," mumbled Fenberg to himself. "I am off-balance; I am way ahead of myself. I am rushing things. I'm going to embarrass myself and get slapped and laughed at." What would Abigail Van Buren say?

Dear Off-Balanced,
   My! It certainly is nice that you have these feelings for this young, pretty and capable lady, and I know your intentions are completely honorable. But good heavens, Mike, wait until she's settled into her apartment!
                                                Signed,
                                                Abby

Boink Abby. I'm going to ask her.

Fenberg rang the doorbell. And knocked. Several times. Finally, he heard a yell to hold on, she was coming, and the shuffling of bedroom slippers.

"Morning," said Fenberg, beaming. "I came to pick you up for the funeral."

Mitikitski blinked stupidly at Fenberg. She was wearing a tattered yellow terry cloth bathrobe, and her thick black hair was matted. There was a crease on her cheek where it had been folded over and slept on. But she looked beautiful to Fenberg.

"Funeral?"

"Uh-huh."

Mitikitski sniffed and looked down the deserted street. "I think you've got this all confused with golf," said Elaine. "While both use rolling expanses of finely clipped lawns, lakes, and a snack bar, golf is played at six thirty in the morning, which is right after dawn. Funerals generally start at tenish."

Fenberg smiled and stood at attention.

"Come in," Elaine yawned and waved weakly, shuffling back inside. "Come in."

Fenberg stepped inside, then hesitated. "God, I woke you, didn't I?"

"No, no," said Elaine, who couldn't stop yawning. "I was going to get up early and do a little duck hunting before the funeral. Blast those little mallards before they had a chance to drink their morning coffee." Elaine folded her arms and leaned against the wall. She had found this apartment her second day in Basin Valley, and Fenberg had helped move her boxes and few pieces of furniture.

"I thought I'd bring you a flower," said Fenberg, producing a long-stemmed rose from behind his back.

Elaine sniffed. "It smells pretty."

"Yeah. They do."

"Are we going in halvsies for the funeral or is this for me?" she asked, rubbing it under her nose.

"It's all yours," said Fenberg. Clifford had counted the bouquet Michael brought home from the florist the night before and noticed there was one extra.

Elaine yawned. "I'm sorry. I guess I'm just bushed. It's been so hectic the last three days, and I really haven't had a good night's sleep. I guess I'm feeling sort of punchy."

Damn. "I think maybe I'd better come back in a few hours," Fenberg said.

"No, no. Stay. I'll make us some breakfast," said Elaine, although she didn't budge from holding up the wall. She looked at the flower then at Fenberg. "What?"

"What-what?" asked Fenberg.

"I've got a feeling," she said.

"What kind of feeling?" asked Fenberg.

"The kind of feeling that you've come here to fire me, tell me something's troubling you, or to ask me something difficult."

"Well . . ." Fenberg stared at his well-shined boots. He had gotten dressed for Darla Behan's funeral at 4:30 in the morning. "There is something I'd kinda like to ask you."

"I'm all ears," said Elaine, yawning.

Elaine had rented a pleasant, spacious upstairs apartment on a quiet residential street. Most of her boxes were still unpacked, but on the high shelf that went all the way around the top of the room a forest of porcelain and stuffed animals sat poker-faced, watching. Fenberg thought they must know a lot about Mitikitski. He stirred the air with a hand. "I, uh."

"Well said."

"Let me lay my cards on the table. This is probably not the best time or even the best way to go about this. I'm not usually this way. I've dated somewhat, and in the last . . . no. I'd like to start over."

Elaine yawned.

"I'd like to preface this by saying that I have no great expectations, and what I'm about to ask you has no bearing on me being your employer and you feeling that you have to go out with me." Sexual harassment suit. That flashed through Fenberg's mind. He went on. "I'd like to ask if you'd like to maybe go out on a regular, boy-girl date. Maybe dinner. Bore each other about our past, embellishing where appropriate. A traditional walk you to the door, thank you for the wonderful evening, please don't try and spoil it date. Maybe I haven't done this very well, but," he swallowed, "would you like to go on a date with me, Mitikitski?"

Mitikitski was catching flies. Her arms dangled, and her mouth was open. She was still leaning against the wall, asleep on her feet. Like a horse.

"Shit," said Fenberg.

Fenberg left her there, walked over to the sofa, and sat down. He drummed his fingers on the arm of the couch, trying to formulate a plan. Shit. This was way too early. This is pushing things. This is acting out of desperation. Man or mouse?—man or mouse?—his brain chanted at him. He thought. He combed his hair. Maybe he should write a note and leave. No. He needed to counter immense stupidity with boldness. Fenberg silently vaulted off the sofa. He stood, frozen, in front of Mitikitski, evaluating how to pick her up. One arm under the legs, the other behind the back, the basic bridegroom carry. Mitikitski was snoring. Fenberg gingerly carried her to the bedroom, neatly dodging lamps and doorways. He tucked her under the covers, and she snuggled and smiled contentedly, and Michael smiled too. She was so damn pretty. He sighed and shook his head, torn between two urges: 1) to kiss her on the squeaky clean cheek, the unfolded one, or, 2) to take a pen and blacken one of her front teeth and leave a quarter under her pillow. Fenberg compromised. He kissed her gently, then left forty-seven cents on the pillow close to her ear. Fenberg picked up the fallen rose and tiptoed out of her apartment, lightly closing the door behind him.

THE FUNERAL

Elaine Mitikitski spent most of the funeral looking confused. She'd look up at Fenberg. Fenberg would look straight ahead.

"Were you in my apartment this morning?" Mitikitski whispered.

"Shhh," said Fenberg.

It was the day before Christmas, and, yuletide or not, people still died and had to be buried. Cases in point, the Behan girl in front and a few rows down elderly Mrs. Villareal. It was a contrast in style.

The Reverend Tuller shrugged helplessly, casting an apologetic glance over wire-rimmed glasses at M. J. Behan and his wife. There was nothing to do but wait until the noise died down. The Villareals and Lopezes, Basin Valley's two premier Hispanic families, were out in force. Cause of death was unspectacular—old age. Still, close to eight thousand pounds of ancient, toothless women dressed in basic *National Geographic* black competed in their sorrow, moaning and beating their breasts with rosaries as the proud young priest paid final respects in Spanish. He ended the service with a sign of the cross and a nod. Men lowered the coffin by rope into a dark rectangular hole. As a final upstage to death, one woman screamed and fell awkwardly backwards, her arms flaying as if she were trying not to fall into a swimming pool. She grabbed her husband by the tie, taking him down with her.

Reverend Tuller held the Bible rigidly in front and cleared his throat.

About twenty-five yards away, on an elevated knoll hidden by ratty scrub oak and brush, the creature, the one that had earlier chased Elaine Mitikitski through the woods and pulled on her ankle, lay on his stomach, hands cupped under chin. He absentmindedly kicked his heels together. He wasn't much of a monster, or even a maniac. Indeed, he looked more like a young Oliver Hardy, with a flat, catcher's-mitt face. He watched the proceedings with interest.

"What is the divine plan that would steal such a young girl in the flower of youth?" Tuller asked heaven. Heaven did not respond. "We cannot question. We can only . . ."

The creature had been to funerals before. On this particular day he had been sauntering through the neighboring woods and, with his keen sense of hearing, picked up the sobs and whimpering from the two large groups. He had been attracted. He sensed the remorse. It raised questions. His huge, hairy rib cage heaved with a sigh, and he wiggled to get comfortable. Basin Valley's version of Boot Hill was nestled among the grassy, rolling foothills a few miles out of town. There were trees and overgrown shrubs in this lush little valley, which provided plenty of camouflage and easy access to the graveyard. Funerals intrigued him, although he didn't know what they were. Maybe he was sad because everyone else was.

"Darla was a good girl," said Tuller, nodding his head. "A comfort to her mother and father. A real . . ."

Trooper? thought Fenberg.

Credit to her race? thought Mitikitski.

Team player? thought Bean Breath Brown.

There were close to a hundred people in dark clothes surrounding the white casket, most from Behan's new congregation. But what had really attracted the creature's attention was a tall, willowy woman with nice calves in the black dress and big hat. The creature thoughtfully sniffed his hand and made a soft, whimpering sound. She was wearing a veil, but the creature could tell, even through the crowd, that it was the woman he had chased. The creature breathed deeply, feeling the pressure in his chest. He had been having this strange shortness of breath lately and didn't know why.

"We must pray diligently for her salvation and equally hard for the salvation of the misguided soul that took this young woman's life. . . ."

A breeze stirred up leaves, and veils fluttered in the wind. Everyone looked at Fenberg.

". . . for what does it profiteth a man to pray for his brother and not his enemy? It is a prayer that will not be answered in heaven."

The creature had the gift. He was intelligent. Not as smart as Mike or Elaine, but certainly sharper than the Magonogonovitch brothers. From his vantage point, the beast had a clear picture of Elaine. She was standing next to a man in a three-piece suit, and in front of him were two boys, the taller in black leather and earring, the shorter with flattened red hair and ill-fitting sports coat. Elaine looked up at Fenberg and smiled. Fenberg raised an eyebrow and smiled back. The creature deduced that Fenberg must be her mate. The hairy voyeur raised up on elbows to get a better look at the man, and his eyes narrowed. His upper lip quivered, and he uttered a low, guttural growl. Then he sniffed, dismissing Fenberg as small potatoes.

The Bigfoot had no idea there was a body in the shiny white box. Likewise, he didn't know that Darla Behan's body had been subjected to numerous probes and cuts in a lengthy autopsy that only brought more questions than answers.

The coroner's office hadn't issued a statement yet, though everyone had an opinion. Half the citizenry believed John Tuberski had finally gone screaming yellow bonkers and had mistaken Darla and the Duffields as hors d'oeuvres. M. J. Behan and his new following of loyal charismatics held to that theory, spicing it up that Tuberski was the devil come-to-Earth and should be skewered over a low flame. Fenberg disagreed, though he admitted such a stunt would boost circulation.

Some people, who had seen or heard of the clump of hair

clutched in Darla Behan's hand, held to the bear-gone-
berserk theory. From the amount of flesh consumed and the
bite radii, it seemed a reasonable possibility.

That's when the FBI threw a monkey wrench into the
works. Because there was the possibility that Tuberski may
have crossed the state line, the FBI was called in twenty-four
hours after the discovery of Darla's body. Their lab team
released these disturbing facts.

The tuft of hair wasn't from a bear, and it wasn't Tuberski's.
Too long, too straight, too thick. Wrong color. The hair sam-
ple found in Darla Behan's hand was black with silver tips. It
didn't belong to any known species of mammal. It did pos-
sess all the properties of human hair, yet, it wasn't human.

"Did you come over early this morning?" Mitikitski finally
asked, whispering out of the corner of her mouth. She stared
piously at her black high heels.

"No," Fenberg whispered back.

Mitikitski looked troubled. "I had the strangest damn
dream."

"How was I?" asked Fenberg.

A few mourners threw darted stares across the grave.

"It wasn't that kind of dream," she said, not moving her
lips and looking straight ahead.

Tuller continued. "And as we lay to rest the body but not
the soul of this young woman . . ."

Early that morning, three days after Darla made her transition, a little baby girl came back into the world. Fenberg,
who had hours to kill after sneaking out of Mitikitski's apartment, visited the infant. It was one of his favorite pastimes,
peeking through the big glass window at the hospital nursery. Tuberski, who believed in reincarnation, said that God,
in his infinite wisdom, made it so that people could come
back as little soft babies. It gave them a chance to be loved
and held. It allowed them time to rest up from the previous
life's heartbreak before they went at it all over again. It was a
comforting private thought to Fenberg.

"Amen," the Reverend Tuller said. He pushed the button
on the hydraulics that gently whirred and lowered the casket

into the ground.

Mitikitski looked across the grave. It was a gray December morning, as if the day didn't feel like going to work. M. J. Behan was glowering at the hole in the ground. He fiercely clenched a handful of dirt, but wouldn't throw it on the coffin. His mouth moved rapidly, and Elaine guessed he was praying. Shrunken by grief, Behan looked gaunt and tired in his big overcoat. He still wore the glazed look of shock and rage, and behind him were five score darkly dressed mourners. No one stood with Elaine, Bean Breath Brown, and the Fenberg brothers. Them against us, thought Mitikitski.

"I'm going to pay my respects," said Fenberg. A line was forming of other people doing likewise. "Say, listen," said Fenberg nonchalantly. He and Elaine took a small step forward. "It's Christmas Eve tonight and, well . . ." They moved closer to Behan. "If you don't have any plans, please come over. There'll be plenty to eat, and the boys would love to have you. I'm cooking. I don't know if that's a deterrent or not." Mitikitski felt like holding his arm, but no, that wouldn't be appropriate in public.

When it came Fenberg's turn to offer respects, M. J. Behan slapped him. Actually, because he was older and weakened by the trauma, he *tried* to slap Fenberg but ended up wafting the top of Michael's head. It caused quite a stir. Behan collapsed to the ground, letting out a pent-up torrent of anguish and crying that he had killed his daughter. By his own hand, he had killed his daughter. Fenberg bent down next to Behan and rubbed his back, just the way he'd done for Angry Joe and Tuberski that week when it seemed everyone had died.

"It's no big deal," said Fenberg. "He's just crying."

A few yards away in the bushes, the Bigfoot lowered his eyebrows, sniffing the air as if trying to glean through scent some understanding. There was the sadness smell. That he recognized. But there was another odor riding the air that disturbed him. Oh, well. He couldn't place it. Remember, he had no tail, hated dogs, and liked to go to the movies. The drive-in, actually. His internal clock told him it was Wednesday, and tonight they would be changing features.

12

CHRISTMAS WITHOUT TUBERSKI

There was a light snowfall Christmas Eve. Smoke content-
ēdly puffed starward from the Fenberg chimney. A rare gray
fox, in thick winter coat, grumpily trotted across the front
yard to the woods beyond and while those closest to Fenberg
were either dearly departed, or crazy, at least for tonight God
was in heaven and all was right with the world.

Elaine Mitikitski sat in the bed of Fenberg's parents. She
wore Fenberg's soft faded red flannel logging shirt and her
long legs were tucked under the cozy blanket. She thoughtfully tapped her pen on the lined note pad Clifford had lent
her, and wrote:

Dearest Sister Mol,

*I believe when we last spoke, I was reporting about the
actual sighting of men with muttonchops. Well. Since
then, my darling Kamali Molly, a lot has happened.
Right now, I'm writing you from the bed of my employer,
and all I've got on is his shirt (just like in the commer-
cials). But before you raise a well-plucked eyebrow, my
trampy sibling, I want to assure you everything's on the
up-and-up, no pun intended.*

*I spent most of the day here and I must say, I can't
remember ever having such a fun, free time. On the
minus side, Sis, I'm feeling that god-awful goddamn*

gravitational pull again. Yes. It's true. The, spit, L-word. But we'll get into that later. Why am I in my boss's shirt?

Innocent and boring. He and his brothers (the two that aren't missing) and our noble sports editor, one Mr. Brown, and yours truly had a take-no-prisoners snowball fight. I was drenched, exhausted, and more happy than I can ever remember being. I was called a dyke by the youngest of these Fenberg men, and I made the little red-haired hermaphrodite eat slush.

And how are you? Spending another holiday in a swank four-star hotel tanked to the gills with yet another nameless Samoan lifeguard, I trust? Sigh. You know, I really, really miss you, Sis. I wouldn't say you'd like it up here, but you'd like Michael.

He is so full of life and pain.

And, of course, Mol, he's cute.

I was helping him wrap presents earlier in the day. Christmas here, is, by the way, an assault on the senses. There are four generations of decorations literally covering every square inch of the house, which is sort of a to-scale version of the Ponderosa. The place lacks, or at least has misplaced, the woman's touch. There's a slate fireplace that covers a full wall, and they've got a black-and-white cowhide sofa, and I suspect they don't know how much it's worth. There are enough twinkling bulbs to light a casino, and the late Mrs. Michael Fenberg had sewn green-and-red elf costumes for all these Teddy bears.

I must find out more about her some day, Elaine thought, pausing.

I can't be certain, Sis. But I think my boss asked me out on a date.

Earlier in the day, Mitikitski had helped Fenberg wrap his brothers' presents. Fat logs crackled and snapped in the fireplace, and Mitikitski eyed Fenberg with suspicion. And a certain measure of veiled mushiness. Fenberg was wearing a white cowboy shirt with the sleeves rolled up around his bulging biceps. He wore jeans and expensive boots, a festive reindeer sweater vest, and an obnoxious green-and-red light-up battery-powered bow tie. During the afternoon, Clifford and Joe had been locked in the tack room of the barn, a time-honored tradition due to the fact that their presents were always wrapped at the last minute, due to the fact that if Fenberg ever brought home a present early, they'd find it, no matter where it had been hidden. But the two boys had been released for the festivities. Clifford attacked Fenberg, and Fenberg effortlessly held him at bay with one big arm. He caught Elaine staring deeply at him. He half-smiled, half-smirked, the light from the fireplace making him look somehow fatherly, sexy, and dangerous all at the same time.

Elaine's and Mike's heads were only a foot apart. It would be the most natural thing if they kissed. Elaine had wondered what the first would be like. It would be a nice one. A soft kiss. No tongues. Tongues would make her sneeze.

And Mitikitski had sneezed.

"Ah-choo!"

"Godzilla," Fenberg had said.

"A-choo-choo!"

"Godzilla-Godzilla." Mitikitski sneezed three more times, then stopped.

"Here. Blow," said Fenberg, providing her with a clean hankie from his back pocket. Michael's thick, wavy hair hung whimsically over his collar and curls peeked around his ears. He held the hankie to her nose. She smiled apologetically through watery eyes. She and Michael had looked at each other, with the two boys looking back and forth between the staring adults. Mitikitski felt that attraction. She sneezed again. And again. And again.

It had started.

" 'Scuse me," said Elaine, standing and sneezing. She zigzagged her way out of the living room, providing her own exploding sound effects as she exited.

"Godzilla," said Fenberg, slapping at Clifford's small hand

trying to tear at some paper.

Fenberg had attributed Elaine's nasal expulsions to allergies, and he wasn't far off.

Mitikitski never had much luck with sex and subconsciously decided that to sneeze made a larger statement than just saying no.

Mitikitski considered sex a bizarre and frivolous pastime. How would you describe sex to a person from another planet? "Well, the girl takes off her clothes and sort of gets down on her back like this, and the guy . . ."

She could imagine talking to the android Data from "Star Trek," and he would look at her with that curious one-raised-eyebrow expression.

". . . and while the guy is doing what he's doing, pumpetta-pumpetta, the girl breaks down in tears and continuously sneezes," she'd say to the robotic commander.

Sneezing.

It had started the last time Elaine Mitikitski had had herself a man, the last time she had made love to her husband, Norman the Mormon. At first, sex had been great. There had been that heightened, narcotizing electricity present that Elaine ironically thought she'd never fall prey to, and after experiencing that Mitikitski was cursed. In the beginning, she and Norman would get away for long weekends and never leave the room, or rendezvous at odd hours and places with Mitikitski afterwards sporting the telltale signs of beard burn on her face, glassy eyes, and appearance askew. *Sex is what's ruining our country*, wrote Elaine to Kamali. Elaine looked out at the light snowfall.

They were married, and Elaine loved Norman passionately, ignoring his endless character flaws. Norman the Mormon lost no time cheating on Mitikitski. Elaine came home early from work one day and discovered a nubile freshman in her birthday suit gleefully bouncing up and down with this person with whom she had exchanged these rather lofty vows. Norman told her to close the door on the way out. Fearing some supernatural curse for being twenty-five and divorced two times already, Elaine did her damnedest to make the relationship work. Norman, charmer that he was, apologized for past indiscretions and promised great promises involving the turning over of new leaves and the putting forward of best feet. Yet he continued to sleep around, and when she called him on it he slapped her and made fun of her sterility. He came home drunk one night, stinking of beer and cigars. He forced himself on Mitikitski. She sneezed on him.

Which was all well and fine, except that Elaine couldn't stop sneezing for two days after that. And that's when Norman had gone through her purse, taken her keys, and held up that convenience store. *Oh, Molly. I'm lost.*

Elaine had written nine pages to her sister. Dinner would be on in ten minutes, and Mitikitski wasn't dressed and still sported the dreaded pre-dinner tangly hair.

> *There's something wrong with me. And life. There's something wrong with love. Some magic word, huh? "I love you." I've said that to at least three men, with deep sincerity at the time. They've all, in their own way, looked at me as if I had said some terrible swear word and maybe I did. All I know is I can't stand one more disappointment in life, Sis. And this damn guy Michael I'm afraid could hurt me to the quick. No. No more for me. I think he and I can be friends, but if he asks me out again I'm going to turn my hat backwards and read him the riot act. Gotta run. Let's talk on the tele.*
>
> *Your smarter and prettier sister,*
> *Elaine Mitikitski*

*   *   *   *   *

Christmas Eve went off without a hitch. Mitikitski didn't sneeze or read anyone the riot act, and Fenberg didn't panic. Neither could remember laughing so much. Elaine overate, a rare indulgence, and spent the rest of the night with her jeans unbuttoned underneath the oversized sweater she had borrowed from Fenberg. The three Fenbergs, Elaine, and Bean Breath Brown sat in the living room by the roaring fire, and, at midnight, opened presents. Bean got a new camera lens and a gift certificate to the local dentist. Angry Joe actually smiled and managed a sincere thank-you to Michael when he shredded the paper off a new electric Fender Stratocaster with a Mesa/Boogie amp. Just like the kind the real Billie rockers use. Clifford liked to play army, taking hours to set up his men, then destroying both sides with dirt clods or the garden hose in a five-minute Wagnerian crescendo. As Clifford had bitten off the heads or burned most of the old set, Fenberg gave him twenty-five packages of Army men—the good kind—and a high-powered water nozzle for the hose with the warning that he not use the nozzle to topple the foundation to the house or any solid structure on the property. Fenberg also threw in a wig, a ghastly Halloween mask, two puppets, and a framed, autographed picture of Anthony Perkins.

Mitikitski got a real cowgirl belt, tooled leather, silver buckle, the whole marianna.

"Thank you," she said, awkwardly tapping Fenberg on the knee. She didn't know protocol in this situation and didn't want to risk a hug for fear of sneezing.

Mitikitski sank back in the big tan corduroy chair, and looked around the living room. It was a cozy home, remarkably orderly, with the heavy hand of a man's touch a little too evident in the decorating. Yes, the place could use a little color here and there. Maybe make that window a little larger. More houseplants. Elaine's eye wandered to the huge oak mantel where, lodged between all these ancient football and basketball trophies, was a framed photo of Mike and John in their younger years. Butch haircuts. Tuberski was grinning and had his arm around Fenberg. Buddies.

By 1:00 A.M., Angry Joe, guitar in hand, was silently bouncing off the walls in his room. He had his headphones plugged into an MTV radio simulcast in stereo and was launching himself off the bed, doing the splits in midair.

In the living room, Bean Breath Brown had passed out from a sugar overdose and lay spread-eagled on the floor with an eight-quart stainless steel bowl over his head. Clifford had fallen asleep on Elaine's lap, and Fenberg, ever planning for the future, made sure he was next to Elaine when she fell asleep so she could nuzzle into his chest.

As the fire died to a few glowing embers, Fenberg smiled. Elaine filled his arms nicely. Michael looked up at the mantel, and Tracy smiled back. Fenberg felt the moisture rising in his eyes. He shook his head violently and looked away.

13

YOUR CHECK IS IN THE MAIL

By New Year's, no one else had been killed or eaten, but the search for John Tuberski continued.

They couldn't find him.

They couldn't find a single clue, though in the past week several tracking dogs had been thrown into the lake.

Although she was 0-for-6 in trying to sneak *"It was a dark and stormy night. . . ."* past Fenberg into one of her leads, Elaine was learning the ropes to this newspaper business. Tuberski wasn't the only story in town. There were other dramas, real life adventures, and current events for the mighty *Bugle* to cover.

Arlene Gullfoil, a cocktail waitress at the Timbermoon Lanes, Basin Valley's only combination bowling alley and night spot, had bludgeoned her sweetheart Rocky Hortman to death with a ball peen hammer. Mitikitski rushed to the scene, steno pad in hand, to ask for motive. Arlene took a puff off her cigarette and calmly told Mitikitski that she just hadn't particularly cared for Rocky's attitude anymore.

There were stories about several auto accidents that had occurred on the ice-slick highways, accompanied by a Bean Breath Brown modern art photo of unrecognizable twisted metal, and the senior citizens' mobile home park had once again been rinsed away down the wash during a vengeful four-day rainstorm.

Elaine checked her watch and sprinted around the office.
She was late meeting Fenberg and still had to close up shop.
It was exciting being in the middle of a newspaper war,
though it was hard to tell who was winning. Everyone still
read *The Bugle*. It had a dramatic, mystery-radio style to its
hard news stories and a folksy, humorous touch to its features. M. J. Behan's newly formed *Christian Clarion* was
pompous, filled with PR for the sanctimonious. No one read
it. But because Behan offered ridiculously low advertising
rates, he was stealing customers by the busload. After his first
week in business, Behan, by offering such things as twenty-
four-inch color TV's with every eighth-page ad, had taken
twenty-three percent of Fenberg's ad lineage away.

"Turn off the Xerox, leave on the UPI," Elaine mumbled to
herself as she scampered around editorial.

But at least for Mitikitski, today had been a milestone. She
had dummied and laid out the entire paper. Some of the girls
in pasteup commented it was one of the nicer looking edi-
tions, and Fenberg begrudgingly grumbled, "Yeah, for a girl."

Mitikitski nervously checked the clock and gasped. "Late.
Late." She was supposed to meet Fenberg for a seven o'clock
movie at the Northern Savoy.

She locked the front door of the office and jogged across
the damp street, her high heels tapping each step. It wasn't
hard to spot Mitikitski in the dark. She was wearing an oversized bright yellow wool Perry Ellis sports jacket with huge
shoulder pads, white blouse, dangling Alliklik silver jewelry,
and skintight Guess jeans. Most of the ensemble had been
sent by Kamali Molly as a fashion CARE package.

Elaine was half-running, half-walking, digging through her
purse for money. She wasn't looking where she was going.
Two fat hands grabbed her by the arms.

"Oh!"

Lom Magonogonovitch held onto Elaine. His brother,
Luther, was standing next to him. Each weighed about the
same as a tuna boat and smelled about as fragrant. Both were
about five feet seven and so overmuscled their arms couldn't
touch their sides. They wore bib overalls, no shirts, logging

boots, no socks, and thin-hooded sweatshirts for jackets. Lom grinned inanely, leering at Elaine.

"I'm sorry for bumping into you. You can let me go now," said Mitikitski evenly. She wondered if a stain would be left on her new yellow jacket from where Lom's filthy hands were clutching her.

"Pretty lady not watching where she's going," jeered Luther, touching a wave of hair on Elaine's forehead. Elaine pulled back. His stained mouth was filled with the dark juice of chewing tobacco.

"Shouldn't be walking the streets alone," said the other brother, pulling her closer, staring at her cleavage. "Why don't you let me walk you home?"

Elaine looked at the alley Lom had gestured toward. No. I don't live in that direction, thank you. Elaine was going to scream and/or kick the brother in the groin with a cruel-yet-fashionable high-heel pump when a voice barked behind her.

"Let her go!"

Elaine turned. It was Behan.

"Now!" he said.

The brothers obediently stepped back.

"I'm sorry," said Behan, touching her. "I hope they didn't hurt you."

"No, I'm all right, thank you," said Elaine, checking the coat for smudges. She caught herself before saying a "goddamn it" in front of Behan. The jacket was indelibly stained.

"You'll have to let me replace it," said Behan. "I feel responsible," he added, looking at the two Magonogonovitch brothers. They couldn't hold his gaze and looked uneasily away. "I've taken these two lost souls into my employ. They're helping us with work on the new house, and at night serve as my companions and bodyguards, what with all this dark murderous work about. . . ." He gestured, avoiding the mention of Fenberg's brother.

"Perhaps a trip to the cleaners is all that's needed," said Elaine, politely disengaging herself.

"Nonsense. You're too kind. I'm a Christian. I must make restitution," he said, smiling. He looked deeply at Elaine.

There was a masked longing there that made her uncomfortable.

She had been bumping into Behan a lot lately. At the gas station, in line at a store. It seemed every time she turned around, there was Behan. His face was paler, and the black and silver hair seemed greasier and thinner. The eyes were red and rheumy, and Mitikitski sensed the loss of his daughter must have affected him physically. Whatever the reason, he looked like he was decomposing, and every time they would "bump into" one another, M. J. would find some excuse to put his hand on her shoulder or against her back, not a pleasant experience coming from a square-headed man who seemed to be in a state of decay.

"Thank you," said Elaine. "Let's just try the cleaners first. I'm sorry, but I'm meeting someone, and I'm very late."

Behan smiled chivalrously and pointed with his cane down the street. The Magonogonovitches walked where he pointed. "Good evening to you then, Miss Mitikitski."

Elaine watched the limping figure for a few moments and shivered. The last two times they had met, he had offered her a job. At twice what Fenberg was paying. Elaine pulled up the collar to her coat and sneezed.

*   *   *   *   *

Mike and Elaine walked back to her apartment in a lazy cadence after the show. They had stayed for both features, and it was after eleven. Fenberg was feeling hopeful, happier than he'd been since the murder of Darla Behan. The FBI had a lead on Tuberski and was confident of finding him by tomorrow morning. For this, Fenberg was grateful. At least John was alive. Elaine was looking forward to meeting this controversial brother of Michael's. She didn't mention Behan.

"You mind a personal question?" she asked. The streets were still lit from the holidays. The town would be somber tomorrow with the decorations down.

"You want to know how much I make," said Fenberg.

"No. Well. How much do you make?"

"About fifty bucks a week, before taxes. We all had to take a cut in pay when you came to the paper."

"Money well spent."

"Would you like to go on a date?" Fenberg asked.

Elaine hooked her arm into his. "Fenberg, you probably haven't noticed, but since I've moved here, we eat all three meals together, work at least eight hours a day together— with some of us not getting overtime. We have this habit of falling asleep at each other's houses."

"In separate rooms," added Fenberg.

"More often not."

"Instead of you dogmatically insisting we split all expenses, I suggest sometime you let me buy you, say, cups of herb tea and fancy dinners for four consecutive days."

"Why four days?" asked Elaine. His arm felt strong, secure.

"Appearances. Protocol. The thrill of the chase. And then, on say the fourth day, you'd be morally and financially obligated to let me perform unspeakable sexual atrocities upon your person."

Elaine felt a tingle. "Do you have a for-instance?"

"Something between baby talk and begging in leather," said Fenberg offhandedly. "Would you like to go a few rounds of 'naughty Indian princess and stern park ranger'?"

"You're traditional. Old-fashioned. I like that in a guy, Fenberg. Except I don't pelv around on the fourth date."

"I'm cute and a good kisser, too," said Fenberg.

"Who's been filling your head with these tales?"

"Ten thousand Chinese women can't be wrong."

"What happened to your parents?" asked Elaine.

Fenberg stopped, and Elaine with him. "Screech!" he said. "I get it. We're changing subjects."

"Uh-huh."

"Why do you want to know?" asked Fenberg.

"Curiosity," said Elaine. "Besides. It's a step toward asking about your wife and that picture you always carry in your right shirt pocket."

"If I tell you about my wife, will you go out with me?"

"Maybe."

They walked.

"From a negotiation standpoint, that's not very good," said Fenberg. "I'll have to have something more concrete."

"Okay, then," said Elaine. "I'll tell you about my three husbands." Five steps together. Fenberg stopped again.

Shock, then the suspicion nurtured by living in a house with practical jokers sharpened his features. He stared deeply into Elaine's eyes. Something in her voice . . . She wasn't kidding. Fenberg smiled largely. "Well, I'm going to talk fast, because I've got a feeling your story is much more interesting than mine. No kidding? Three husbands?"

Elaine smiled and nodded.

"Wow. Good hustle, Mitikitski."

Fenberg quickly summarized how his parents were still lost, fanny-up, somewhere in an Arctic glacier—one of those European trans-North Pole flights that didn't quite make it. Elaine held on to Michael's arm and buried her nose from time to time in Fenberg's sheepskin collar for warmth. And she listened.

Yes, they really were named Roy and Dale. They never liked each other, at least for as long as Fenberg could remember. Together, they were poison and ironically, inseparable. Fenberg remembered vowing with Tracy that they'd never allow it to get that bad. But he didn't tell Elaine that part. He described his mother's chronic hypochondria and flair for theatrics. His father's stoicism and solitude. How he could see traits from each in all the brothers.

Fenberg went on. He told her about the fights at home. Him and Johnny running away. The arrival of Angry Joe and later, another mistake, Clifford, the Nitro Kid. All the stars were out as Fenberg and Elaine walked, and the occasional dog barked in the distance.

Elaine told Michael about Larry, Moe, and Curly Joe, aka her three husbands. Fenberg listened with interest, without wisecracks or judgment. And when she had finished, a great load had lifted. She had never felt so close to a man before. Never felt it could be this easy or frictionless. They were at her apartment.

Elaine pulled off a mitten with her teeth and searched for the key.

"You're a neat guy, Fenberg. A good friend." She hugged him fraternally. "Make you a cup of tea?"

And I can fall asleep on the couch? By myself? Again?

"Actually, I've got to pick up the boys over at Malulu's."

They looked at one another.

"Date?" asked Fenberg.

Elaine sighed. "Can I have the night to think about it? Come by. We'll go out for breakfast in the morning, okay?"

Fenberg nodded. They said good night, and Fenberg found himself facing the closed door. He knocked, and Elaine opened it. Fenberg turned his head to the side and tapped his cheek lightly. Elaine shook her head, smiled, and went to peck Fenberg on the cheek. He turned quickly, kissing her full on the mouth. Fenberg half-smiled, half-smirked. He gave Elaine a two-shake wave and walked away.

"Oh hell, goddamn it," said Mitikitski, wrapping her arms around herself. "Here I go again."

* * * * *

By phone, Mitikitski polled those closest to her.

Kamali Molly voted yea. Go out with the handsome newspaper editor with the curly hair and lumberjack suit. Mom, Dad, and Elaine's therapist handed in negative votes. A date with her employer was a one-way ticket to the honeymoon suite of Heartbreak Hotel, and, in general, a bad idea. Elaine had bad dreams all night, first of Fenberg taking a picture of her out of his shirt pocket and setting it on fire while maniacally laughing. It was a side of him she didn't like. There was a brief intermission while Elaine tossed and rolled her top sheet into a ball, followed by the standard repeat tied-to-the-stake-with-monsters-coming-in-at-twelve-o'clock feature. Then she dreamed of M. J. Behan tilting his head to the right and tapping his cheek, turning at the last minute so she, *ooh*, kissed him full on those grotesque thin lips. She sneezed from three to five, had cramps and started her period forty-five minutes later. She fell asleep at eight, woke up at quarter after, lethargically slid to the bathroom, saw her face in the mirror and didn't like it. Mitikitski had an oatmeal pack on her face and curlers in her hair when Fenberg came to the door.

Fenberg blinked, counted to two, and raised his hand solemnly in greeting. "How," he said.

"I am a fight waiting to happen," announced Elaine. She glowered, establishing territorial dominance, then stormed off to the bathroom.

Fenberg's mouth ovaled to the size of a Cheerio. Okay. Just where I want to be, he thought, walking on the carpet as though it were made of eggshells. He didn't notice that she had started repacking her boxes.

"I'm late," said Mitikitski, popping her head out the bathroom door. Want to make something about it? And what's the fucking idea of setting *my* picture on fire last night, Mister?

"If you don't mind, I'll just make myself a cup of tea while you're getting ready," said Fenberg, walking cautiously toward the kitchen. His back to her, he smiled carefully. The bathroom door slammed. I see. This is what happens to Donald Duck when he gets wet.

Fenberg was dipping a tea bag when Mitikitski trounced into the kitchen. The curlers, robe, and oatmeal mask were still there, and Mitikitski was brushing her teeth. "You are what those in the dating business call a keeper," said Mitikitski, pointing a frothy toothbrush at Michael. "I'm not in the market right now for a keeper. We've known each other for a few weeks, and I find myself getting pulled in closer and closer to you. Damn it. I like you. I respect you. You're the nicest man I've ever met." Elaine paced in the slippers, with the toothbrush in hand. She stopped in front of Michael. "I have sexual problems."

Fenberg broke off a large formation of oatmeal from her nose. "Midgets?"

"What?"

"Your sexual problem. Does it have anything to do with midgets?"

"No!"

"Dog collars?"

"No."

"So far, I'm relieved."

"I sneeze when I engage in, or think about, sex." She folded her arms.

Fenberg nodded understandingly and dropped the oatmeal globule into the sink. He got close to her face, squinted, and yelled, "Foreplay!"

"Fenberg. Why did you shout at me?"

"I was just testing."

"I sneeze when *I* think about sex. Not when *you* think about sex."

"So don't think about sex. Do what I do. Think about ballplayers."

"You're not taking this seriously," said Elaine, wrapping her arms around herself.

"Geez, Elaine . . ." Trying to be consoling, Fenberg took a step toward Mitikitski. Elaine wiggled away from the arms that reached for her.

"God! Why do men always think that whenever a woman shows a little emotion it's their cue to run in and do the manly thing by grabbing them. I hate that!"

"Backing off, see?" said Fenberg, holding his hands in the air. I don't think I've ever had this response before when asking out a woman. "You know, I'm not looking to borrow money, Elaine, all I wanted to know is if you wanted to go out on one innocent little date."

"Why couldn't we have just stayed friends and left things the way they were?" she asked. "Why did you have to go and ask me on a . . . date?" She punched up the word, giving it a smelly-fish connotation.

Fenberg shrugged lightly. "It's a tough world out there sometimes. We're not Zen masters, and we get lonely. I think you do. I know I'm lonely."

"Then buy a dog, Fenberg."

Woof. Fenberg winced almost imperceptibly. This lady is strict. He thought they were supposed to go out a few times, and then maybe have a fight, not the other way around. He was also beginning to suspect that Mitikitski might be a little crazy, which frightened him more than her remark, because the thought of Mitikitski being crazy, oatmeal pack and all, was actually attractive to Fenberg.

And then he saw the boxes.

Fenberg felt sick. Mitikitski said a few things she shouldn't. He couldn't hear she was controlling her voice, forcing down the hysteria that would follow. She was scared, and just wanted Fenberg to promise something no man could deliver: that he would never hurt her. Of course, she didn't say this. She said she'd repay Fenberg the advance for the moving expenses.

Then, she quit.

Fenberg shifted his weight and considered. Swell, the first reporter of the year and here we go again. Mitikitski wanted her therapist or her sister or even her mother. But most of all, she wanted to run to Fenberg and break down, crying that she was sorry.

But Fenberg had taken his jacket and left.

* * * * *

Fenberg slammed the front door to the ranch house. The screen door echoed in collision. He had stopped by the paper on the way back from Elaine's. The FBI report from the night before had been a bum lead. Federal agents had mistaken a tall Indian, fishing in a remote part of the national forest, for John Tuberski.

"How's Elaine?" asked Angry Joe, taking a bite out of a bologna sandwich.

"Shut up," said Fenberg, steaming past. Joe made a compression chamber face and inched nonchalantly for the door.

Fenberg ground it into reverse. In a rare display of terror, Angry Joe stared silently at the grungy mail sack. "What the hell is that?" Fenberg demanded.

The smell of execution was in the air. "I didn't do anything!"

"I didn't say you did. What's in the bag, Joe?"

"Mail. For John," he blurted. "There's another sack just like it in his room. The mailman delivered them about an hour ago. He said John had a post office box that had been running over the last couple of weeks. He said he had to deliver it."

"I'm sorry I snapped at you," said Fenberg, through gritted teeth. Fenberg grabbed the heavy mailbag and carted it off to Tuberski's vacant room. He tossed it on the bed with the other mail sack. Fenberg stopped at the doorway and lowered his head.

The obvious question arose.

Why would someone without a career or fan club be getting that much correspondence? Fenberg sat down on his brother's bed and tilted his head to the right. No. He looked away. Sanctity of the mail, an individual's right to privacy, and all those things that made this country great which Fenberg enjoyed writing editorials about. No. He wouldn't open his brother's mail. But it wouldn't hurt to just pull out a few envelopes and check return addresses.

Fenberg's brow lowered. He quickly pulled out a handful of letters. And then another handful.

It wasn't exactly mail.

Outside, Angry Joe had made a beeline for the farthest boundary of the Fenberg ranch. Clifford was busy terrorizing a kitten under the barn. They both heard a bloodcurdling scream coming from the house, the kind a man makes when he cuts off his hand with a Skilsaw.

Fenberg screamed again, clutching the letters and twisting them into a pulpy mass.

They were bills.

Or more accurately, hate mail from credit card companies.

Using what looked to be the official letterhead of the American Nazi Party, dozens of letters from various banks with bloodred lettering on the outside reminded the addressee: THIRD AND FINAL NOTICE! with a silent but implied, "Consumer Shvinehoont" at the end of each envelope. Fenberg dumped the contents of both bags on Tuberski's

Alliklik woven comforter and frantically sifted. It was mostly junk mail and catalogs because what happens when someone has seventeen major credit cards is that he automatically becomes implanted into the computer banks of every store and junk mail house in the free world.

It took an hour for Fenberg to piece together the awful truth. Tuberski had forged Fenberg's name as cosigner onto each and every one of those seventeen cards. One Gemco, three American Express gold cards, six MasterCards, two Visas, a Diners Club (were they still in business?), Sears, Abercrombie & Fitch, Pep Boys, and the slender, hard-to-get, Neiman-Marcus plate.

Fenberg added the totals. The tale of the white tape was crippling. With loan shark interest rates and various penalties ranging from tardiness to being right-handed, Tuberski owed a whopping, make-your-knees-buckle, punch-in-the-stomach grand total of $45,096.34.

Fenberg sat on the bed, limp, with a concentration camp stare.

The phone rang.

It was his banker. He apologized for calling on a weekend, but wanted to discuss the penalty for the early withdrawal Fenberg had accrued on his high-yield savings account.

What . . . early . . . withdrawal . . . ?

The early withdrawal that your brother, John, made . . . as a matter of fact, the day he disappeared. Gee, Mike. It had your signature.

My signature?

Yeah. You closed the account, took out the entire twelve thousand dollars. And oh, by the way, don't forget the final payment on the ranch was due this month. Yes. I don't have the exact figure in front of me, but I think it's around fifteen thousand and change. See you at Rotary. 'Bye.

Fenberg hung up the phone. In a trance, he calculated . . .

$45,096.34—credit cards. 'Kay. Plus . . .

$15,221.42—ranch balloon payment. Due in three weeks. 'Kay. Plus . . .

$714.98—penalty for early withdrawal. Grand total of,

say 'kay, ding-ding-ding . . .

    $61,032.74—thank you for shopping at K Mart.

Because *Fenberg*'s name had been forged on all the applications, *Fenberg* now owed a whopping, make-you-hyper-ventilate grand total of $61,032.74, past-due-now-even-as-you-take-this-very-breath, don't-forget-to-sign-the-check, make-sure-our-address-is-in-the-little-plastic-window-on-the-envelope-and-your-account-number-is-on-the-outside, thank-you-and-sorry-about-the-threats-and-for-implying-you're-an-asshole-on-the-outside-of-our-stationery.

Neiman-exhorbitant-Marcus.

Fenberg ransacked the house, confiscating all of John Tuberski's pictures, including frames, which he loaded into two big cardboard boxes. He put the boxes in his truck. Fenberg then walked steely-eyed to the stalls where he unlocked a rusting maximum security box that contained one deer rifle and several cases of shells.

"Where you going?" yelled Clifford from across the yard. He had a rope and was trying to lasso the yellow tabby hiding under the barn.

Fenberg strode purposefully toward his black pickup, the rifle slung over his shoulder. "I'm going to find a tower," said Fenberg. "I'm going to climb to the top. I'm going to shoot innocent bystanders."

"Can I come?"

"No."

Fenberg drove for twenty minutes to a deserted dump yard and purposefully set up a line of John Tuberski's grinning pictures. He paced twenty-five yards away, aimed for the nuts, and fired.

PART II:

Three Months Later . . .

—14—

DEAD BUNNIES

Fenberg pulled off the road onto a paved turnout where the tourists liked to park and ogle. Tourists. Nuke 'em, thought Fenberg. He was glad none were around today. Fenberg climbed from the cab of his gargantuan black pickup and zipped up his jacket. It was cold on the unprotected granite overlook, and a wind from a distant storm was blowing Fenberg's hair. You could see five thousand square miles of mountain ranges and fog-shrouded valleys and, of course, lots of trees. A half-day away, a schizophrenic storm was brooding, punching through the charcoal gray cloud mass with spiny fingers of lightning. It was too far away to hear any thunder.

Fenberg was on his way to the Zoo Bar for a beer and burger. He wanted to be alone. Odd, he thought, when that's all he'd felt these past months. Alone. And coming apart. And like biting someone.

Fenberg sat on the hood. It was warm, like sitting on an electric blanket, and he rested his back against the windshield. He pulled out the picture of Tracy and the baby, thoughtfully rubbing the worn edges. Tracy had high, rounded cheekbones and long, wavy blond hair. She was a fifth-degree heartbreaker, and she and Michael had been Basin Valley's Nick and Nora Charles in jeans, always laughing, always bantering, always with a beer in hand. Fenberg would crack jokes or tickle her just to make her cheeks climb even higher and rounder before he kissed them. Baby Fenberg had the same cheekbones. Fenberg used to sit his son on his lap and play motorcycle, all the sound effects included. The noisy ride would conclude with a spectacular crash, sending Michael and son rolling off the sofa and onto the carpet. This, to Baby Fenberg, was high entertainment, and he'd giggle like an idiot, mimicking his father's motorcycle noises.

"You're going to break the baby," Tracy would say, coming into the room, playing the role of disapproving mother.

"The guy's indestructible, see?" Fenberg would point out, bending the boy's limber body at odd angles and holding him upside down. Tracy would gasp, and Fenberg would scoop up the child like a fumbled football, making two-cylinder and siren noises with Tracy in hot pursuit. Invariably, Tracy would corner the two in a distant part of the house, and Fenberg would fend her off, threatening to drop the toddler. Once Baby Fenberg was recaptured, Michael would corner Tracy, whispering the suggestion that they put the child down for a nap and go off and make another.

It had been three months since the Darla Behan murder, and Fenberg had yet to fully resign himself to the fact that his brother, Norwood Z. Fenberg, alias John Tuberski, was dearly departed.

Honestly, the way things had been going these past three months, Fenberg had ambivalent feelings about the loss. He reached into his jacket for a Hav-A-Tampa and stuck it, unlit, in his mouth.

The credit card scam irked Fenberg, as did the forgery at Basin Valley First National Fiduciary. Both seemed so out-of-character for his brother. Although his own bank hadn't gone so far as to call Fenberg a welfare slug or a liberal, or send a vice president in white shirt and bland tie in the dark of night to spraypaint "DEADBEAT" on Fenberg's house, they were making uncomfortable but insistent coughing noises. Fenberg was eighty-four days overdue on the balloon payment. In six days, they would foreclose. Fenberg had tried getting another mortgage or loan, normally financial child's play. Except with his name X-ed on seventeen credit cards, all long overdue, Fenberg had a TRW rating lower than Neal Bush. As collateral, the paper was untouchable because he had borrowed a sizable amount last year to finance new printing presses, and the bank was already worried about that loan payment because as a business, *The Bugle* was nearly dead.

M. J. Behan had taken off after Fenberg and *The Bugle* with a vengeance, and his newly formed *Clarion* had lured eighty-one percent of *The Bugle*'s business. Already Fenberg had been forced to lay off six people on a fifteen-person staff. With gifts and cash rebates, Behan was practically giving away ads. Behan was right. He would bury Fenberg. It was only a matter of time. Fenberg had been editor of *The Basin Valley Bugle* all his adult life. There were the boys to think of and a ranch to pack. Where would they go? Thirty-thousand dollar jobs with perks didn't grow on the surrounding trees.

Fenberg lit his little cigar and took a drag, looking at Tracy. "I guess I'm not doing such a hot job down here, babe."

Fenberg had investigated the possibility of cashing in on John's insurance policy, a paltry thirty-two thousand. But the insurance company didn't believe Tuberski was dead. Few people did, except for Fenberg. Most thought John was still out and about, killing and eating people.

Someone, or something, had murdered and mutilated ten people in Basin Valley between the New Year and the end of March. Two teenage lovers—the Rapporport boy and Charlene Hittleman—were unceremoniously yanked from their parked car on a starlit overlook in January. Terminal *coitus interruptus.* Twenty miles away, the next evening, right in the middle of town, the elderly hippie woman, Edith Mooney, was killed at the all-night coin Laundromat. That sent the town into a tizzy and normally would have meant a land-office business for *The Bugle*. There wasn't a household in Basin Valley that started their eggs and coffee without first reading Fenberg's staccato Walter Winchell accounting of what neighbor had been the latest entreé. As a photographer, Bean Breath Brown was an idiot savant; his graphic photojournalistic accounts of the crime scenes were worthy of a

Pulitzer. While everyone *read* Michael's newspaper, no one bought any ads. "He gave me a free VCR with remote, just for running a lousy little quarter-page," one businessman told Fenberg, not able to look him in the eye. "I'm sorry—I needed the recorder. I've got kids. It's only a temporary thing, Michael. The town's behind you."

But they weren't.

Sheriff Bubba Fenberg instigated a curfew with which everyone in Basin Valley was happy to comply. Twenty-eight days of nerve-wracking quiet passed before the killer struck again. Then, in February, the partial remains of two still-warm corpses were found steaming by the side of the Interstate in the early morning dew. They were hitchhikers, both young, strong men in their early twenties, added to the list that included the Duffield family and Darla Behan.

The *modus operandi* was identical in each homicide. The victims were all literally torn apart by something with great strength, partially eaten, then buried. They were all killed at night.

M. J. Behan took each murder personally and publicly blamed Tuberski. And Fenberg. And after each murder, he'd lower his advertising rates.

With the FBI and the National Guard called in, it was a natural for national media coverage. Fenberg couldn't blame them. The hike out to Basin Valley earned most reporters and news crews a small fortune in travel expenses and also gave the newshounds the chance to use "CANNIBAL KILLER" in a headline. The manhunt on a grand scale for John ended in March. Interest waned when no one, not even Fenberg, could find a trace of John Tuberski. Fenberg had checked hundreds of square miles and all their boyhood haunts. No. Tuberski was dead all right, Fenberg figured. He felt that even if his brother had killed and eaten everyone from San Francisco to the Bering Strait, John would have at least had the decency to call. And despite the possibility of guilt, despite John's taking the money, Michael would have loved to see him.

Fenberg wiggled on the hood of his truck, trying to get the circulation going in his rear end. The Hav-A-Tampa was smoldering all the way down to the birch tip. He extinguished the last bit of glowing ember on his boot heel and flicked the butt into a nearby trash can.

Fenberg put the photo away. He raised his eyebrows, slowly filled his cheeks with air, and considered his few options. He could get drunk. That was easy. He could get laid. Highly doubtful. Perhaps a fight? Perhaps a combination of all three?

A car with Kansas plates pulled onto the overlook and parked next to Michael. The back end was low to the ground, stuffed with luggage. Doors opened, and children clambered out, screaming and blowing off steam. The husband grunted and swung out of the driver's seat. He was wearing a Hawaiian shirt, shorts, black shoes, and black socks.

"Cold up this high," he said, rubbing his forearms and grinning. "We're tourists!"

Fenberg still sat quietly on the hood of his truck with his arms folded. Is that so?

"Could I impose on you to take a snapshot of me and the Missus and the kids, kinda with the mountains in the back?" he asked, offering his cheap camera to Fenberg.

"Sure," said Fenberg. He made them stand in a tight formation, then take four little steps to the right, four little steps to the left, two steps back, now everyone squat down just an inch or two. Fenberg arranged them perfectly centered in the viewfinder, half-smiled and half-smirked, then raised the camera a couple of inches so only the sky and the tops of their hair would show when the prints came back.

Click.

* * * * *

"Whiskey and fresh horses for my men," said Fenberg, dully, straddling the barstool.

A hundred dusty taxidermied animals, one bartender, and one eleven by fourteen framed photo of Phoebe Cates silently regarded Fenberg. Using just his tongue, the man behind the bar switched the toothpick from the left side of his mouth to the right. His name was Herb, and he was the owner of the See 'Em Dead Zoo Bar. He was bald, fiftyish, and had big ears. From the back, he looked like a Volkswagen with the doors open.

"Yeah. Sure, Mike," said Herb. He slapped a hamburger onto the grill and submerged a basket of fries into boiling oil. He poured Fenberg a beer. Sometimes Fenberg ordered prime rib and Lowenbrau, sometimes it was melon and yoghurt, charged to his suite. Herb would just smile and say, "Yeah. Sure, Mike," and bring Fenberg a cheeseburger, fries, and beer. It was all the Zoo Bar served.

Fenberg took his tankard to the end of the long, knife-pocked bar and sat next to the Indian.

"Been looking for you," said Fenberg.

"That's what they tell me," said Charlie Two Eagles Soaring Johnson, immersed in the basketball game on Zoo Bar TV. Charlie's long white hair was braided in a ponytail and dangled out the back of his black Stetson. He wasn't very big, and the plaid shirt and jeans draped loosely on him. A beefy borax worker, sitting on the stool next to Fenberg's, made a disgusted face. He took his beer and walked away. "I hear you're not very popular," said Charlie.

"Not with some. Nope." People had been avoiding Fenberg lately. Mothers moving their children to the other side of the street. Former softball cronies ignoring his greetings. "I guess they're afraid I'll eat them or something."

"That's kind of humorous."

"I came by your house a couple of times."

"I wasn't home."

"Just wanted to know if you'd heard anything about my brother."

"I hear he hasn't been around," said the Indian, not looking away from the set. "I myself have been in the hills. Never could understand this game. I think my ancestors played something like this, a long time ago. Or maybe it was lacrosse."

"Is he dead?"

"Can't say."

"Why?"

"I'd rather not get into deep conversations in the middle of a ball game, Fenberg. But there is no such thing as death," said the Indian. "Don't you read your Bible?"

"Not much." Tuberski used to be the Bible reader in the family. "I don't know, Charlie. I'm clutching at straws, I guess." Michael pulled out the picture and leaned it against his beer. He put his chin on his hand, slouching on the bar, staring at Tracy and the child.

"She was a hell of a girl," said Charlie Two Eagles.

"That she was," agreed Fenberg.

"Nice hips. You ought to give her up, Fenberg."

Fenberg nodded.

The Indian looked at the blonde and the baby. "I don't know what to say that will help you, Fenberg. You have a great poison in you that you mistakenly believe is your friend. I truly wish your brother was here to counsel you. He has much wisdom."

Fenberg perked. "Has?"

The Indian shrugged. Has, had. Tense is for white men, and Charlie switched the conversation to one of his favorite topics: why his grandson never got much playing time on the state championship basketball team. Fenberg reminded him that his grandson had the tendency to make spectacular steals, drive the length of the court, and throw the ball over the top of the backboard on his lay-up. What about John?

"Your brother was to be a great light-of-the-world. God talks to all men. Few are given the precious gift to hear. While God lovingly poured wisdom into your brother, he also created him to be easily distracted. And John had his own hurts to deal with."

Fenberg sat up.

"Charlie, what are you trying to tell me?"

"Fenberg. Don't ask me questions I don't want to answer. If I were you, I would be more concerned with other matters."

"Like?"

The bartender brought Fenberg's dinner, along with a bowl

of industrial-strength jalapeno peppers.

"The *Mandrango*. It is nearing his time. This next full moon, I figure. He is coming for his bride. No power on earth can stop him."

Fenberg made a bored face and shook his head. He was getting fed up with all the stories and opinions. Someone had even sent him a silver bullet at the paper with a note saying ". . . rub this in garlic and shoot through the heart. It is the only way the killer can be stopped."

"*Something* has been killing and eating people, Fenberg," said the Indian.

"That something wouldn't have anything to do with my brother, would it?" asked Fenberg, not dropping the subject.

Charlie avoided looking Fenberg in the eyes.

"Your brother is . . ." Charlie stopped, staring past Fenberg's shoulder.

"Yes?"

"Speaking of death . . ."

The front door of the Zoo Bar exploded open, and a blast of Arctic air knifed through the little dive. The Zoo Bar was half-filled with regulars—loggers, cowboys, borax workers. No one yelled to close the door. The taxidermied animals that lined the See 'Em Dead Zoo Bar walls seemed to be snarling.

"I think I will be going," said Charlie, grabbing his beer and quickly sliding off the stool.

The Magonogonovitch brothers stood silhouetted in the doorway, leaves and dust whirling in a small storm behind them. An odor of dead animals whiffed into the bar as the two men filled the entranceway, exposing tobacco-stained teeth and tiny eyes filled with hate and stupidity. They had played on both Fenberg's championship teams, anchoring the offensive line. Lom and Luther lived in the dark part of the forest in a rusting mobile home abandoned on concrete blocks. Before working for Behan, they had poached, selling the bear pelts they trapped in the national forest to tourists. They sold drugs and committed petty crimes to support themselves. Normally, they avoided the Zoo Bar.

It was four in the afternoon. Both were already stinking

drunk. Lom, his eyes bloodshot and piglike, took in the sights of the See 'Em Dead, staring at the customers, who kept their faces down, noses into their beer. Lom noticed Fenberg and tugged on his brother's overalls to follow. He pushed three lumberjacks out of the way en route.

"Give us beer," Lom ordered, hoisting a meaty thigh onto the stool next to Fenberg. The bartender eyed the thick ash axe handle he had hidden under the bar. He hesitated, then brought two full glasses of draught.

Lom regarded his drink, held between dirty index finger and blackened thumb, before turning the glass upside down and pouring the beer on the counter. It flooded over onto the wax paper holding Fenberg's cheeseburger.

"Give us pitchers!"

Luther laughed and dumped his beer likewise. Lom was the older brother and did most of the talking.

Fenberg sighed. He pulled out a few singles and set them on a dry part of the bar. "Thanks for the burger, Herb. Kind of runny this time." He stood to leave. A thick, scarred hand forced him roughly back onto the stool.

"Where you going, faggot?" asked Lom.

Fenberg clenched his fists. He was no tiny person, but the Magonogonovitches were the next truck size up. Each weighed almost a hundred pounds more than Fenberg. They were capable of murdering someone just for the pleasure of watching him die.

"Your brother pushed us around," said Luther.

Oh great, thought Fenberg. Another Tuberski hen come home to roost.

The Magonogonovitches took turns voicing their grievances:

"You always thought you were big stuff in school. . . ."

". . . and with your brother to protect you."

"Mr. Big Quarterback."

"Mr. Popular."

"You got all the girls."

"That's because girls are for dating, not eating," said Fenberg. He flinched, thinking Luther was going to sock him in the back. Luther was, but stopped. He laughed through gritted teeth.

"Faggot. I'm going to buy you a drink." Lom leered at Fenberg, not quite focusing.

"Thanks, but I've got to get going."

"You too good to drink with us?" He jammed a fat, deformed finger into Michael's sternum. Fenberg looked down at his chest, then up at Lom, mapping out a vulnerable place to strike. There wasn't any. He could feel the other brother's putrid breath down the back of his neck.

"Another time," said Fenberg, standing. He roughly shrugged off another attempt to seat him.

They laughed at him as he walked toward the door. They hooted and called him a coward.

"Hey, Fenberg!" shouted Lom. "You're pretty cool—just like your wife!"

Fenberg stopped.

"Hey! How *is* the wife and kid?"

There was a dizzying rush that flooded, angrily pounding on the dam that was Fenberg's eyes. With no outlet there, it rushed through the ears, screaming a deafening silence. Fenberg felt paralyzed, his feet not his, just roots in a wooden floor. He scanned the faces of the men in the bar and saw them as the bright, hopeful children he had grown up with. They all looked helplessly away.

"Your wife? She was a fine tail. I hear she don't drive so fuckin' good in the snow!" Lom fiercely gritted his teeth. Luther belched out a laugh.

"Hey, Fenberg!" shouted Lom. "How old would that little boy of yours been? 'Bout five years old by now?"

Fenberg was white.

Things didn't seem to matter anymore.

They laughed at Fenberg as he walked back to the bar.

"Maybe I'll join you for that beer now," said Fenberg, smiling at Herb and grabbing a full pitcher. He kicked Lom's stool out from underneath him, quickly spinning to whack the other brother full-force in the middle of the nose with the base of the heavy glass pitcher. Unlike in the movies, the pitcher didn't break. It made a sick, dull thudding sound. Also unlike in the movies, Luther didn't fall down, knocked out. He staggered stupidly, knocking over tables and patrons, blood gushing from his head as he held his face. Lom reached up, tearing Fenberg's shirt, viciously punching him as he pulled him down. Fenberg grabbed a bowlful of dripping jalapenos, grinding them into Lom's face as the men fell to the sawdust-covered floor. Insanely, Lom screamed as the pepper juice ate at his eyes. Fenberg pulled himself free and stood. He felt the bottom part of his face disconnect. The other brother had recovered to land a running boilermaker.

"Mike, look out!" yelled Herb.

A portion of Fenberg's brain that was not swimming toward unconsciousness acknowledged with a yeah, thanks.

Luther flayed wildly, pinning Fenberg to the bar and punishing him with vicious body punches. Fenberg could feel blood vessels breaking and ribs crunching. He head-butted Luther in the nose again and rolled his way along the bar to get free. Bloody, and hydrophobic with pain and rage, Luther made a second charge. Fenberg awkwardly sidestepped it.

From behind the bar, Herb tossed Fenberg the axe handle and later at the Zoo they would say it was one of those who-let-all-the-air-out-of-the-Kleenex-boxes Reggie Jackson strike-out swings. Fenberg kept his shoulder up, had perfect extension and extreme wrist speed when he connected squarely on the back of Luther Magonogonovitch's thighs. Everyone at the bar agreed that 1) it had to sting and, 2) Luther wouldn't be going to the beach with welts like that on the back of his legs. The force of the blow sent Luther crashing into the edge of the thick wood bar, where he left a small portion of his scalp before passing out.

Half-blind, weaving, Lom pulled the knife to make that one last banzai assault. He would put it through Fenberg's ribs and twist. Only Fenberg didn't go along with the plan. He took another baseball swing, cracking the brother on the bicep. He hit him again on the top of the shoulder, and the knife spun across the floor. Lom fell to his knees.

The light had left Fenberg's eyes.

Fenberg grabbed Lom Magonogonovitch by the hair and roughly forced his head onto a chair. He raised the handle high over his head like an executioner's axe and aimed for the pate. Ten men rushed him and saved him from murder.

Claustrophobic, still strengthened by the bloodlust, Fenberg yanked free. He threw the handle to the ground, looking with disgust at the men who had watched him in his frenzy. He backed toward the door and disappeared into the storm.

The regulars said it wasn't a fight the same caliber as his brother's Zoo Massacre of years earlier, but Fenberg had to be given some credit. He wasn't nearly seven feet tall. He didn't weigh almost three hundred pounds and wasn't as quick as Tuberski. Besides, Fenberg had always considered himself a lover, not a fighter.

*　*　*　*　*

In between quitting six times, a staff record in the long and checkered history of *The Basin Valley Bugle*, Elaine Mitikitski ran from things. She ran from pain. She ran from the memory of three stinko husbands. She ran from Mike. But for all her firm protestations, her occasional tantrums which were a smoke screen, her long and involved letters of resignation which kindly removed all burden of responsibility from other people's shoulders and firmly placed it on her own, Elaine Mitikitski had become Michael Fenberg's true heart sweetie.

Mike and Elaine had created this perfectly charming, flirtatious, supportive relationship of fun, friendship, and romance. Elaine Mitikitski had been a reporter at the mighty *Bugle* and Mike Fenberg's girlfriend for about three months now.

Ninety days ago, the first time she quit, Elaine had unrealistically figured she could pack her belongings, load a trailer, get her mail forwarded back home, and complete all the other nagging errands involved with moving *and* getting out of town all in one day. In her eyes, the day a partial failure, she vowed to be on the road bright and early the next morning before she had a chance to do something stupid again with *spit* another *spit* man (i.e. Fenberg). Fenberg, who at times bordered on Machiavellian, had earlier secretly confiscated Elaine's house keys and had duplicates made. He showed up in the middle of the night in Mitikitski's bedroom. Still half-asleep, Elaine got up on one elbow to see Fenberg undressing and slipping under the covers next to her. He wiggled around for a moment, trying to get comfortable, closed his eyes and pretended to snore while Elaine stared at him with a look of understandable query. Fenberg opened his eyes.

"Fire," Fenberg said. "Destroyed the entire ranch. Smoldering ashes, charred timbers, twisted metal, my two brothers, appropriately burnt black as weenies. It was terrible."

Elaine rubbed her eyes and nodded understandingly. She collapsed back down, then climbed back up on one elbow.

"This may sound old-fashioned," said Mitikitski. "But if I find out you're sleeping with anyone else, I'll kill you."

"Agreed," said Fenberg.

"I'm serious."

"I believe you."

"I mean *I mean it.*"

"I think I get your drift."

Damn it, thought Mitikitski. "Hold me."

One thing led to another, as they will with two naked grown-ups lying next to one another. And then Mitikitski said, "Time out. I can't do this." Fenberg took a deep breath, hit himself in the forehead a few times and rolled off. "Okay." He asked why. Elaine began the lengthy story of her involvements with peculiar men, told him how she fell in love easily, and about her allergy. "Sex makes me sneeze," she said. Fenberg suggested a good college try.

"I can't," Mitikitski apologized, wrapped in Fenberg's strong arms and laying her cards on the nightstand. "If I make love to you, I'll start sneezing. The last time, I sneezed for three days, and it wasn't very pleasant. Worse, I think I'll probably fall in love with you, and if this one doesn't work out, I'll die. It's as simple as that."

Fenberg agreed, saying he didn't have much use for a dead

girlfriend-slash-managing editor. Do you consider me your girlfriend? Mitikitski asked. Hell. Sure. Mitikitski thought that was sweet. Fenberg kissed her on the cheek and promised that as far as he was concerned, he'd like her just as much if they never made love. Elaine thought that that too, was sweet and snuggled asleep in his arms. In the dark, Fenberg stared off in narrow-eyed, sinister contemplation. He made plans for the next night to get Mitikitski stinking drunk and screw her brains out.

Mitikitski was slightly tipsy that following evening, leaning against the kitchen counter at Fenberg's ranch. The boys were sequestered at Malulu's. She had orders to kill them if they tried to escape. Fenberg started with the ploy of rubbing Elaine's shoulders after a hard day's work, which moved to stronger caresses, which advanced to kissing and heavy petting, proving that those films they show in sixth grade health class aren't entirely inaccurate. Michael expertly undressed the two of them and slowly led the naked Mitikitski toward his bedroom by gently tugging on her nipples and kissing her while they walked backwards. At the door, he picked her up and carried her through. Vivaldi played impishly. The room flickered with several strategically located candles, and at every corner of the bed and on every flat surface were boxes of Kleenex Softique tissues, pink, Elaine's favorite color.

Fenberg liked his chances.

But as things grew steamy, he had to whisper the delicate yet gentlemanly question. "While I'm sure we'd create the world's most charming and erudite baby, my darling, are you, um, practicing any method of, um, are you on the pill or diaphragm?" Mitikitski said she didn't need a diagram, she remembered how. But then she cried, and Mike gently asked her what was wrong. Elaine blurted that she was as sterile as a fruit fly in a nuclear reactor and couldn't have babies. Ever. Fenberg held her and said there-there, honey-honey and all that and considered that there were always babies arriving every week at the hospital nursery, and in the candlelight he told Mitikitski that he would love his managing editor to pieces sans kids or with. She cried herself to sleep in his arms. Again.

The next day at the office, Fenberg was dizzy. Being that close, two nights in a row, after about three hours sleep in as many days, Fenberg felt the early symptoms of genital and brainial damage. At the end of shift, Elaine rubbed Fenberg's shoulders, kissing him appreciatively on the cheek. He said please don't. If I get excited again, I'll implode. She kissed him again and left him a folded-up note:

> *I'm naked in the UPI room. Meet me there in fifteen seconds and I'll make you harder than Chinese arithmetic.*
>
> > *Best wishes,*
> > *Elaine Mitikitski*
> > *Managing editor*

Mitikitski did fall in love with Fenberg, so much so that she did everything except write Michael's name with hearts and arrows on the front of her reporter's steno pad. They were good together. Slow dancing. Arguing over movies. Gossiping. She took a lot of the pain and sharpness out of Fenberg's brothers, and they clung to her in a polite and veiled desperation whenever she was around. Mitikitski missed feminine companionship and Kamali Molly. But she was also beginning to fall in love with the small town pace and scenic grandeur of Basin Valley. There was an acute peace here that came from doing hard but honest outdoor work, when it seemed that neither time nor space existed. It was experiential, and Mitikitski could never find the words to explain to Molly the tranquility found in brushing down a horse, or fixing a busted fence in the rain, or chopping up a downed tree for firewood. Not that Mitikitski was becoming a rube. There was the Basin Valley Community Theater where local artisans staggered around stage holding the backs of their hands on their foreheads as though affixed there with Velcro, yelling, "Stellah! Stellah!" and Cougar Playhouse (as an eighth grader, Angry Joe played the lead in *Bye Bye Birdie* for his school play). And once every two weeks, Fenberg insisted they dress up and dine formally, if only by candlelight at the ranch. Fenberg, she was surprised to find out, owned his own tux. They had a million things in common, from monkeying with each other's typewriter margins to holding each other all night and just gazing into one another's eyes.

It was all so perfect.

Ergo, something had to be wrong.

A little fire alarm slowly clanked in a distant part of Elaine's mind. That pattern. For three months now, whenever they made love, afterwards, there was something a little strange, which was probably nothing, she reasoned. But . . . something came over Michael after they made love. A subtle change of coloring. A distancing. Claustrophobia.

* * * * *

The outer fringes of the storm sprinkled over Basin Valley. Most of the fury would miss the local mountains, dumping its swollen cargo of a billion-plus gallons of rainwater on the unsuspecting desert to the east.

Elaine Mitikitski was boarded in for the night, ready for a quiet evening at home. She had all the necessary ingredients: tea, lots of pillows, cookies, though a fat lazy cat would have been nice and keeping in theme of the way she had been feeling lately. Tired. Actually, Elaine had been riding an emotional roller coaster lately, woman's hormones and all, feeling sometimes giddy, sometimes depressed. She averaged twelve hours sleep a night and woke ravenous.

Light music played on her stereo, and the raindrops tapped a narcotizing code on the metal grating outside.

Elaine sat on the floor, using the sofa for a backrest. She was reading a trashy novel, one featuring lots of airline trips, a sullen hero bent on revenge, some Nazis, and lots of fashionable people drinking to excess in European restaurants. To be a woman and get into this book, one had to be at least a D-cup. There were lots of steamy "I-love-you-I-need-you-suddenly-he-was-in-her-take-that-and-that-and-that-oh-God-Larry-they-smoked-afterwards-where-have-you-hidden-the-list-of-Western-agents-in-Soviet-Russia" sex scenes.

Elaine squirmed and continued to read.

There was one particular scene which Elaine had to skim over, moving her lips slowly as she read. She put the book down and juggled two invisible puppets, trying to imagine how the hero and the heroine had managed their sexual acrobatics. Elaine gave it up to artistic license. Mitikitski read for an hour and was about to call it a night when she heard the front door buzzer. Someone was leaning on it.

"All right, all right!" God, I'm coming. "Yes?"

"My knuckles hurt. And my ribs. And I think I've lost valuable IQ points and perhaps a molar."

Elaine nearly gasped, but controlled herself. It was Fenberg. There was a cut on his left cheek, and his shirt was ripped open at the collar, revealing another gash. He stood under the dim yellow porch bulb in a light drizzle. Steam rose from his heated body and tousled curly hair. On this day, life had not been kind to him.

"I'm sorry I'm such a mess, but can I just maybe rest on your floor for a couple of minutes?" Fenberg asked. There was a mouse welling up under his eye.

Elaine compassionately hugged Fenberg. He made a funny noise and gently pushed her away. His ribs hurt, and his feelings, and he was very, very angry.

"Mitikitski."

"What?"

"Be nice to me. I'm having a very bad life," Fenberg said.

"Oh, sweetie . . ."

* * * * *

Elaine had gingerly treated Fenberg's abrasions, but as is the case in the early stages of dating when two people can't keep their mitts off one another, Mitikitski and Fenberg found themselves in the unstoppable gravitational pull of lovemaking. But on this night, something was wrong. Mike was not Mike. Ever alert for trouble signs, real or imagined, Elaine noted that this particular joining lacked the tender, caring touch of which Fenberg was usually so conscious. Fenberg was controlled weariness tonight, and it wasn't from the fight. Mitikitski squeezed him out of reflex, then winced. She forgot about his sore ribs.

"Sorry."

"Oh, that's okay. I'm just a little tender. I'll be better tomorrow after some sleep."

Elaine counted to ten.

"Can I ask a personal question?" Elaine wondered. They sat on the living room floor. Her head was on his chest, and they snuggled on the carpet, leaning against the sofa. Fenberg reached up and pulled the white and yellow Hudson Bay blanket down to cover them.

"It's not about how much I make. You already know that. It's not about the fight." Fenberg was silent for a long minute. "You want to know about my wife and baby," he said, quietly.

Elaine looked up. "Is that tacky? I mean, for me to ask?"

"I'd just chalk it up to morbid curiosity."

"So I'm morbidly curious," said Mitikitski. She had frequently noticed Fenberg stealing glances at that snapshot that never left his shirt pocket.

"Curiosity killed the cat."

"Satisfaction brought him back," answered Elaine, "and besides, you've pestered me about my past indiscretions."

"Tracy was not an indiscretion." There was just a little edge on that. Fenberg feigned joking. "That's because women should be completely open and honest about all their foibles while men have the right to be quiet and secretive. It's the male mystique."

"It won't work, Fenberg," said Elaine, hugging him. God, she was suddenly hungry. She had this craving for a relish sandwich on Wonder bread and a creamy A & W root beer float. "Would an exchange of information interest you?"

"You're not going to drop a fourth husband on me, are you?"

"Something even better."

Fenberg didn't answer. He didn't realize he was holding his breath.

"If this is too hard for you, Michael, I can certainly understand." Elaine craned her neck to look up at Fenberg. He was staring at the wall, narcotized. It was a soothing peach color, and he found a temporary escape just looking at it. A deep breath came, and he shook his head, refocusing on the rest of the room and the raven-haired editor with the delicate splattering of freckles.

"You know, I haven't talked about this, I guess, ever," he began. Elaine started to say he didn't have to, but Mike shook his head. "It's funny how you associate a few scenes so vividly with a person. I always think of Tracy on horseback. Her folks moved away after the accident. They had a good-sized horse ranch about ten miles from here, and I probably owe them twenty thousand dollars in meals. They bred Arabians, not the people, but the horses. Small heads, nasty tempers."

Fenberg glanced down at Elaine's flowing hair, partially covering him up and cascading onto the blanket.

"She could ride with the best of them and won all sorts of ribbons and trophies for show and jumping. She wore my varsity letterman's jacket for four years during high school. We were together almost every day since we were fourteen, through braces, a combined twelve-inch, 146-pound growth spurt, and fights, and reconciliations, and proms. It was high school nirvana. We even split apart for several years, dating other people. There was college and an ad agency for a few years for her. She was back here visiting her folks when we started it up again, stronger than ever. So strong. I felt that nothing, not all the gods in heaven, could break us up this time.

"We were in our mid-twenties when we had the big goof, and it was the happiest shotgun wedding on record. Damn nice girl," said Fenberg. He half-smiled at the recollection. "She was aggravatingly sane and well balanced. I've never met a person who laughed so easily and had such a rosy outlook on life. She was so perfect. This soft honey and buttermilk skin. Large, perfect breasts . . ." Elaine started to look down at her own. "Itty-bitty waist. Natural athlete and outdoorswoman. So pretty, and artistic too. She had this long, wavy blond hair that sort of fell over her eye like Veronica Lake. She had a devilish laugh and . . ."

Mitikitski rolled her eyes, smiled, and shook her head.

". . . was one of this century's great wise guys. Like Kipling's monkeys, we meant to do great things with our lives. Own our own paper and ranch. Travel. Open a restaurant in San Francisco. Had it all mapped out for the next sixty years, right down to giving the grandkids rides on the tractor and building special wings onto the house for our brothers and their wives to live in, though now, if she were here, we'd probably remap that last one."

Mitikitski imagined she would have liked Tracy.

"Anyway. The baby came, and he was a guy."

"What was his name?"

"He had several. Jack was on the birth certificate. We called him Dutch after Tracy's dad. The little guy had his mom's thick blond hair, my curls, her blue eyes, and someone's smile, we couldn't figure out whose, probably his own. John called him Champion Jack. Champion Jack Fenberg. My brother has trouble leaving things with their appointed names."

Mitikitski listened while Fenberg described the day of the accident, which ironically fell two nights before Christmas, five years ago. It was during one of those unforgiving cold snaps where the windchill factor dipped the temperature well below zero. It was a record-breaking cold throughout the state and especially biting in Basin Valley. Trees exploded, and cattle were found frozen to death standing on their feet. The sheriff thought it was a drunk driver that forced Fenberg's wife off the road. She and the baby would have lived, the doctor said, had the driver called to report the accident. But no one called. A full twenty-four hours passed before a search party found where the station wagon had careened over the embankment. Both occupants were dead, not from injuries, but from exposure. Mitikitski listened quietly, a little dazed hearing Fenberg talk about the accident, the funeral, and especially about packing away the baby's things in boxes.

Fenberg stopped talking, putting a quick cork on anything uncensored that might race to the surface unchecked. There are some things that hurt too much to be shown the light of day, images he falsely worshiped. Fenberg feared that if he ever began to let out the grief, it wouldn't stop, that it would all rush out and there would be nothing left of him.

"Hey, come here," said Elaine, sitting up and putting her arms around Fenberg. "I'm the one who should be holding you."

Fenberg concentrated on the wall and the color, focusing to control the great screaming monster in his chest. Lately, he had been having dreams, not the Tracy and Baby Fenberg Show, but dark dreams, of being held by the arms by hairy guardians. He would look over his shoulder and see a light— comfortable, secure, friendly—but it would only be a glimpse. And his attachment to his pain would lead him away from the light.

"Ah, Mike, if I haven't told you recently, I'm telling you now. I'm crazy about you." Although Mitikitski was tall, not quite five-nine, there was a certain round theme to her body, her breasts, the curve of her legs, the stomach somewhat. She held Fenberg close, running her fingers through his hair, reassuring, soothing. Fenberg pulled away.

"I'm sorry," said Fenberg, sitting up, "it just makes me feel a little claustrophobic."

Elaine smiled lovingly and started to touch his back, then dropped her hand. "Do you want to talk about it anymore?"

"No."

Elaine leaned against the sofa and hugged her knees. "I want you to know. If you ever need to talk about her, or anything, I'm here for you."

"Thanks."

They sat in distant silence on the floor, their backs to each other, Fenberg not wanting to move, Elaine wondering how she could tell him what she had to tell him. Maybe just wait. No. She had already waited too long. Any longer would be dangerous.

"I, uh . . . sort of think I could use a friend right now

myself," said Elaine to Fenberg's back. "You still in the friend business?"

"Open twenty-four hours," said Fenberg. He wanted desperately to be anywhere but there. Swallow it.

"You are such a dear friend to me, and much more, Michael. I am crazy about you." She thought about the word, 'crazy' and laughed. "I'm sorry you went through so much pain. And I'm sorry I don't make it any easier by quitting six times. But I get real scared. Every relationship I've had blows up in my face in a spectacular fashion. I suppose I try to run out before the next bomb goes off. I know this isn't the best time to bring this up, but we're at sort of a big crossroads in our relationship. Do you sort of know what I mean?"

He didn't.

"I've never met a fella like you. You make me feel so damn special. And corny. I feel like such an idiot around you sometimes, and yet, at the same time, very centered." I am about to win some sort of Congressional Vagueness Award, she thought. Maybe I should write a letter. No. "Have you ever considered having a more serious, uh," she closed her eyes, "commitment-type of relationship with me?" Mitikitski's pulse jumped. She wasn't asking the question for herself. "I'd like to talk to you about where our relationship is going and what we're going to do about some dead bunnies."

Mitikitski desperately hoped Fenberg would turn and look at her.

"I don't know if I could ever love like that again, Elaine. It just hurts too much."

Elaine felt the constriction in her throat.

"I guess for all my talking and looking, when the chips are on the table, I don't know if I would ever want to be attached to a woman and family. Ever."

"What are you trying to tell me?"

"It's just that we've had this terrific, best-behavior romance these last couple of months. . . ."

"Three."

"Three months. I feel I'm under a lot of pressure. That the world is coming down around me. I'm not being honest with you. God." Fenberg shook his head. "I feel I could just use a year. One year of rest and no problems and no brothers and no paper and no . . ."

It dangled in the air.

"Me?" asked Elaine softly.

"I can't think of a way of saying this without it sounding like a cliché."

"Please try. I'll make an appropriate wisecrack afterwards."

"I'd like to have some time by myself, no offense, away from everyone, even you, where I can sort things out."

"How long?" Elaine held her stomach.

"How about a month?" Fenberg shook his head. He felt scattered, as if he had climbed out of his body at several bus stops and was running around a strange city, trying to find himself. "Maybe just a week would be long enough."

"No. A month's fine," replied Elaine evenly. "If you don't mind, I think I'll go for a little walk. I need a little 'time and space,' too, as they say in Southern California," she said, forcing a smile.

"If you want, I'll get dressed and leave," said Fenberg, finally looking at her. "I mean, I sort of forced myself on you tonight anyway. . . ."

Elaine stood. She had a strong desire to be clothed. Quickly. "You didn't *force* yourself on me. I enjoyed it. At the time." She did an about-face and disappeared into her room. Fenberg stared at the carpet. He suddenly had the embarrassing sensation of being naked.

"Elaine?" he called to the next room. "Is something wrong?"

Men can be *so fucking stupid!*

"Is anything wrong?" Fenberg asked again as Elaine walked briskly by, tucking her hair into a blue and white stocking cap. She was dressed for a long walk, it looked like. Boots, ski parka, two sweaters.

Yeah. Something's wrong.

"No. Nothing's wrong," she said to the nude man under the blanket. She stopped at the door. "I'm sorry you got hurt tonight, and maybe I'm not being a good friend. But you'd better like me, Fenberg. I'll see you through anything, but you'd better like me. We could be the best thing to ever happen to one another. You would miss me very much if I were gone, and I know I'd sure miss you, and I'm not just saying this stuff just for me. . . ."

"What is wrong, Elaine?"

"Nothing." She walked out the front door and slammed it. On the porch, she clenched her fists and vented a mime's roar of exasperation. Maybe it was the fresh mountain air. Or maybe it was Fenberg's high cholesterol diet and particular gene package. Whatever the reason, despite all those safe years of non-protected sexual recreation and dire head-shakings by medicine's finest, Elaine Mitikitski was going to have Michael Fenberg's baby, and she considered him an insensitive stupid man-guy ignoramus for not somehow knowing it.

15

NO PETS ALLOWED

The door slammed. Sitting wrapped in a blanket, alone in a peach-colored apartment with posters of dainty ballerinas, houseplants, teapots, and stuffed animals, Fenberg felt out of place. He also thought about punching himself in the nose. Should he wrap a towel around his fist first, to soften the blow, or favor the other extreme and use brass knuckles?

Maybe a simple apology would do, if it weren't too late.

Fenberg climbed up to the sofa and got dressed. The last boot was tugged on slowly, since Fenberg really had no place special to go. It was after ten, and the boys would be out of the movies soon. He'd have to pick them up at Malulu's, and the thought didn't make Fenberg want to do any Cheetah-the-chimp backflips. But it would probably be the polite thing to do, pick them up before they did something heinous.

Maybe heinous acts ran in the family.

What was happening to him? He felt so out of control, and tonight, in the bar, he'd been close to losing it. Losing what? He didn't know, and that was the scary part. For some reason, he was mad at Mitikitski. Why? She hadn't done anything, and she sure as heck was right. He would miss her if anything happened. He liked her. He really liked her, on a smooth, everyday basis. But what was going on?

The Fenberg genes. Michael shook his head knowingly.

The dreaded Fenberg genes.

He was finally going crazy, not even colorful, but crazy.

"I wish I could be in love with you, Mitikitski," Fenberg said out loud to himself. One hundred percent. I wish you were the one. I wish we could run the tape back tonight, and I could tell you how much I cared for you. I'd also like to tell you that you scare the hell out of me, Mitikitski, because no matter what you say about being there, I have this deep premonition that you won't. Everyone in my life who was close to me is either dead or nuts. I have this gut feeling you're going to break my heart, and I won't be strong enough to come back this time. And on top of everything else, I miss my wife and baby, and I wish I didn't.

Fenberg tucked in his shirt and walked over to the sliding glass window. He peeked out through the drapes. The storm was clearing. Clouds raced through the open sky, like ghosts darting to get home before dawn. The moon would be full tomorrow night.

Someone knocked on the door, a familiar shave-and-a-haircut knock. Fenberg strode across the room, ready to read Clifford and Joe the riot act for wandering the streets at night with a maniac around. Fenberg opened the door. He saw a brief vision of something filling the doorway, huge, hairy, with yellow fangs staring down at him. It growled. Fenberg slammed the door and leaned on it. He blinked. Yes. It was true, his worst suspicions confirmed. Fenberg was going crazy. He was hearing things. He was seeing things.

"Oh geez. I've got to see a doctor," said Fenberg weakly.

He held his breath. He listened. Through the walls drifted a curious, muted voice. Familiar, it sang a childhood jingle.

"McDonald's is your kind of place. They steal your parking space. They feed you rattlesnakes. The last time I was there, they fried my underwear. But really, I don't care. It wasn't my best pair." The singing stopped. The doorbell rang.

Fenberg heard a familiar voice that made him jump.

"Buddy. Buddy-buddy. It's me, your buddy."

Fenberg looked through the peephole and saw a distorted face. Stretched out of proportion was the tiny head on huge shoulders in a tight white T-shirt.

"*Norwood!*" yelled Fenberg, flinging open the door. Tuberski sheepishly stepped inside and held his arms out.

"It's John," he said. "I changed it."

With some effort, Fenberg grabbed his little brother around the waist and hoisted him in the air. "Goddamn it, I missed you!" Fenberg yelled. He dropped Tuberski for inspection. None the worse for wear for being gone three months. He couldn't have been living in the woods and come out looking so clean, Fenberg deduced. "Where in the hell have you been?"

"In the woods," said Tuberski.

Fenberg shook his head slowly, happy to see his brother. Fenberg closed the door and hugged Tuberski again. "I thought you were dead. Do you know everyone in the world is looking for you?"

"Sure do. That's why I was hiding, Mike." Tuberski sported an infectious grin, but he looked awkwardly away. "I would have called, honest, but there's lots going on that I just couldn't involve you in. I didn't want you to be an accessory. Geez, Mikey. It's real good seeing you, too. I was getting pretty homesick."

"I thought I was going crazy," said Fenberg, leading his brother to the sofa. Tuberski craned his neck, looking back at the door. "How have you been? Where have you been? God, you must be hungry. I'll see if I can scare up something to eat, but I don't know because Mitikitski doesn't keep real food in the house. Where have you been?" Fenberg asked again, not able to stop grinning.

"Who's Mitikitski?" asked Tuberski, still looking uncomfortably at the door.

"She's this incredible woman I'm . . ." Fenberg wanted to say ". . . in love with," but something stopped him. "uhhh . . . dating. I guess she went out for a walk. You'll love her."

"Buddy, I've left something in the hallway that I think I probably really ought to bring in," said Tuberski, nervously rubbing his hands on his jeans. Michael walked with him to the door.

"God, you know,. when you knocked, I thought I was going crazy? I opened the door, and I had this hallucination some—thing—was standing in the doorway. I mean, it was something you . . . *painted whores of Babylon!*" shrieked Fenberg, crouching.

"Mikey, lower your voice a few octaves," whispered Tuberski. "And quit standing like that. You'll scare him."

Fenberg did scare him. Or it. It ducked into the hallway. All Fenberg could see was the dimly lit hall and the steps outside.

"Come here," Tuberski urged something. "Come on! Don't be afraid, it's okay. C'mon. . . ."

A hand, or hairy paw, timidly reached around the door frame. Fenberg shrieked again and literally jumped backwards. The hand was the size of a Thanksgiving turkey.

Tuberski clicked his tongue, as if he were calling an unruly horse. "C'mon, will you get in here, you worthless pelt?" Tuberski urged, grabbing the thing by the wrist and tugging. Tuberski, it should be noted, who could bend steel in his bare hands, was having a difficult time pulling whatever was attached to the rest of that wrist.

"This, Michael, is my protégé," said Tuberski, beaming and gesturing magnanimously upwards. Fenberg couldn't close his mouth or take his eyes off the man-thing that had to duck and bend sideways to enter Elaine Mitikitski's apartment. "And, may I add, our meal ticket to prosperity? This is my brother, Mikey. Say hello to my brother."

Tuberski's protégé ignored Fenberg. The creature's neck turned, and his nose quivered from an overload of scents and sensations pulsating from Mitikitski's apartment. He looked around and nodded appreciatively. It was cheery. It had a light touch, and it was certainly decorated better than his dark cave. The thing stood in the living room, knees slightly bent because his pointed head was scraping the ceiling. If Fenberg weren't in a state of mild shock, he would have quickly deduced the thing was a few inches over eight feet tall. There would be other details Fenberg would fill in later when he composed himself: weight—nearly a half-ton; hair—

lots of it, all over, light brown, matted, and shaggy; eye color—hazel; occupation—creature. He was a big boy. And he smelled.

"Say hello to my brother. Go ahead," said Tuberski, poking the thing in the ribs, an aggravating habit John had inherited from his mother.

The thing looked down at Fenberg and scowled. He had seen lots of humans before, but the face on this one seemed familiar. The beast lowered his eyebrows farther and sniffed. A faint vision of the funeral floated by—this was the tall man who had been with the woman who had the well-turned ankle that he had chased and fallen in love with.

"Foof!" It was a cross between a sneeze and a bark and Fenberg overreacted.

"I don't think he likes you, Mikey."

The thing ignored Fenberg, not wanting to grace him with his attention any longer. He moved easily past him, towards the fireplace and mantel.

"He won't hurt you or anything," said Tuberski, tossing a thumb in the beast's retreating direction. "Playful as a kitten. Got a heart as big as all outdoors."

Fenberg cautiously stepped closer to Tuberski. The monster spun and crouched.

"Buddy. He thinks you're trying to sneak up on him."

The creature's eyes locked on Fenberg's. Fenberg could hear a low, guttural growl deep from within the eighty-five-inch chest.

"If you'd like a little advice, you might want to stop acting like you're sneaking around the corner of a building in a bad spy movie," said Tuberski. "He'll think you're trying to sneak up on him or that you want to play. Either way, he might bite you."

"Bite me?" repeated Fenberg, trying to figure how to act natural while frozen in midstep.

"I can't seem to break him of it," said Tuberski, putting his hands on his hips and shaking his head. "Every once in a while, he'll take a little nip at you. Nothing serious, just annoying. A bad habit, I guess."

Fenberg put his leg down and smiled, looking at the jaws that had probably devoured ten people. Bites. The creature's growls increased, and he feigned a short lunge at Fenberg.

Tuberski sighed.

"You want to see Charlie?" John asked. The creature pretended not to hear him. "You see this?" Tuberski asked again, showing the beast a fist. "You want to see Charlie?" The man-thing looked uncertainly between Fenberg and Tuberski. To save some dignity, he threw a disdainful "foof" at Fenberg then sniffed at something on the mantel.

"I sock him in the thigh and give him a charley-horse when he doesn't listen," said Tuberski. "It's not exactly enlightened John Bradshaw, who, as you know, is one of my heroes, but it works." He engulfed Fenberg in a bear hug. "Michael, I've missed you and the boys and the ranch so much. You really won't believe what's been happening the last few months. Boy, have I got some stories, and, most importantly, this time our ship has come in," grinned Tuberski. He patted his stomach. " 'Kay. I'm hungry. This new girlfriend of yours got anything to eat?" John walked into the kitchen and yelled from in there. "What did you say her name was?"

The creature turned his head quickly and glowered at Fenberg, who had the sensation of being a very small boy in a fenced yard with a very large dog. Fenberg cautiously tucked his hands into his jeans and didn't move. He had no idea what the hell the thing was or how well it listened to his brother. Reality, of some sort, was coming into focus. Fenberg tried to piece together some sort of reference as to what was going on. Tuberski looked the same. The face was still too small for the body, and he was maybe a little more gaunt, but Tuberski didn't look that bad for having been living in the woods for twelve weeks in the dead of winter. Which didn't make sense. Fenberg knew that his brother consumed something like seven thousand calories a day, putting away a half-dozen burgers and as many orders of fries in one sitting, washed down by Coke and malts. And Tuberski was so *clean*. You couldn't live in the woods for three months without getting dirty. Tuberski was even freshly shaven, and

Fenberg could smell the waning odor of his brother's trade-mark aftershave: Virgin Islands Bay Rum mixed with Polo. And speaking of odors, that thing the size of two gorillas sitting in the middle of Elaine's living room literally *stunk*. Fenberg's eyes were watering.

"This woman friend of yours eats like a mouse," said Tuberski, coming out of the kitchen with a loaf of Wonder bread and a jar of relish. "I've never seen such a collection of stuff. She's got all this health food, and her trash is lined with a bunch of Baby Ruth wrappers. Must be a Gemini. Or maybe she's pregnant, heh-heh. Well, we gotta be going. . . ."

"What!"

"I was just kidding. How's your pal, Behan?" asked Tuberski, dipping a slice of bread into the relish. "I wish she would have left a candy bar."

"Behan's still around, kicking big dents in *The Bugle*." Fenberg was spellbound. Something on the mantel had caught the creature's attention. It lightly touched a framed photograph of Elaine and made a small, whimpering noise. "Why is he making that noise?"

"I don't know." Tuberski ambled over to look. "Here. Let me see. Whatdya got there?"

"Ooooh," said Tuberski's protégé, gently showing John the photo. Tuberski chewed and thoughtfully regarded Mitikitski's picture. The creature made a move for the bread, and Tuberski lightly slapped his hand away.

"Mike. She's gorgeous. Absolutely gorgeous."

"Yeah, she is, isn't she?" admitted Fenberg.

"I take it she must be a newcomer. Someone who looks like this couldn't stay a secret for long living in Basin Valley."

"She's Henry Darich's replacement."

"Better looking than Henry," said Tuberski, handing the frame back to the monster. "You know what? She reminds me of somebody, and I can't quite place it."

Snow White, thought Fenberg, but he didn't want to get into that. Monster or no monster, there were a few thousand small points that had to be cleared up with Tuberski. Like where he had been, why had he forged Michael's name on all those credit cards, what happened on the night of the murder(s), and what was that monster doing in Elaine Mitikitski's living room, just for starters.

"I guess you're kind of sore at me," said Tuberski.

"I'm a little too numb to be mad at you, but give me a minute." Fenberg grabbed a dining room chair and straddled it. The creature didn't pay any attention to Fenberg, and Michael was beginning to feel that at least with Tuberski present, there would be little if any danger. "The beginning."

Tuberski gave a slice of Wonder bread to the monster, who sniffed it before swallowing it whole.

"First off, how did you find me?"

"Truck's parked outside. Seeing that this is a duplex and the one downstairs is empty . . ."

"John, do you have any idea how much trouble you're in?"

"Bunches?"

"First off, you are wanted as the prime suspect in ten murders." Fenberg glanced at the creature.

Tuberski made a face. "Geez. Ten?"

"Yes, ten. I've been keeping track. And what on earth prompted you—*Get off that couch!*"

The creature flinched when Fenberg yelled at him, then bared his teeth defensively. He was leaning on the sofa on his elbows, sniffing the cushions. The light maroon-colored couch was creaking under his weight.

"He's going to break the couch if he doesn't get off it," said Fenberg, half getting out of his chair. "Get off!"

The creature was awkwardly lying on his back, half on the sofa, half off, in a supine position, his upper lip curled in a slight sneer.

"Goddamn it," said Fenberg.

Any further confrontation, however, was interrupted by a knock on Elaine Mitikitski's well-worn front door. Tuberski jumped, and the monster quickly vaulted to its haunches, almost in a sprinter's position.

"She must be a popular girl," whispered Tuberski. He silently mouthed, "Get rid of them," and led the beast into Elaine's bedroom, closing the door behind them.

"Just a second!" said Fenberg.

The knocker pounded again, this time more insistent.

"I'm coming, hang on!" yelled Fenberg, checking to see if there were any telltale signs of his company. "Who is it?"

"Open up, please. It's me, Cousin."

Great, thought Fenberg. Just great. He reluctantly opened the door, holding his arm on the frame to act as a barrier.

"Hi, Bubba. Stereo on too loud?"

"Hi, Mikey." Sheriff Bubba Fenberg smiled, revealing the spaces between his teeth. With his fatness and beige suit, he looked like a handyman with a gun. "You know, it's funny," Bubba said, rubbing the back of his neck. "You stay in this job long enough, you'll hear just about everything."

"I want to thank you for coming over at this time of night to share that," said Fenberg, swinging the door shut. Bubba casually blocked the move by sticking his hand in the door-jamb.

"There's more to it."

"Oh?"

"I got a call from an elderly lady across the street."

"Mrs. Cowling?"

"That'd be she."

"Nosy lady."

"A bit of a pain, at times," said Bubba. "We get a call once a month from her, complaining of prowlers and rapists. Wishful thinking, I suppose."

"I'm sorry," said Fenberg, "if that helps."

"Thank you. Only tonight, she calls and says she sees a big guy in a white T-shirt tiptoeing across the street hand in hand with a giant gorilla."

It's a monster, not a gorilla, thought Fenberg.

"And she says she saw both parties knock on this door and enter. Where's your girlfriend?"

"Out. Taking a walk. You wouldn't be calling my girlfriend a gorilla, would you?"

"And I suppose you've been here all night?" asked Bubba, ignoring his cousin's question.

Fenberg half-smiled. "I was over at the Zoo, earlier."

Bubba chuckled. "So I heard. So I heard." He wrinkled his nose and sniffed. "That Miss Mitikitski own a cat?"

Fenberg nodded sympathetically. "Cat odor and cigar odor. You just can't get them out."

"Smells more like skunk."

"Elaine's eclectic, but she doesn't own a skunk."

"I think I'd like to come in and check around, if you don't mind."

"I guess I ask the generic question: search warrant?"

"And this is where I take out my service .45," said Bubba, doing just that. Fenberg let him in. Bubba glided past Michael, his eyes darting back and forth for a possible ambush. He spotted something by the sofa. Bubba picked up the blue and white plastic bread wrapper and discarded it. Then he picked up a long, shaggy hair. "Sort of long," he said, holding it out to Fenberg.

Fenberg shrugged. "She's got long hair."

Bubba examined the thick strand. "Tell her to use a better creme rinse. You want to open that door for me, cousin?"

"Well, I was sort of fibbing when you came in," said Fenberg, smiling man-to-man. "You see, Elaine didn't go for a walk, she's still in the bedroom, and, well, you know . . ."

"Open the door," said the sheriff. "Worst thing that'll happen is I'll have to apologize."

"Okay," said Fenberg. He raised his voice. "Honey! Make yourself decent. We've got company! It's my cousin!"

Fenberg opened the door and peeked. There were two indentations where his brother and the creature had been sitting on the bed. It was easy to see where they'd gone. Mitikitski's sliding glass door was open, and the standard-issue beige apartment drapes were blowing in the breeze.

"See?" said Fenberg. "Like I said. She went for a walk and doesn't own a skunk."

Bubba quickly walked to the window and crouched. He slid the door open all the way, checking to see if someone was on the narrow railing outside. No. He checked under the bed, then carefully opened Elaine's closet. Just clothes. No monster, no Tuberski. Bubba holstered his gun and pointed two chubby fingers at Fenberg's nose. "You're getting deep into something that will cause you grief. And it'll all be for nothing." With that the sheriff left, closing the door behind him.

Fenberg was tempted to double-check the closet, but then dismissed the idea as ridiculous. He walked onto the tiny balcony where Elaine had a couple of hardy plants. Fenberg looked up at the roof. It was too tall for even the creature to reach. Fenberg spotted the footprints in the moist soil about ten feet to the right, and then the dogs started barking. First two, a block away, Fenberg thought, but couldn't pick out which direction.

Then the rest of Basin Valley's yard hounds joined in the cacophony, barking, yelping angrily, throwing themselves against their leashes and chain link fences. Avoiding the light from a distant street lamp, Fenberg crept through the long shadows next to the apartment, following the trail to another backyard. He checked for dogs, then climbed the rickety fence. A clump of matted hair stuck in a splinter, and Fenberg wondered how the rotten wood could hold the beast's weight, then decided he'd probably jumped it. The spoor wasn't difficult to follow. Fenberg saw muddy footprints emerge from the front lawn onto the sidewalk and progress onto the street. They disappeared in the grass in the yard of a corner home.

"What in hell is going on out there!" A screen door crashed and an elderly woman stepped onto the porch of the Victorian-style house.

"Gas company," said Fenberg. "Just checking the meter!"

"Ten o'clock on a Saturday night? I'm calling the police!" barked Mrs. Cowling.

Fenberg lightly jogged across the street. There were no lights on in the corner house, and the wet lawn offered no more hint as to where his brother and the monster had gone. Fenberg slinked along on the edge of the grass, trying to find mud or hair or a boot print on the sidewalk.

"Psst!"

Fenberg looked around.

"Over here!" Tuberski stepped from the shadows and waved frantically.

Fenberg looked quickly up and down the street for patrol cars or snoopy neighbors. He stepped carefully into the dark, trying to see where the creature was standing.

"Mikey, we've got big trouble."

"Yeah, I know. In case you didn't hear, that was our cousin at Elaine's, the one with the badge. Some old biddy spotted you going into the apartment with the 'Creature from the Black Lagoon.' He's probably somewhere on this block looking for you right now. Where's the thing?" Fenberg asked, looking around.

"That's sort of the problem."

"You mean, he's loose in town here?"

"That's close, but that's not really the problem."

"John, we don't have time to play twenty questions. What *is* the problem?"

"He sort of kidnapped some lady who was walking down the street."

"He fucking *what?*"

Tuberski held out his hands, trying to placate Fenberg. "When we climbed out the window, he got a little bit of a jump on me. I lost track of him, then I saw him scoop up some woman about a block away."

"What?"

"Well, he sort of jumped out in front of her, and from what I could tell in the dark, she sort of fainted, I guess. And he sort of scooped her up and ran off with her."

"Stop saying sort of."

"Okay. He did."

Mitikitski. Oh God, thought Fenberg.

"Was this woman wearing a yellow ski parka and a blue and white toque?"

"A what?"

"A toque. A cap, goddamn it!"

Tuberski thought for a moment, then nodded his head. "Yeah, I think. It was dark, but I remember the yellow. The cap, I can't remember, except it was striped. I yelled after him, but he galloped off in that direction," said Tuberski, pointing to the dark hills.

"Shit!" Fenberg bit his lip and paced, trying to compose himself and think. Think. It wasn't working. He slugged his brother in the arm instead.

"Ow!" said Tuberski, holding his bicep.

"We've got to get her back," said Fenberg. It seemed every dog in the world was barking. Fenberg could hear the growl of high-powered engines and the screech of tires the next street over. He and Tuberski sprinted in the opposite direction, but ran into the blinding glare of high beams and spotlights. Over a loudspeaker, an automaton voice, emotionless, ordered them to halt. In less than three seconds, Fenberg was standing in the middle of the wet street with his hands up. He turned to tell his brother how embarrassing this was going to be, except his brother was no longer there.

"Halt!" barked the deputy, crouching low with both hands on his revolver, elbows locked. Tuberski ran directly at the deputy, screaming, and stepped on the hood of the patrol car, launching himself over the roof. The deputy followed his arc through midair, shooting him squarely in the small of the back. Fenberg saw his brother grab his spine, then land. Tuberski's legs went out from under him, and he rolled several times before trying to stand. He couldn't. Tuberski fell forward, arms outstretched, and lay still on the cold, wet pavement.

No thoughts entered Fenberg's mind, just reaction. He sprinted toward the deputy who had fired the shot. The deputy turned, shock and fear on his face. Fenberg figured the man wouldn't have time to turn his gun all the way around before Michael could get his hands around the deputy's throat. But something distracted Michael's attention. A collision. A dull ache. He didn't feel the rifle butt hit him in the back of the neck, but he felt suddenly very light. His head seemed to be traveling in a direction separate from his body, his eyes taking in the tops of the trees and stars, then men in brown shirts, and finally he saw the wet sparkle of the road and a pair of polished black shoes with water drops on them. And then, darkness.

16

JAILBIRDS

Bubba Fenberg was proud of his jail, and justly so. It was escape-proof. It was 131 years old, a minimalist white concrete and adobe bunker that sat on the lawn of the town square, begrudgingly housing the other county offices. The great sugar cube eyesore had been specially constructed to incarcerate Lupe Valdez, the famed claim jumper and bank robber who'd terrorized California during the Gold Rush. Lupe's bloodthirsty gang had attempted a jailbreak of their leader, and the bullet holes from their unsuccessful attempt were still lodged in the thick walls as a memento and warning to those who would assault justice.

Through stealth and violence, more desperate men than the Fenberg brothers had tried and failed to escape the Basin County pokey. Tuberski didn't even have the distinction of being the first cannibal.

Arthur Mantooth, the legendary Indian trombone murderer of 1931, terrorized the valley one dusty Depression summer. Mantooth, a deranged and walleyed Alliklik warrior, preyed on young and old alike, beating his victims to death with a trombone and then eating their fresh, warm hearts.

"It gives Mantooth much strength to eat the hearts of his enemies," Mantooth had told a distant Fenberg relative and editor of *The Bugle*, little realizing that it was the Aztec, not the Alliklik, who practiced this savage rite. He made three attempted prison breaks, the last two being halfhearted efforts of lunging through the bars at a deputy who was a safe twelve arm-lengths away. Mantooth was lynched.

Nearly twenty-five years later, Basin Valley fathered another mass murderer, the quiet and demure high school honor student, Toddy Honeycutt. Toddy poisoned everyone in the 1953 Cougar homecoming parade. It was an unforgettable sight as captured on the yellowed pages of a *Bugle* back edition. Around the dirt track surrounding the football field, a quarter of Basin Valley's teenage population, still in formal gowns and tuxedos rented from ninety miles away, lay awkwardly strewn in overturned floats and stalled convertibles. It was one of the nation's worst high school disasters.

The last mass murderer of Basin Valley was the transient Carlos Cauderno. During an Easter vacation in the sixties, Cauderno got drunk and climbed to the top of Rocky Point overlooking Rocky Point Park. Eight hundred feet above the picnic area, after several more bottles of cheap wine, he became enthralled with the idea of loosening the fourteen-ton Rocky Point boulder. Cauderno caused the boulder to bounce down onto a Methodist picnic below, killing six and squishing many others. Mantooth, Honeycutt, Cauderno—and better men than they—had all tried and failed to escape from the Basin County Jail.

* * * * *

Tuberski awoke to the uncomfortable feeling of a damp, dirty pillow. He heard the sounds of steel swishing and men grunting in combat. Tuberski had been drooling in his sleep. Mouth open, and half his face buried in the well-used prison-issue pillow, Tuberski surveyed his familiar surroundings. Holding cell number two.

Across the way, on the top bunk, Charlie Two Eagles Soaring was asleep on his side, his back to John. Charlie was snoring off a monumental drunk. Shaking on the floor in the corner, a gray blanket pulled all the way up to his pitted glasses, was Bean Breath Brown. In the cramped center of the cell, Fenberg was nimbly dodging the knife thrusts of the weasely Red Dog Rassmussen.

Tuberski blinked and yawned. He and Fenberg had already been awake that morning at six, had breakfast and been informed that they were in trouble. Bean Breath arrived shortly after ten.

Fenberg was not speaking to Tuberski.

Tuberski groaned and sat up stiffly. He stretched and tried to rub the small of his back where the rubber-tipped expanding riot bullet had hit last night.

"Sort of state of the art in crowd control," Tuberski had explained first thing to Fenberg, who hadn't asked. Fenberg seemed disappointed. "Doesn't penetrate the body, just sort of knocks you out with no supposed side effects, except my kidneys hurt, and I think I've got a bruise."

Tuberski's legs dangled over the sides of the top bunk. He smacked his lips. His mouth felt as if he had been licking newsprint. Tuberski quickly jerked his legs out of the way as Red Dog slashed high at Fenberg's face. Fenberg ducked. The blade jammed into the wooden corner post of Tuberski's bunk.

The hatchet-faced part-Indian's expression quickly turned from triumphant bloodlust to whoops, sorry. There were footprints on Fenberg's muddy shirt, which was also torn at the sleeves from where Red Dog had slashed at him. Dried blood stuck in his ear, his hair was mussed, and Fenberg had a migraine. He fiercely gritted his teeth and pounced on Rassmussen.

Tuberski sighed. He slid off the top bunk and walked to the elevated barred window, stretching as he went. Outside, it was a clear blue morning. Spring was near. Inside, Fenberg had Red Dog by the throat and was banging him against the bars.

"I've got to hand it to you," said Tuberski. He could see most of the town square from the window. "Most people find it difficult to adjust to prison life. You seem to have picked it up just ducky."

Slam-slam-slam against the bars, Fenberg bounced the sinewy half-breed.

"It's like that in the big house," said Tuberski, philosophically.

Slam-slam. Red Dog's eyes were bulging, and his tongue was turning a grotesque blue.

"The strong pick on the weak. The large prey on the little." Slam.

Fenberg, still gritting his teeth, reluctantly looked at his brother. He took a deep breath and straightened Red Dog's collar.

"This is the second time he's snuck up and tried to kill me," said Fenberg, holding up two fingers. "Second time!" He wiggled the knife free from the bedpost.

Tuberski's expression brightened.

"And I'm still not talking to you," Fenberg said. He threw the knife at Bean Breath Brown. It stuck, quivering, in the wood floor next to him. "And I'm not talking to you, either." Bean had snuck the knife through the window that morning. Unfortunately, he had handed it to Red Dog Rassmussen. Bean was apprehended shortly thereafter.

Bean offered a passive smile.

"Just goddamn it anyway," said Fenberg, to himself. He walked back to his bunk, sidestepping Red Dog. Red was bundled in the fetal position, clutching his throat. His breath came in hacking stabs and hisses. Fenberg told him he was a discredit to real Indians everywhere, then went to his bunk to sulk.

Tuberski meandered to his brother's cot and sat next to him. The bunk creaked from the weight. Fenberg wiggled so they wouldn't be touching.

"I'm sorry," said Tuberski.

Silence from Fenberg.

"Are you still not talking to me?"

More silence.

"You know, you can't *not* talk to me forever. I mean, you have to talk to me sometime. I *am* your brother."

There was a groan from the upper bunk. Charlie Two Eagles Soaring moaned and tried to get up on one elbow. The attempt failed.

Tuberski stared at Fenberg. Fenberg slowly rubbed his palms together. Tuberski smiled hopefully, waiting, like a puppy for a kind word. Fenberg patted an unruly cowlick, and Tuberski quickly offered his black plastic comb. Fenberg took it, spit on it, and handed it back.

"You're still sore, aren't you?" Tuberski asked, wiping the comb on his jeans.

Michael looked at John. Huh? Sore?

Tuberski dearly wished that Fenberg would yell at him, or hit him, or give him that icy, sardonic smile that meant, some-how, somewhere, Fenberg would get even with some satanic, inspired practical joke. Like the time in high school Fenberg had stapled him to the garage door for the weekend. But Fenberg just stared straight ahead, rubbing his palms. Tuber-ski did the same.

An hour later, Fenberg spoke.

"Dead bunnies . . ." he said, straightening.

"What?"

"She said, 'dead bunnies.'" Fenberg pictured Elaine's angelic face, the hair stuck at the temples from the sweat of their lovemaking. The bright, light blue eyes and that biteable lower lip.

"*I'd like to talk to you about where our relationship is going and what we're going to do about some dead bunnies.*" Miti-kitski's words came back to him.

"Ohhh, God! How could I have been so stupid?" Fenberg said, still frozen.

"What?" asked Tuberski. "What, what?"

Fenberg's eyes darted back and forth. He had gone through this before. With Tracy. He should have remembered. Elaine had been going through these wild emotional swings, up and down. Little things setting her off, making her cry. At other times, she'd get the giggles. The time off from work. Getting sick in the morning—what do you need, Fenberg, a goddamn caveman to chisel the message on your forehead in reverse and hold a mirror to your face? Elaine had been gaining weight, her breasts were getting larger, and coming right out and saying, ". . . dead bunnies"?

Christ. The rabbit died. She's going to have a baby.

"This still doesn't mean I'm speaking to you," said Fenberg to his brother. "But somehow, some way, we've got to break out of here."

"No one's ever broken out of here," said Tuberski, looking at the bars. "The concrete's a yard thick; the bars are solid steel."

"I'm getting out, John. Today. Are you coming with me?"

Tuberski looked at the bars again, then at his brother. "Let's do it."

Fenberg put his hands on his hips and paced. A plan. They needed a plan. And then they needed to find Mitikitski. Where the hell could she be?

* * * * *

Elaine was in the woods.

She was lost.

The creature wasn't.

Elaine had been minding her own business the night before, taking a brisk walk through Basin Valley's tree-lined residential district, thinking bad thoughts about Fenberg and how she'd have to start looking for those god-awful circus tent maternity clothes. The hell with him. She'd have the kid by herself, Elaine planned. Maybe staying six months until it really started to show, embarrass that son of a bitch Fenberg in front of everyone in town, then move back home to have her little girl. Elaine knew it was going to be a girl. She already had the named picked—Katie Scarlett O. Mitikitski.

It had been a nice night for a walk. Brisk and damp, but refreshing. All the trees and houses had been washed clean, and there was that invigorating smell of mountain water and pine. She didn't think anything about all the dogs barking. There was no one on the street when Elaine decided to walk through the deserted town square. She rounded a tall bush and bumped squarely into what she immediately categorized as a yak. It was big enough to be a yak, and had that musky yak odor, but, of course, there were no yaks indigenous to

Basin Valley. Only monsters.

Tuberski's creature stood in front of Elaine, whimpering and holding onto his left arm, as if asking for help. But Elaine didn't notice that. She looked up and saw two photosensitive eyes, glaring red and looking somewhat sinister, blinking down at her, and that was that. Mitikitski crumpled to the ground. She didn't feel the large, calloused hands reach down to pick her up as if she were only a kitten.

During the first ten miles, Mitikitski had been aware of the rush of cold air and the pounding footsteps at a subliminal level. She thought she had been sleeping and had been awakened by one of those California earthquakes, but it was Tuberski's creature running and walking through the woods. He carried her over his shoulder, fireman style. He smelled to the dickens, and it's strange what a person thinks about in times of stress, Elaine noted. She was wondering if the dry cleaners would be able to get the stench out of her clothes.

She watched the back of his heels picking up, one after the other, and the ground sliding constantly backward, like she was in the back of a station wagon and being hypnotized by the steady pulses of the dotted white line of the center divider. They effortlessly ate up mile after mile of some of God's most unforgiving terrain. The creature walked straight up mountains and ran down the other side. He splish-splashed through gentle, babbling streams, and she screamed as he picked her up over his head, twelve feet in the air, as he forded a major river. Occasionally, he would switch her from shoulder to shoulder and at one point, crossing what she imagined to be a meadow, he carried her like a demon groom would carry his doll bride and ran. The biting of the cold wind and the sensation of speed were pleasant at times, a dreamlike state of shock.

They traveled all night, and Elaine had to worry what effect the jostling would have on the small, slowly spinning seed inside her that would someday be, knock on hairy back, Baby Katie Scarlett. Through her grunts and groans (she was afraid to hit), she had communicated to the creature that she wanted to be put down. Which he did from time to time. But then, looking worriedly behind him, he would scoop her up and start off again for points unknown.

Just before dawn they reached their destination. It was a cave, nestled in the side of a hill and hidden from view by two small scrub oaks. The opening faced eastward. Elaine shivered and happily greeted the warming rays of sun. The creature had dumped her, gently but unceremoniously, then left.

At first Mitikitski sat in a ball, hugging herself. She was so caught up at the moment in being cold and somewhat grateful about touching the non-moving ground that she didn't consider escape.

But slowly she warmed. She uncreaked her legs and twisted her neck and back, languidly stretching and cracking. Nothing broken, although she knew she'd have a dandy black and blue mark on her side. She patted her tummy. No. Her little friend inside was okay. There was a spotlight of sun from the entrance, and as she sat in it, Mitikitski realized that this cavern was surprisingly warm and dry. Dry was one thing. Warm was another. It shouldn't have been that warm. Elaine leaned over and felt the walls of the cave. They were emanating a comfortable heat. Her eyes were used to the dark now and Mitikitski thought about maybe exploring a little. No. No, thank you. *I don't particularly want to go play touch-feely in a dark cave that is probably populated with bats, poop, corpses in various states of decomposition, and quite possibly, other monsters, thank you very much,* she thought.

Mitikitski spotted a pinpoint of light, peeking around a distant corner of the cave. Another entrance? It might be good to know, she thought, rubbing her hands together and blowing on them. Elaine lurched her head forward, trying to pick up a noise. It sounded like water running. Possible, of course. No. It was more like bubbling or crackling in the distance. Elaine found herself inching her way along the wall before she caught herself.

"What am I doing? Get a grip, Elaine," she said out loud. "You can play Explorer Scout some other time."

The creature had left. She figured it wasn't a monster, just an elusive Sasquatch. An elusive Sasquatch that had eaten ten people. Elaine chided herself for thinking about that. She had read they were nocturnal. Maybe he had gone someplace to sleep all day. God. Elaine shook her head and actually smiled. That would be too easy. Just walk out of the cave and . . .

And what?

Head west, she thought.

What if he's out there?

You won't know till you stick your head out and find out, will you?

Adrenalin.

Mitikitski moved forward. She heard the sound of something heavy moving outside in the underbrush. Elaine threw her back against the wall and waited. She heard a grunt, and the light at the mouth of the cave was momentarily snuffed out by the silhouette of the man-thing. Elaine slowly retreated into the cave. She could see the eyes, red and glowing. She knew he could see her wherever she went. He gestured and, that failing, took Mitikitski by the wrist, leading her outside.

Mitikitski shielded her eyes from the sudden bright light. The thing pushed her down into a sitting position and pointed to a flat rock in front of her. There was a squirrel lying on the rock. It was dead. The creature sat across from Elaine and motioned to her, then to the squirrel.

Mitikitski stared at the dead rodent, not wanting to look up into the hairy, catcher's-mask face or at the yellow tusks. The creature touched the squirrel with a black, leathery index finger, then poked Elaine.

I think he's trying to communicate, thought Elaine.

"Me Elaine. That's a squirrel," said Mitikitski, managing to look up at the thing for the first time. He cocked his head sideways and whimpered. Elaine said shit and looked back down. He was larger, uglier, and dirtier than the undercarriage to a 1958 Buick Roadmaster.

The creature's brow furrowed. He looked confused, a little frustrated at not being able to communicate. He poked the squirrel again, then touched Mitikitski in the stomach. She laughed uncomfortably and drew back, holding up her hands.

"Oh, I see! This is breakfast!" she said, smiling. "Thank you. Thank you very much," she said, intoning as if she were talking to a child who had offered her a mud pie. "But I'm not very hungry right now." She gingerly nudged the squirrel back on the Bigfoot's half of the dinner table rock. "Why don't you go ahead. I'll probably just have the salad bar."

The creature took a long breath through his nose. He lightly tickled the deceased rodent under the chin, spun it slowly in circles on the rock, then nonchalantly pushed it to Elaine's side of the table. She thought maybe he was smiling. It was hard to tell. The creature clicked his molars together and pointed to his open mouth, then to the squirrel.

Mitikitski pushed the rodent back a few inches with a twig. "No, thank you. Squirrels are out of season. Why don't you go run and get another, and I'll make you a nice set of earmuffs?"

Her suggestion went over the monster's head.

He pushed the squirrel farther, so it limply hung over the edge of the rock, as if in a swoon.

Mitikitski smiled and said no thank you again, I'm a vegetarian.

The creature mumbled something that was predominantly an "R" sound. The he screamed at Mitikitski, pounding the piece of slate and causing the squirrel to jump in the air like it was popped from a toaster. That's it. Coronary. Mitikitski began sobbing with her mouth open, and tears splashed into her lap. She was mad, scared, tired, lonely, and had to go to the bathroom. She wanted Fenberg and her room and her mother and her sister. She picked up the squirrel and flung it at the monster. It bounced off his chest.

"I'm leaving!" Mitikitski stormed off, crying, intending to walk all the way out of the forest to someplace or be killed in the process. Perplexed, the beast watched her disappear, then bounced after her like a Saint Bernard puppy. He didn't know it at the time, but he was a sucker for a strong woman.

Mitikitski was taking long strides downhill and tried to shoo him away, but he just picked her up and took her back to the clearing in front of the cave. It was then that Mitikitski believed she was really in trouble, because the creature caressed her cheek with his knuckles and made embarrassing cooing noises. What was it they used to write in the old dime romance novels? she found herself thinking. A fate worse than death?

"God, I can sure pick 'em," said Mitikitski.

* * * * *

"Hello, Malulu."

The little bell on the door of *The Bugle* mindlessly dingled as the large woman dressed in generic polyester with the Attila the Hun bun ushered in four unfriendly, soiled children between the ages of three and seven.

"Hello, Vanessa." Malulu reluctantly looked up from *Family Circle.*

"I want to buy an ad in the classifieds," the woman said, waddling to the counter. "I'm having a garage sale."

"They're giving ads away free across the street," said Malulu, not moving.

"Yeah, I know. Already placed one. But no one reads that paper." The woman looked around the office. Something unfamiliar but not discernible troubled her. "What's different here?"

"The new reporter. She came in one weekend and cleaned. Brought in some houseplants." Malulu stood with apparent effort. She licked her fingers and dug out an ad blank. "What do you want the ad to say?"

"How about 'Garage Sale' in capital letters at the top?"

"Clever. And original." Malulu patted the back of her head. She had just gotten a new, short spring hairdo. It made her look like Jack Webb.

"Speaking of that new reporter woman, did you hear?"

Malulu made a face. Of course she'd heard. Wasn't this Basin Valley, where Malulu Jean MacClean was the reigning black hole of gossip? Mikey and John were in the hoosegow, and Mitikitski had been kidnapped by the giant cannibal monster. Big deal. That was old copy. Vanessa, who was a walking compendium of other people's business, straightened triumphantly. She casually asked if Malulu heard that M. J. Behan had exploded.

"Like in spontaneous combustion?"

No. Well, first, word had it that M. J. Behan, married and with kids and all, had been courting Mitikitski. Sending her presents. And flowers. Which was supposed to be an incentive for Elaine to come to work for his newspaper, but who in the hell did that old codger think he was fooling?

Malulu leaned forward on the counter with interest. Vanessa took a vicious swing-and-a-miss cut toward one of her children's heads, then snarled at the quartet to go sit down on the bench over there where they wouldn't be underfoot.

Vanessa glanced across the street, as if the employees at the other newspaper might be able to hear.

"I was in there when it happened!" she whispered. "I was placing an ad, and the place was pretty busy. Up drives Mr. Behan himself in that Rolls-Royce. I guess he'd been out of town on business, or whatever. But in he walks, giving everyone these warm good-days and all. His wife, you know, the one that looks like Jackie Kennedy's older sister who drinks? Well, his wife tells him the whole story about last night. About Mikey and his brother getting arrested and . . ."

Malulu waved her hand. Yeah, yeah. She knew this part already.

"Well, Behan gets this big cat-eats-the-cream smile on his face. And then she tells him that eighteen people saw this monster thing carry off the woman reporter out of town last night over its shoulder, bold as brass, down the main drag."

"I know that part," Malulu said again, impatiently.

"His wife tells Behan the reporter girl is missing, and he hits the ceiling! I mean, first, he's real quiet, staring at the floor like he can't believe it, like they were real close or something. Then he starts pulling out his hair. I mean, Malulu Jean, he starts pulling out the *hair* from his *head!*"

"You're kidding me!"

"No," said Vanessa, solemnly shaking her head. "He throws this tantrum, knocking everything off the desks, kicking over typewriters, pushing people. Then he struck his wife, frail thing that she is. I would have walloped him with the generous end of a skillet had he come at me like that, and no court in the land would vote me guilty."

"He hit her?"

"Knocked her down! Then he started hitting himself, and saying to himself that . . ." Vanessa squinted, trying to remember his words. "He said, 'After so long, it can't be true, this can't be happening to me.' Says he's got to go out there and find her. Bring her back. Kill that devil monster. Then he slapped his wife again. Now if that doesn't sound like an old fool of a man in love with a younger woman, I don't know what does."

"Peculiar," said Malulu Jean, staring off into space for a moment. "Two-ten, and it'll be in this Wednesday, if we still have a paper to put it in, Vanessa."

Vanessa thanked Malulu for the ad and said the garage sale money would come in handy, as she was expecting her fifth. Malulu looked at the four filthy children and chewed the inside of her cheek. Kids. Which reminded her. She was keeping Angry Joe and Clifford while their brothers were in County. Joe played his guitar sometimes until three in the morning, and Clifford insisted that she call him Norman, Norman Bates. Malulu Jean MacClean dearly hoped that Michael Fenberg and John Tuberski would not be sentenced to life.

*   *   *   *   *

Tuberski tried not to look at his brother. He had offered Fenberg a capsulized version of his past three months hiding in the rugged wilds of Basin Valley, the explanation of which only made Fenberg sigh like a weary and disappointed Lyndon Baines Johnson.

Fenberg lay on his back, hands behind his head, thinking dark Hamlet-thoughts, Tuberski figured. At times, he fright-

ened John. Lying on his back in the jail cell bunk, he wasn't
smiling. The gray eyes took in the intricate freeway of details
of the cheap springs that held the top mattress above him,
and Tuberski knew the unblinking eyes were calmly calculating solutions to every problem, right down, should it come to
that, to funeral arrangements for Elaine and what he'd tell the
boys. Fenberg was stronger than John was. But if you looked
long enough, and below the surface, you could see the tur-
moil and pain, and if Fenberg felt you saw it, he'd turn away.

Tuberski methodically chipped at the concrete holding the
iron bars into the window. He used Red Dog's knife, not
punching too hard. He'd already worn down the blade. Bean
Breath Brown stood by, obediently cupping his hands to
catch the debris. Immersed in his work, Tuberski wasn't paying much attention to the two Indians that shared his cell.
Rassmussen was perched on a top bunk, hunched over like a
stoic vulture. He had finger marks on his throat. Underneath
him, the old Indian sat cross-legged, his unbraided hair nearly
touching the cold wooden floor. Charlie Two Eagles had
been chanting in a bass, almost inaudible pitch for over an
hour.

"You said you were asleep," Fenberg quietly said, breaking
his long silence.

Tuberski stopped his excavation. He was standing on his
tiptoes, reaching out from the bunk to the window. "Huh?"

"You said you were asleep," repeated Fenberg, stretched
out in the bunk. "And right before that you threw in something off-the-wall about your monster. Remember?"

"No," said Tuberski, puzzled. "Oh, yeah. I remember. I said
he had a bad ticker."

"A bad ticker," repeated Fenberg, relishing the way the
words rolled out of his mouth. Bean looked over and grinned.
"A heart condition."

Tuberski resumed his excavation, somewhat buoyed now
that Fenberg was speaking to him. "Yup. From the signs, it
looks like angina pectoris, the kind mom used to get."

Fenberg nodded understandingly. "A monster with a heart
condition." Fenberg swung out of the bunk and stood. Tuber-

ski stopped working, and Red Dog straightened as a matter of protective reflex. They watched Fenberg. He looped his thumbs in his pockets, lowered his head, and slowly paced. Fenberg's pacing was slightly out of sync with Charlie's chanting. "I want to get this straight."

"Which part?" asked Tuberski.

"I'll settle for any part," said Fenberg. "On the night of the murder of Darla Behan, your ironclad alibi is that while she was thirty feet away, being brutally murdered, you were asleep."

"Uh-huh." Tuberski's tone was more placating than positive.

"And fearing wrongful accusation, you fled into the hills, eluded one of the nation's largest manhunts, single-handedly captured an elusive half-ton Abominable Snowman who just happened to be standing outside the drive-in theater waiting for the show to start, then you lived in a cave with said creature for three months, returning last night because the thing has a heart condition and needs medicine."

"It doesn't sound very airtight when you present it that way, does it?" agreed Tuberski.

Fenberg paced and shook his head no. "Would you like to share why, with evident and careful premeditation, you decided to turn my name into a TRW curseword?"

"I beg your pardon?" Tuberski chiseled away faster. He had been waiting for this one.

"Credit cards, John. Sears, MasterCard, American Express-don't-leave-your-cave-without-one? Not even Leona Helmsley could spend an average of fifteen thousand dollars a month living in a cave. Would you mind telling me just what the heck you bought on a forty-five thousand dollar shopping spree?"

Tuberski stopped chipping. "Most of it went for my safari."

Fenberg smiled with melancholy. Safari. There was another one of those words he liked.

Tuberski leaned against the wall. "Forty-five thousand?"

"Yeah. You mean you didn't know?"

"I didn't know it was that much." Tuberski stared in consternation. Fiscal irresponsibility was one of his strong suits. He hadn't ever bothered to sit down and total his purchases, nor did he consider the skyrocketing shyster interest rates. "Well. Let's see. I had to buy some nets, the heavy-duty kind for catching large animals. Then I bought a cage. And some bear traps. A canteen. A tent. A special rifle that shot tranquilizer darts and then I had to buy the tranquilizer darts themselves, and they weren't cheap. Had to send away to San Diego for those. A few other things. This expedition stuff all adds up, you know."

Fenberg smiled and strolled as if in front of an invisible jury. "But while you captured this creature relatively early during your leave of absence from civilization, you didn't bring it home for three months. Why?"

Tuberski chipped away at the bars. "It took me a while to gain his confidence. And he sort of ran away a lot."

"When you were with him, why didn't you throw the net over the monster, attach a pair of bear traps to its feet, blast it full of tranquilizers, wrap it in the tent, and roll it downhill in the cage?" He left out the Mr. Tuberski.

The bottom line was that Tuberski didn't have the heart to shoot the beast. John had grown attached. "I tried, several times. Either he gave me these pitiful looks and started weeping, or he bit me."

Fenberg took a long, deep breath through his nose. Seven steps to the wall. Seven steps to the front of the cell. Fenberg put his hands behind his back and played his ace.

"Neiman-Marcus."

"I beg your pardon?" Tuberski pretended to be lost in his work.

"Neiman-Marcus. What . . . did you buy . . . at Neiman-Marcus?"

"A sports coat." Tuberski resisted the impulse to call his older brother Mr. Fenberg.

Fenberg stopped.

"When you see a black cashmere sports coat, size sixty, extra-extra long, Italian cut for a guy with a thirty-four-inch waist on a special display, you buy it."

Fenberg nodded. Okay. He'd give him that one.

Tuberski grimaced. He tugged on the bars. They gave, a little. Fenberg resumed his pacing.

"We seem to have a time element problem here. We've established that you purchased forty-five thousand dollars worth of . . . safari equipment . . . that you never ended up using."

"I kept the receipts. We might be able to send a lot of it back."

"Well, there's a cloud parting. But still, why did you draw out the twelve thousand from our savings the day of the Darla Behan murder?"

Tuberski considered this. "I'll have to back up a bit. Remember, for quite some time we'd been hearing about this creature around the outskirts of town."

Fenberg nodded. He had been running articles on sightings for about a year.

"Well, actually, I saw it. Several times. Always in the same spot. The first time was a full two months before Darla's murder. The last was the night before. It was the evening I came into your room and explained my plan."

"Where did you spot the creature?"

"At the back of the drive-in."

Fenberg took a labored deep breath. He looked long at his baby brother.

"You're not going to hit me, are you?"

"No. This is actually getting interesting. Keep working on the bars. What do you mean, 'the back of the drive-in'?"

"You know the hill behind it?"

"Yes."

"The one that overlooks the screen? It's fenced off with barbed wire to keep the kids and pikers from sneaking up there and enjoying a free silent movie."

"Go on."

"So anyway, I'm at the drive-in proper. It was about six months ago, I think it was *Drop Dead Fred*," said Tuberski, "with Ms. Phoebe." He grimaced, grabbing two steel bars and leveraging against them. They bent, a little. "Anyway. I'm

with Teri Winston, Bob and Quanch's daughter? Teri, as I'm
sure you know, has had more hands up her skirt than a Muppet. We're in the back row. The night's young. She's beautiful. I like my chances. I've got her blouse off, and as I'm
turning back to unfasten her . . ." Tuberski stopped. Bean
Breath and Red Dog were leaning forward with lascivious
interest. "As I'm leaning forward to give her a big, friendly
Western welcome, I'm distracted.

"I catch more than a glimpse of something strange up on
the hill. It was the creature. I watched it for a full five minutes, moving around. I climbed over the fence and tried to
sneak up on it, but by the time I got there, it was gone. The
next day, I went up to the hill in daylight. There was plenty
of evidence showing that something other than a drive-in
cheapskate had been there. Footprints, hair samples, indentations, and the like."

"So."

"So, I get the plan. The very next night, I borrow your
camera. I got a little closer this time and snapped a few shots
of the thing. It ran off. But still, I had the pictures."

"You took pictures of the creature and didn't tell me?" said
Fenberg, thinking of the feature story that would have made.

"I didn't want to start a public furor. I figured that we could
make millions if we captured a genuine Abominable Snowman. I didn't want to run photos of it and have every lunatic
Sasquatch hunter in the free world roaming Basin Valley and
jumping our claim."

This was actually beginning to make sense to Fenberg.
Which frightened him.

"So, I suppose like Wile E. Coyote, I start sending away for
stuff to catch the thing." Tuberski stopped tugging on the
bars. "Did you ever wonder why Wile E. Coyote never just
used all that money he spent sending away for things to buy
some mail-order food?"

"The food wasn't important. He was driven," said Fenberg.

"I suppose. Anyway. That night I came into your room, I
had come an inch away from catching the stinker. But I
slipped in some junk. Turned out that he had gotten into the

trash and pulled out sacks of cast-off food. I went chest-down into a batch of secondhand hot dogs, hence the mess on my shirt that night. Anyway. He escaped."

"Why did you withdraw the twelve thousand?"

"I was cash-poor. I had decided to go after the thing full steam. I needed the liquidity for emergencies, more supplies, food."

"How much do you have left?"

"Right now? About fifteen hundred," said Tuberski, lowering his voice and returning to his anti-masonry work.

"*What!*"

Tuberski looked up and shrugged meekly.

Fenberg stood with his mouth open. Tell him there are giant monsters lurking with heart conditions. Tell him the mother of his child has been kidnapped by said creature. Tell him someone has eaten ten people. But don't tell him that you could spend ten grand living in a cave. Fenberg held both hands out, like an enraged Phil Donahue. "What . . . could you possibly . . . I've got to get myself together here," Fenberg said, shaking his head and looking at the ground. "What did you buy out in the middle of nowhere for ten thousand dollars?"

Tuberski pretended to be absorbed in his work. "Oh, food . . ."

Fenberg calculated. "You ate almost a thousand dollars a week in food?"

"No. It was for the creature."

"The creature evidently managed quite well all these years living on roots and berries," said Fenberg. *And people*, a small voice finished Michael's sentence. "What else?"

"Camping supplies."

"You said you bought those with the plastic."

"And I sort of bought a truck." Tuberski's voice lowered more.

Fenberg put his hands on his hips and laughed. Not that he thought any of this was funny. There were Chekhovian themes here. To the wall. And back.

"Why didn't you lease?"

"Bad credit rating, Mike. Had to pay cash."

Fenberg listened intently as Tuberski relayed how he had stayed in a cave with the creature, teaching it various tricks. Fenberg was more than surprised to learn that Charlie Two Eagles had been in on the scam, how he had used the truck to secretly drop off supplies. Charlie never looked directly at the creature. The Indian believed that if he locked eyes with it, his soul would be doomed to walk the netherworld for eternity.

"The night of the murder . . ." prompted Fenberg. "There are certain things that don't gel here, John. On one hand, you lived with this thing. You tell me how gentle, kind, considerate, nonviolent, and compassionate it is—a veritable Saint Francis of Assisi in a fur coat. On the other hand, we have the undeniable fact: ten people are dead."

John folded his arms and looked down.

"Not only are they dead, but they were dismembered and eaten by someone or something of great strength. Did you kill or eat anybody?"

"Of course not."

"That leaves your creature. Think back. The night Darla was killed. What the hell happened out there?"

"She was supposed to come out to the ranch that evening," Tuberski said, folding his arms. "I had caught up with her the morning after the protest, you remember, after that fight she'd had with her father?"

Fenberg nodded.

"She and I got to talking. As soon as I saw her up close I knew she was just a sweet kid. Had a lot of problems with her dad, which I could understand. I told her to come out to the ranch tonight if she could make it, we'd put some logs on the fire and talk. It was nothing sexual," Tuberski recollected, raising his eyebrows.

Fenberg sat on the edge of his bunk and listened.

"She was going to drive up around seven," Tuberski went on. "I finished my work around the house about five. The boys weren't home yet, so I took a nap. I overslept. I remember because I looked at the clock. I fiddled around the house a minute then looked out the window, because she was very late. I saw her car, but no Darla. That's when I went outside, and there she was." Tuberski stared into deep space.

"On the lawn."

"Yes. Geez, Mike." Tuberski tiredly leaned against the wall. "It was all so damn gruesome. I stood over her and felt this wave of helplessness. She was wearing a white dance dress, I remember, with sweats underneath. She was just a damn kid, and I remember looking down, thinking how frail and broken she looked." The feel of walking on the damp grass, the cold night air, Darla, it was a night Tuberski would never forget. "And then the horses went absolutely crazy. I heard them whinnying and kicking against the stall doors. I remember this strange feeling. It was beyond fear. Beyond terror. It was a high-key resignation to death. I felt as if I had entered into a hypnotic conspiracy to be a victim. The air literally jumped on my back. I felt like slapping at it. There was something out there, very close, watching me."

"Your creature."

"I . . . don't think so." Tuberski shook his head slowly. "But it was something huge, and powerful. I could feel a hunger. The word 'evil' comes to mind."

"Okay. You're standing over Darla . . ."

"Yeah." Tuberski shook himself again. "I heard the horses just throwing themselves against the paddock, kicking and screaming, and I figured I'd better get over there before one broke a leg. As I'm running over there, I feel like I'm in a trance. I jog a few steps and stop."

Tuberski didn't tell Fenberg about hearing the Voice. It had warned him. "I just stopped. Something pulled me away from going into the barn. I knew. I knew down to the center of every cell that . . . that something was in there, waiting for me. I ran to the house, locked the doors, and prayed. Then I called the police and took off."

"After the monster?"

"Oh, no. No way. I went in the opposite direction," said Tuberski. "I guess the sheriff picked up my trail later that night. I just jogged for an hour, I remember, putting a few miles between me and the ranch. I headed over the first two sets of hills up to the Timberlane Meadow, crossed it, and circled the lake to that little general store. I called Charlie Eagles. I figured everyone would blame me for killing Darla, when I knew all the time it was . . ."

"It was what?" coached Fenberg.

"I don't know."

"The creature?"

"That's what I thought at the time," Tuberski went on. He looked at the knife in his hand, wiggling it back and forth limply. "I mean, I set out with the intention of bringing it back so I could clear myself. At the time, I thought it had murdered the Behan girl. I called Charlie Eagles that night and told him to meet me. I gave him the money. He bought the truck and started bringing me food, supplies, clean changes of clothes, and the like."

Tuberski stared at the old man, his white hair untied and draped over his shoulders. Charlie's eyes were closed. He rocked back and forth slowly, the same deep, primitive mantra emanating from the wrinkled brown throat.

"He's trying to invoke the spirit world to come to the rescue of your girlfriend," Tuberski said quietly.

Fenberg thoughtfully rubbed his palms together. He'd take any help he could get. "So you were camping out. Where?"

"By Webster's Leap. There's an old fire trail that hasn't been maintained very well. Later, when I captured the creature, he led me to a cave with a hot mineral springs inside. Worked out great. With so much hot springs activity in that region, I guess they couldn't spot me from the air at night with their infrared devices. But you know, the damnedest thing . . ."

"What?"

"Every once in a while, every few weeks or so, I'd get this eerie sensation that the thing that killed Darla was around somewhere, looking for me."

"When you'd get these"—Fenberg rolled his hand in air, looking for the word—"feelings, I guess, was the creature with you?"

Tuberski lifted his head quickly. "No."

Charlie Two Eagles opened his eyes, ending his chant. Michael and John stared at him.

"Soon will be the final three nights of the full moon of the Nagomo cycle," he said simply. "In two days, the *Mandrango* will crawl from the earth and make his final transition from monster to great man-demon wizard."

"What's a man-demon wizard?" Fenberg asked.

"I have no idea," said Tuberski.

"It is an order of the Dark Brotherhood," Red Dog Rassmussen interjected, speaking for the first time. "It is very evil and very strong. It is man from animal." And that was all Rassmussen said. Charlie Two Eagles gave him the creeps. All the old Indians with their secret rituals and magic, making the wind pick up or bringing back the dead, gave Red Dog the creeps. He rolled over on the bunk, his back to his cellmates.

"In order to make his transition, he must take his bride of destiny," said the white-haired Indian.

Mitikitski, thought Fenberg.

"It came to me in my trance. It is clear what we must do," said Charlie. "We must escape. We must find and kill the *Mandrango* with a spear of pure silver. Run it through the creature's heart and out the other side. Then bury him in herbs."

Tuberski's brow furrowed. "We're talking about a monster, not old lasagna. Maybe in his trance he picked up an Italian cooking show somewhere instead of the spirit world."

"I have had my vision," said Charlie, with finality.

Tuberski shook his head to the contrary. "Listen. I lived with the thing for three months. I'm telling you, Mike, he's as playful as a kitten. Wouldn't hurt a fly. Got a heart as big as all outdoors."

Fenberg looked back and forth between the two seers.

"If we do not get to the woman in time," Charlie Eagles continued his prediction, "the *Mandrango* will enter her with his great stallion's staff. . . ."

Fenberg's legs involuntarily tightened and closed.

". . . He will enter her over and over again, by the rays of the full moon, entering her again and again, savagely, depositing his seed not once, but over and . . ."

"Yeah-yeah," interrupted Fenberg, holding up a hand. "I think I get the picture." Fenberg winced. He swallowed. Geez. At least the old medicine man could have had the politeness to leave out a few of the over-and-over-agains, thought Fenberg.

17

THE BIG BUTT MONSTER

The creature leaned against the boulder above the cave, sitting, his hands lazily behind his head. One hairy leg crossed a hairy knee as the beast watched the fading palette of oranges, reds, and yellows in the late winter sunset.

The creature didn't have an easy face to love. The head was bullet-shaped and the face flat. He had an eyebrow ridge the size of a two-by-four, and two bowling-ball-size holes that twitched for a nose. Starting at the other end were shaggy clown's feet, the soles as hard as bone. The massive legs and buttocks were out of proportion on his frame, like a retired NBA center who had let his weight get out of hand. But the eyes gave the creature away. They were beady, and somewhat bloodshot. Beyond that was a light, intelligent and searching.

Despite being overweight compared to the norm of Abominable Snowmen, this creature was still athletic. Though weighing nearly a half-ton, he was still faster than the fastest human sprinter. There was no lumber to the monster, no knuckle dragging gait. When it walked, it had a natural out-for-a-brisk-summer-stroll swing to its arms.

Mitikitski's kidnapper had always been a little different than the rest of his small nomadic band—different than any of the several rare creatures of his kind that shyly hid from man on the fringes of civilization, from northern Los Angeles

County to Canada and Alaska and beyond.

He had been the youngest of a tribe that consisted of six females, the dominant male, three beta males and the lanky youngsters. Like the gorilla, because of their great size the Snowmen spent most of their waking hours foraging. They nibbled on bark, roots, and berries, they captured small rodents and animals, or stole from trash bins and outlying farms. This monster was born curious, later developing an attitude problem categorized as aloof.

As a child, he would pass away the hours by the banks of a pond, head on hands, watching the fish swim. By wiggling his hands and making a curious, whining noise, he'd ask his father how fish could swim—a question beyond the realm of comprehension for the old, yellow-tusked male.

As he grew, there were countless mysteries in the forest that intrigued him. Where was the wind going? How come he couldn't see what he could smell? How did water fall from the sky, and how did it get up there in the first place? Where did the sun go at night? The moon, with its changing shapes, absolutely baffled him. When he was eight, his first confrontation with humans baffled him further.

The first three lessons a young Abominable Snowman learns are: 1) do not pick up rattlesnakes; 2) don't pester the bears; and 3) do not fraternize with humans. Humans were hot-tempered. They always were. They probably always would be. His race had learned that lesson a hundred thousand years earlier, crossing the great land bridge that briefly connected the continents of Asia and North America.

Humans. Yapping, screaming, always afraid, always aggressive, poke-you-with-a-sharp-stick-just-as-soon-look-at-you humans. Each one comes equipped with a built-in inferiority complex, which makes them doubly dangerous. The Snowmen couldn't take the competition and slowly faded into the green curtain of forest not only in America, but on every continent. Later, the humans would pronounce them extinct and solemnly dub their old bones as *giganpethicus*.

When he was eight, the creature learned lesson number three the hard way. He innocently walked into a campground, looking for someone to play with. What was he expecting? Smiles and greetings? Shared food? He was over six feet tall and quite thin. The campground wasn't filled with the standard mosquito-bitten suburbanites out for a two-week picnic. It was the beginning of deer season, and the clearing was packed with hunters. They saw the young Sasquatch and opened fire. He heard loud explosions and the ping of bullets ricocheting off ground and trees. Had the hunters been more sober and less afraid, or had not the old graying male unceremoniously reached out from behind a pine and yanked him back by the scruff of the neck, the monster would have been history.

"That which does not kill us makes us stronger," Nietzsche once said. So did the producers of the movie, *Conan*, which the creature had seen at the drive-in and immensely enjoyed.

The lesson served to give the young Snowman a healthy respect for humans and their weapons. From the tangy smell of gunmetal and the astringent scent of sulphur in the gunpowder, he had learned to tell at a safe distance whether a human was armed or not.

Sometimes even then, it didn't matter.

Because of a chance throwing together of genes, or the creative whim of a Cosmic Consciousness at work, or, more likely, the latter influencing the former, the creature was blessed with an unusually high intelligence. In the human world, he wouldn't be smart enough to teach physics, or even work retail, but maybe with a little luck and knowing the right people, he could have worked in television. At any rate, his intelligence went undirected, and, as is often the case, his energies were funneled into other endeavors, such as monkey business. He developed a sense of humor.

Dogs were his first target.

He loved to sneak up on them.

He'd come from downwind, stealthily crawling across a front yard on his belly like an infantry commando. Closer and closer, and closer, to the unsuspecting Fido. He'd move his face to within an inch of the sleeping dog, then, filling his lungs, blast the air with an ear-piercing maniacal scream. The lucky ones would yelp, jump up, and hit their heads on the roof of their doghouses. A few had heart attacks and seizures. Some would later die of insomnia, too frightened ever to risk sleep again. Some of the meaner or dumber mutts would take out after him, and he'd lead them on a merry chase through woods and underbrush. When they were out of breath and lost, he'd backtrack on them, throwing them by their tails into the nearest body of water.

The creature had a variable voice box—he could make guttural, throaty noises, growls, grunts, and whines. He made a gargling noise when he was happy or preoccupied. He also had a repertoire of hideous, bloodcurdling screams, his favorite being a pathetic moan that seemed to rise from under the earth to ride the night sky like an icy blast of wind. When he was angry, his howl/scream was dual-pitched, a cross between someone dragging his nails across a blackboard and sheet metal ripping. The creature barked and could say the word, "foof." Tuberski would say, "Foof, indeed," and go back to teaching him how to say "John." The best the creature could manage was "Don." Disgusted, Tuberski gave up.

Next to Tuberski, the most influential occurrence of his life was the discovery of the Timberlane Drive-In one sultry summer night. He was on the prowl with two females and a lesser male, when he looked down from a ridge and saw it in the distance—the glowing apparition: a huge, animated face wiggling its lips and eyebrows, coming out of what looked like a giant window only with no house attached to the window.

The beast was shocked.

The creature barked crisply, but with uncertainty. The entourage stopped. He pointed worriedly to the silver screen. His comrades followed his outstretched arm with their noses. They peered into the distance and sniffed, and listened, then moronically returned to their grazing. Nothing there that concerned them. The creature whined and pointed, running in turn to each. Are you kidding me? Can't you fucking see that there is a face . . . wait, look! Two faces now! Two faces of human beings over there, and from the size of their mugs, these people have got to be over four hundred feet tall!

His three companions did not make the equation. Anything they couldn't shred and stuff down their gullets was of no consequence. They left without him.

Cautiously venturing closer to the theater, he sat a mile away. Hours later, when the movie let out, he was still enthralled with the visions in the distance. Something pulled at him. Something told him to keep away. There was the feeling of claustrophobia there, everywhere, in fact, surrounding the world of humans. They lived their lives penned in. Penned-in houses, penned-in cars, in those funny leaves and furs with which they covered their bodies. The creature had a feeling. Without any sophisticated language to translate his feelings into explanation, the creature still had a premonition. That choking claustrophobia down there would someday kill him. He would die at the hands of man. A broken heart, half-broken for living out his days in some straw-lined cage, half-broken for never having had anyone with whom to share his life.

But who can resist the movies?

Gradually, he worked up his courage, getting closer to the big screen each visit. Weeks passed. His boldness grew, and he studied the topography around the drive-in in the day-time, searching for an advantageous spot, one with a good view, yet somewhere where he couldn't be seen. There was a bluff about one hundred fifty feet behind the drive-in, and underneath the bluff was a ledge with a protective overhang. Barbed wire surrounded the top of the hill, discouraging cheapskate lovers from enjoying the view. The barbed fence was no barricade to the beast. He just jumped over it. His reconnaissance also discovered the nearby trash bins, and he learned to pluck out the large plastic trash bags which were filled with half-eaten hot dogs, candy bars and remnants of hot buttered popcorn.

He learned a lot at the movies.

Quest For Fire was his favorite film, especially the part about how they learned the missionary position. He found himself grinning stupidly during that scene, although, come to think about it, he found himself grinning stupidly during

most of the romantic parts of every movie. He was a sap. He
liked all the *Planet of the Apes* pictures, although it took him
a while to get used to the gratuitous violence. Explosions
were beyond his realm of comprehension. They were like
quick sunsets, only noisier. He loved *King Kong*, though he
didn't care for the ending, and he was perhaps the only
viewer in America to be smiling when the dog in *Old Yeller*
died.

Movies were great. They *moved*. Constantly. Well, most of
them. And they were in color. Most of them.

There was, as always in the human scene, the other side of
the coin.

Monster movies scared the bejesus out of him. Here he
was, a full-grown male Sasquatch, capable of pulling a tree
out of the ground, yet how scared he'd get. Something would
frighten or repulse him, and he would squirm under that
ledge, a melting Baby Ruth bar in one hand and a previously
owned hot dog in the other, forearm shielding his eyes,
except of course, to peek to see if it was okay to look yet.
Sometimes monster movies would affect him so much, he
wouldn't leave the safety of the overhang until right before
the loving rays of dawn. He even developed a series of brief
phobias from things he didn't know existed.

Jaws affected him that way.

For a two-week stint, during the day, he wouldn't go in the
water, but he did crouch on a large boulder on the edge of a
pond. Giant gnarled club in hand, he pensively stared at the
water, waiting for a toothy great white to rear its ugly head so
he could whack it one. He clubbed no sharks, but did startle
some catfish.

He didn't like Joan Crawford. He cried at the end of
Beauty and the Beast and couldn't follow *Victor/Victoria*. He
liked Sean Connery, *Flipper*, and *Bambi*, at which he also
cried at the end. *Snow White* was on his all-time great list.
Maybe that's why, later on, he developed a crush on Mitikitski.

The movies were always fun, although they seemed to
raise more questions than they answered. Formless queries

arose, desires that whispered and disturbed, yearnings he couldn't understand let alone fulfill. He was well into his sexual prime, but had never mated. His own kind shunned him as being, well . . . odd. There was race panic and a developing ego that frightened him. Would he pass from this parenthesis in eternity leaving nothing behind? No little Bigfoot to carry on the family name? The sexual drive in his kind was not very strong, but it was there, nonetheless. During steamy movie scenes, he would feel a stirring. Once, after watching *American Gigolo* he tried a couple of moves on a budding light-haired Sasquatch. He looked into her eyes and lightly massaged her breasts, and she gave him this I-beg-your-pardon look right before she smacked him, exiting in a huff. He watched his own kind make love (maybe that was his problem—he was a voyeur) and it was entirely different than the silent screen. No romance.

And, to make matters worse, when he was at the bottom of his small barrel, someone had taken his spot at the drive-in. The creature had gone to his favorite seat. Every night, four nights in a row, the same large human was there, dozing in a cocoon or something. Adding insult to injury, the man was surrounded by fresh mouth-watering food. It made the Snowman curl his upper lip. Needed was an idea. The creature formulated a plan, a simple one. He'd just sneak up on the human, just as he had sneaked up on all those dogs. It would be a simple matter to wait until the Homo sapiens was asleep, crawl close, bark, and scare the tamales out of him.

He'd scared the wits out of Tuberski all right. Except Tuberski responded by punching him in the nose.

It hurt the creature's feelings, not to mention his nose. His acute sense of smell was fogged for almost a week, and he had trouble breathing.

Of course, to be fair, Tuberski did apologize later and more than made it up to him after he enticed him into being his friend with the reward of hot food, pizza, burgers, fries, and cola.

Tuberski made the terror-pain in his chest go away one day, when the creature couldn't move his arm or breathe and all the trees in the forest swarmed together in a whirlpool with the sky. He was close to dying, but didn't. Tuberski had healing hands.

The creature learned a lot the three months with Tuberski, although John had failed to convey the intricacies of patting the drum solo from the surf hit, "Wipeout" on one's stomach. There was a lot to be said about being human, and, for the time, he misplaced that sense of being neither fish nor fowl. Even the vague dreams of claustrophobia and straw-lined cages disappeared. He had always thought there was a better life out there, and Tuberski showed him that yes, there was. And when Tuberski sat opposite the campfire, laughing and saying, ". . . millions, billions," the creature smiled too, not knowing what either a million or billion was.

Life was swell. He hadn't a care. Until he went to town and lost Tuberski. On the plus side, at least he now had Mitikitski. On the down side, he didn't know what to do with her.

She wouldn't come out of the cave.

* * * * *

It was a beautiful day, birds chattering with inflated self-importance, the snowcapped High Sierras contrasting sharply against an endless sky. Uncountable acres of trees, ranging in size from blades of hopeful grass to wise, centuries-old monarchs, patiently blew back in the gentle breezes, disappearing into the horizon toward the end of the world. While this was high cinemascope to the creature, Elaine Mitikitski would only sit on a rock in a dimly lit cave and shiver.

The creature didn't know why she shivered. The cave was warm, heated by an adjacent hot mineral springs and thermal activity underground.

Elaine Mitikitski was hungry and had to go to the bathroom. Since she discovered her pregnancy, Elaine "I'm *what?*" Mitikitski had to go to the bathroom every twenty minutes. It was an annoyance. It was all so undignified, when you thought about it. If Mitikitski didn't know better, she'd think Nature was really a man, not a mother, off behind some curtain, sniggering at the fine joke he had pulled on women. Elaine looked around the cavern, gritting her teeth, then staring hopefully at the welcoming light that beckoned from outside.

Every abdominal muscle tight, she stood and bit her lower lip. I do not want to think about Niagara Falls, Sparkletts, or Lloyd Bridges, she thought.

Mitikitski nimbly approached the mouth of the cave, three slender, manicured fingers tightly pressed against her swollen bladder. She had to go to the bathroom. She didn't want to go outside because the creature was there. She wouldn't go inside because, pardon me, this is where I'm sleeping tonight (knock on granite). Elaine peeked out, her black hair falling off to one side. She squinted from the brighter light. It was so beautiful up here. Even in her frenzied condition, she recognized that. It had been a surprisingly mild winter, and normally the area around Webster's Leap would have been five feet under snowdrifts, deeper at the higher elevations. Around the cave were only a few patches of melting snow.

"Hello?" Elaine called out.

No answer. Elaine thought she might burst a kidney.

"Hello?" she cried louder. Mitikitski screwed up her courage. She hesitantly stepped all the way into the retreating sunlight and took an involuntary deep breath. Freedom. Elaine looked around for the beast, but really was more interested in a clump of bushes a few yards away. She gingerly walked toward them. Five steps from the cave, she froze. On a ledge a few feet above her was the man-thing. He was posed on a rocklike lounge chair, disinterestedly sitting with massive arms behind his head, one giant hairy leg crossing the other. He was watching the sunset. He looked lazily down at her. Mitikitski didn't move. Neither did the monster.

"I've got to go to the bathroom," Mitikitski finally said.

The thing sniffed the air, his head rolling around in an arc. He zeroed in on Elaine's pink Nike running shoes and easily rolled off his boulder perch. Without hesitation, he crawled on all fours to her.

"Get away," said Mitikitski, batting the air around him.

Even on his knees, his face was eye-level to hers.

Elaine looked straight ahead, past his nonexistent ears on the leathery bullet head. The creature bent effortlessly, like a jointless chimp. He was on his elbows, sniffing Mitikitski's size sixes, lightly touching them with an index finger.

Elaine's mind and kidneys worked in tandem, like boilers about to explode. She didn't move for fear of enacting grisly expectations, but she didn't want to wet her pants. This great beast of the Pacific Northwest, with one quick bat of the hand, one quick snap of the jaws, could end her life, her baby's life, all before she (they) had time to go to the bathroom.

Mitikitski made a decision.

She straightened, forcing her shoulders back to a dominant position. "I am going to the bathroom, over there," she loudly announced in her best animal trainer's voice, first pointing to herself, then to the clump of scrub oak. "I am going over there. Alone. You stay here."

"Foof," said the creature, watching Elaine's retreating figure striding purposefully downhill and disappearing into the thicket. He sniffed the air and looked around, then attended to an aggravating flea lodged somewhere on his right side. Big deal. Go ahead. You don't need a hall pass from me.

Moments later, feeling greatly relieved, Mitikitski tucked in her shirt and buttoned her jeans. But as the great woodsman Tuberski once said about wilderness survival, if it's not one thing, then it's another.

Elaine Mitikitski was starving to death.

She hadn't eaten for eighteen hours, and although she knew people could live for two and three weeks without food, Elaine was convinced she was starving to death. Maybe not right this minute, but she was definitely in the early stages.

With all that spare time in the cave, she had already painted a detailed mental picture. A search team, led by Fenberg and her parents and friends from college and Kamali Molly (hi-tech green khaki fatigues, patent leather hunting boots laced to the knees, chrome revolver, Japanese headband) would find her, dead, sprawled on her back. The lips blue, the eyes open, as though she were pitifully taking in one last look. Miraculously, she had delivered the baby, and the baby was fine, except very sorry her mother was dead. Fenberg would pick up the little girl, and father and daughter would cry over Mitikitski, lying there, dead. Everyone would cry. They would solemnly carry her down the mountain like a Viking queen, her arms dangling. And Molly and Mike would get married, and they would make perfect parents for her little girl, although Molly would make Fenberg absolutely miserable because she was a witch, and Fenberg would deserve it for not loving Elaine as much as she loved him.

The orange tip of the retreating sun plopped behind a distant mountain, off like a dependable, celestial milkman, bringing light to other people and other lands. In the opposite end of the heavens, the near-full moon was already up. Twilight. The temperature would soon drop into the thirties again, and Elaine's only sanctuary from wind and cold and maybe an unexpected blizzard was the cave. Mitikitski scoured the ground for small branches and twigs to make a cooking fire, sourly noting her hands were getting dirtier. Funny the things you take for granted, like clean, unsticky hands. Water wouldn't be much of a problem. Food would. In the bushes, she had scooped up several handfuls of snow for her dry throat, although it just seemed to make her thirstier. If only she had some sort of container. Elaine thoughtfully patted her stomach, rubbing it reassuringly. She was so happy there was life in there. She was also ravenously hungry.

She thought about the squirrel.

How would one prepare squirrel?

Why would one want to prepare squirrel anyway?

No, Mitikitski, you can't afford to be a prima donna out here, especially when you're eating for two.

Did the squirrel die of unnatural causes? she wondered. Bubonic plague? Rabies? Sickle-cell anemia? Cut it out, Elaine.

Mitikitski made a small circle of rocks, then dragged a large branch over to it. She'd get the smaller wood going, then put the heavier log on top, sliding it over as it burned. All the while, the creature just squatted, arms wrapped around his knees, watching her.

She had gotten over the initial terror of the creature always being around. Lurking seemed to be the right word. It was so amazingly huge, and despite being out in the open, Elaine felt she was locked in a stall with a bull. She was always aware of his presence, and the slightest grunt or twitch on his part sent Elaine's heart racing.

He grunted.

She jumped.

Elaine took a deep breath and resumed her duties. She could make it through the night of course, without eating. She'd be famished, but it was better than eating the wrong thing and getting her sick and the little growing baby upset. Tomorrow, she'd look for something safe to eat. Maybe berries, she reasoned, not knowing berry season was months off. Then, somehow, she'd escape. In the meantime, she'd start a roaring fire that might attract some lonesome ranger or a search party that she was sure was out there looking for her.

Elaine gathered a pile of hand-sized stones of different compositions and spent the better part of fifteen minutes banging and clicking away. Occasionally, there was a spark, but no fire. The creature watched. She needed flint, Elaine thought, but who was she kidding? She wouldn't know flint if she were sitting on it.

The creature grunted again, and this time the preoccupied Mitikitski ignored it. He grunted again, then, sitting erect, barked and vigorously shook his hand.

"I'm making a large bonfire so the search planes will find us and drop napalm on you," said Mitikitski, clicking away.

The creature looked skyward with a furrowed brow, then back at Mitikitski, then at the dry campfire. He walked over to Elaine.

"Hey!" yelled Mitikitski. "What the hell do you think you're doing? Get your mitts off me!"

The creature had lightly grabbed Elaine by the arm and led her into the dark cave. He sat her on the ground. A few seconds later, he returned with the rocks and kindling. Elaine's eyes strained as she tried to see what he was doing. He was reconstructing the campfire. The circle wasn't as perfectly round as Elaine's, and the placement of the kindling and logs wasn't out of the Boy Scout manual, but it was still a campfire.

"You can't make a fire in here, you jerk," said Elaine. "You're going to suffocate me. There's no damn ventilation."

The creature looked up and sniffed, then crawled out of the cave opening. Elaine tried to sneak out a few minutes later, but was greeted with a gruff guttural warning.

Swell, thought Mitikitski, sitting down and folding her arms. Big butt monster.

It was totally dark now, and fear settled in. No frogs croaked or crickets chirped when the creature walked at night. He had been gone almost a half hour. The little bit of dark gray light that came in through the mouth of the cavern was obliterated when he crawled through, dragging something behind him. Eyesight was useless to Elaine. She could only hear and smell.

The creature was rustling through something, and Mitikitski heard a familiar clicking sound she couldn't place. The cave was suddenly illumined by a dim, dancing orange light, and Elaine saw a large, dirty thumbnail reaching into the straw and twigs, holding a Bic lighter. The creature bent down and gently blew on the fire as Tuberski had taught him. Soon, Mitikitski was enjoying a small, but comfortable camp fire.

The creature sat back and watched as the sparks and smoke whiffed upward, back over Elaine's head and out through a natural ventilation shaft at the other end of the cave. He crawled back out, and Elaine noticed there was a grocery bag that had been sitting behind him. She checked the entrance, then scurried over on her hands and knees. There were some metal plates, coffee cups, a pot, a percolator, and frying pan in the bag. Elaine jumped back and tried looking nonchalant when she heard the creature returning. It carried three green-and-white Coleman ice chests.

"This is not reality as I know it," Elaine said out loud. Yet she knew it wasn't a dream.

The Snowman opened the lid to one of the chests and pulled out two large bags of potato chips. He opened one with his teeth and made it a point to show Elaine by shaking his head "no" that the discarded plastic top portion of the bag was not for eating, as Tuberski had shown him. He reached in for a chip and took an imaginary bite, then handed the full sack to Mitikitski. He watched approvingly as Elaine dug into the bag and crunched the chips into her mouth.

Junk food had never tasted so good.

He dug around in the ice chests and pulled out packages of Ball Park franks, hot dog buns, several six-packs of Coke, cookies, and, of course, some Jiffy Pop popcorn. There were more supplies left in the cache that Tuberski had hidden. The creature brought Elaine a Bay blanket with white, green, and yellow stripes, an air mattress, pillows, and a cassette player, no batteries.

Mitikitski thought this would make a hell of a story. Then her balloon settled to earth. Hell. Who would run it? She immediately dismissed most of the major periodicals in the country. Maybe the *National Enquirer*. In the distance, a coyote howled. The creature sat cross-legged across from her, and, with great concentration, just as Tuberski had taught, carefully poked long twigs into the frankfurters and held them sizzling over the fire.

"Foof," said the creature, thinking all that was missing was a good movie. His internal clock told him they would be changing the bill tomorrow at the drive-in. And tomorrow, there would also be a full moon.

18

FENBERG MAKES A STATEMENT

"Who bent my bars?"

"He did," said Fenberg and Tuberski in harmony, pointing at Bean Breath Brown. Bean nodded his head vigorously in agreement.

"Goddamn it anyway," said Sheriff Bubba Fenberg, painfully examining the window. A foot of concrete had been removed, and three of the vertical steel bars guarding the window leaned arthritically. "Why did you have to do this?"

"We were trying to escape," said Tuberski helpfully.

Bubba thoughtfully palmed the pearl-handled revolver in his holster. "Go on, get out of here," he said. Even in defeat his voice was deep, gravelly from cigars and bad coffee. "But I'll tell you one goddamn thing. The repair work on those bars is coming out of your pockets."

Fenberg looked suspiciously at his cousin, then at the open cell door.

"You're free . . . except there's one stipulation."

Bubba Fenberg had been up all night on another saddle-sore excursion into the Basin Valley wilderness. He had found no trace of Mitikitski or the monster. It was M. J. Behan who had suggested mending fences. Tuberski was the only person who could lead them quickly and accurately to the beast, so Behan had put up bail for the Fenbergs, on the stipulation that John and Mike head a posse to bring back Elaine.

The hunters would leave at dawn, and the Fenberg brothers weren't to get any ideas because there would be one hundred armed men with orders to shoot them should either be inspired to deviate from the plan.

Before separating, Fenberg instructed his baby brother to line up all the safari equipment he had charged. Nets, guns, traps, tranquilizers. Fenberg wore a look of pained exasperation as he watched Tuberski disappear out a side entrance with the keys to Mike's pickup. John was a car abuser.

Outside, against the glare of one hundred thousand watts of light, Fenberg pushed his way roughly through a shouting mob of media people. Microphones and TV cameras were thrust into his face.

"Mr. Fenberg! Is it true that you saw a Bigfoot carry off one of your reporters last night?" News had traveled quickly of the daring apartment escape. The press jumped at the logical angle, yeah, *Beauty and the Beast*, Fay and King.

"Were you and the woman reporter engaged to be married, Mr. Fenberg!?"

Fenberg slowly shouldered his way across the town square, across the street to the sanctity of *The Bugle* office.

"Is this the same beast authorities believe is responsible for ten cannibal murders in Basin County?"

"Is it true your half brother lived with the creature in a cave for three months?"

Fenberg stopped in front of the door and faced the throng of blinding lights and rapid-fire questions.

"Be quiet!" someone yelled. "He's going to make a statement!"

Fenberg shielded his eyes from the blinding lights.

"He's not my half brother," Fenberg said, "he's my whole brother. John changed his name several years ago for career purposes." Fenberg turned and went inside, squishing several newspeople in the door who tried to follow.

Meanwhile, Red Dog Rassmussen slithered through the fallopian-tube-sized opening of the bent bars and became the first person in history to escape from the 131-year-old Basin County Jail.

19

MRS. BEHAN IN THE BAR

Under the shade of an overgrown elm, on the corner of
Peachland and Sixth Streets, sat Duberry's Drug Store—open
till seven. It had a marble sit-down soda fountain, a glass-
enclosed cigar case, beads, postcards, double-edged razor
blades, an old-fashioned wooden telephone booth, a rack of
dusty sunglasses, and a nearly complete collection of every
comic book published in America.

Duberry's was Clifford Fenberg's home-away-from-home,
and he waited there dutifully from 2:45 P.M., when his first
grade class let out, until 3:30 P.M., when Angry Joe picked
him up. The druggist didn't chase Clifford away from thumbing through the volumes of the Silver Surfer, Kid Colt Outlaw,
the Fantastic Four, Green Lantern, or Batman. Cliff disdained
the soft core pablum of Disney and Archie. He was into violence and X-ray vision. Monday through Friday, he'd straddle
the stool on the end, reading, sipping Coke through a straw,
absentmindedly kicking his shoes against the counter.

The comics gave him hope, a fantasy that he too could be
cut of the same taut invulnerability, tested but never pained,
invincible to all the bullies and evil of the world. And, above
all, to rise above the rejection. Clifford was much like Tuberski, able to grasp obtuse philosophical and metaphysical con-
cepts and, on the surface, afraid of nothing. But in reality,
Clifford was afraid. While he'd launch himself blindly, flailing

against anything in size all the way up to the ninth grade, in the end he wasn't made of steel. He was just a little boy.

He liked Elaine.

He liked Fenberg, too, although he didn't know quite what to make of him. Other kids had parents. Clifford had Fenberg. Mike held Clifford and read him stories, always using a wide variety of voices. He wrestled, letting Clifford win most of the time. No matter how busy, at paper or home, Fenberg would stop to look Clifford in the eye to answer any question. Fenberg let Clifford cook, let him sit on his lap and operate the scoop on the tractor, and went ga-ga over the simplest Picasso stick figure Clifford created.

But Fenberg didn't have that softness Mitikitski possessed. For one thing, Elaine never had five o'clock shadow, and when you hugged her there was a pleasant resiliency, a softness. She listened intently, like Fenberg, but now when Clifford cried, it was Elaine's arms he rushed for. She'd let Cliff sit on her feet and hug her legs while she read. All the battle walls melted when she brushed his red hair from his eyes, although he wasn't too hot on the way she rubbed hardened food off the corner of his mouth and cheeks with a wet wash towel. When he thought of Mitikitski, Clifford always remembered Christmas and the perfumed baby blue cashmere sweater that matched her eyes.

Clifford studiously turned a page. Hell. He liked them both and considered they made a very complementary couple. But was there something about Clifford that drove people away? Cliff had never known his parents. And really, it had been fortuitous that they decided to leave Clifford at home that week five years ago. Elsewise, he would have ended baby-bottom-up, stuck in some uncharted glacier. He and Tuberski had talked at length about the nature of life, how it just went on, that you never died, you just changed bodies as you would a set of clothes. You'd come back and make new friends. Clifford hoped Elaine was not changing clothes. He was just getting to know her. He especially didn't want Fenberg and Tuberski to change clothes, because that would mean Angry Joe would become his parental unit, and what kid deserves that?

Clifford skimmed the last panel of Superman and closed the comic. His thoughts drifted to theology. Could Superman beat up God in a fight? Probably not. Why would anyone want to beat up God in the first place? Why didn't God ask Superman to beat up the devil? Good question. He'd have to take that up with Tuberski, who was expert in such matters.

"Excuse me, spaz," said Angry Joe, bumping into him.

"Excuse me, spaz," said Clifford right back, shoving with an elbow. It was more a greeting than prelude to an altercation. Joe inspected the comic book from over Clifford's shoulder. Satisfied it was one he had already read, he didn't confiscate it.

"They just let Mike and John out," said Angry Joe, like it was no big deal. "Mike said we're supposed to meet them at the paper."

* * * * *

Fenberg stood, sipping tea and watching the bedlam outside. The reporters were still shouting questions at him through the storefront window of *The Bugle*. The lights, the distorted faces—the scene had a surrealistic quality, like watching an aquarium filled with maniacal, screaming fish.

The flames were lingering in *The Bugle*'s stone fireplace. Malulu had unplugged the phones, and the front door was bolted. She read *Family Circle* and ate chocolate-dipped grahams. Fenberg made a big production of complimenting her on the new hairdo, using such diplomatic phrases as ". . . sporty, must be comfortable, brings out your features" instead of telling her that she looked like the dyke swim coach of the former East German swim team.

"Mr. Fenberg! Mr. Fenberg!" the muffled voice of a reporter yelled through the glass. "Can you shed some light on this utterly fantastic story?"

"Can't you give us any clues?" another pleaded.

Fenberg considered.

He meandered to an ancient manual Royal and rolled in a

sheet of paper. Moments later, he sauntered back to the window. The press corps crowded against the glass to read the note: THE WALRUS IS PAUL.

The reporters' lips all moved as they silently mouthed the words.

Fenberg figured that should give the media something to work on for the next ten to twenty years. He pulled the worn cord on the venetian blinds.

Fenberg heard the haphazard clump of familiar footsteps and spun his tea to avoid spilling it on Clifford. Clifford had sprinted in from the back entrance. He grabbed Michael by the leg and fiercely hung on, sitting on Fenberg's shoe. He told Fenberg he was going to destroy him and flush him down the toilet. Translated, it meant he was very happy to see Fenberg, but didn't want Fenberg to know it. Fenberg looked impassively at the boy on his boot.

"I suppose you want a hug," said Fenberg.

"Yes," said the pale boy with the cheese face.

"Didn't I give you a hug last week?" Fenberg asked, eyeing Clifford with mock sternness.

"Yes." Clifford giggled.

"What did you do with it?"

"I don't know."

"You lost my hug?"

"Yes." The normally anemic Clifford was red. Fenberg reached with his free hand and grabbed his little brother by the back of the belt and lifted. Clifford locked onto Michael's neck. Angry Joe walked in a minute later and struck a pose.

"How have they been?" asked Fenberg of Malulu. The side of her mouth sank fatalistically. While staying with Malulu the past two days, Cliff and Joe had indulged in a little nonproductive resistance behavior. Joseph had convinced Clifford to disguise his voice as a woman. Over the phone they ordered several dozen washers and dryers and had them sent to various Basin Valley residences chosen at random. There were more phone high jinks, involving restaurant reservations for parties of forty, and Joe's Pizza had wasted a tankful of gas delivering pizza to people who hadn't ordered pizza. Angry

Joe and Clifford also had the infamous and fictitious Mr. Less paged at the bowling alley. "Mr. Less . . . Mr. Less . . . Paging Mr. Dick Less . . ."

"They've been regular angels," said Malulu, lethargically stuffing her purse. It pained her to lie. "Dinner's on in an hour. You boys be there by then."

"That's all right, Malulu," Fenberg said. "I'm taking them out to eat." Clifford yelled approval, and Fenberg sent him to get reservations at the restaurant two blocks away. "Get us a table for four." Mumbling it was just as easy to cook for nine as it was for seven, Malulu tiredly ice-skated toward the door.

Joe and Fenberg were alone in the office.

"You got a minute?" asked Fenberg, turning out lights. He scattered the dying logs in the hearth, and the last responded with a burst of flame.

"This isn't going to be one of your touching male bonding speeches, is it?" asked Angry Joe. In the firelight, Fenberg's face had gained a couple of lines.

"What makes you ask that?" Fenberg smiled.

"I recognize the tone of voice." Joe was wearing a black leather jacket and a clip-on earring. Fenberg wouldn't let him get his ear pierced.

"Nah, put your dukes down. You're not in trouble, and if you don't want, we won't discuss anything remotely humanistic. I've just got some business to go over with you."

Joe leaned against a doorway, partially in the dark. He'd never forgiven his parents for dying, or Tracy for that matter. And he watched Fenberg constantly, suspicious that he too, would leave.

"In the morning, John and Charlie and Bean and I will be leaving," Fenberg began. "John's pretty handy in the backwoods. If anyone can find Elaine up there, he can."

Joe wanted to ask Mike if he missed Mitikitski, but couldn't. "Are you going with the sheriff?"

Fenberg laughed. "Oh, no." A posse of a hundred men, followed by twice as many reporters carrying more lights than Las Vegas? No-no. You can put a tent on that circus. Besides, neither Fenberg nor Tuberski relished the idea of walking in the wilds with M. J. Behan or the Magonogonovitch brothers at their backs. "Bubba thinks we're leaving with them at dawn, but we've made other plans. This, of course, Joe, is between you, me, and the walls."

Joe nodded.

"We might be gone overnight, and we might be gone a week. Maybe longer. I want you to take care of Clifford, of course. And except for the crank calls, I think you've done a good job," said Fenberg, stirring the coals. "I'd also appreciate it if you'd run the newspaper while I'm gone."

Joe had a visible reaction, which was lost to Fenberg in the shadows. "Is this some sort of let's-give-the-juvenile-delin-quent-a-lesson-in-responsibility deal?"

Fenberg shook his head no. "I've never considered you a juvenile delinquent. I just need some help."

"You're coming back, aren't you?" It was almost an accusa-tion.

"I always do," said Fenberg. He sighed. It's those others who don't come back, he thought. "You might miss a little school, but not much. I've already spoken with your principal. He thinks it's a good idea. Here," said Fenberg, handing Joe a heavy brown packet. "Instructions on how to produce a news-paper with handy things you have lying around the house. There's also some cash—the absolute last of the fabled Fen-berg fortune." Three hundred dollars. "There are enough sto-ries in overset to last two weeks. Most are timeless features, with accompanying photos in the negative file. Use lots of pic-tures. If you write anything, have Malulu proof it for grammar. Don't use cusswords in print." Michael smiled broadly. "I guess this is one of those manly rite of passage things. Included in that packet is your first inter-office memo."

Joe took the envelope and didn't say anything.

"I want you to run this story, top front page, eight-column banner. I want it set in twelve point type," said Fenberg, pointing to a handwritten letter with red ink instructions for the typesetter. "Both Tuberski and I have insurance policies, but in John's case, I think you have to produce the body and take it into their main office in LA."

Angry Joe didn't laugh.

"I've left a will."

Joe was close to the fireplace. Fenberg could see his brother was confused and scared, and maybe a little teary. He resisted the urge to rub Joe's shoulders and pat him on the back. Joe wasn't a hugger. Fenberg asked if he had any questions, and no, said Joe, he didn't.

Fenberg watched the last embers, resigned to sleep, pulsing. He looked at his brother who was staring at the hearth, that hardened face still very much a baby's. He and Joe were much alike. "I'm sorry you wander the streets some evenings and spend the night in the movie house others. I'm sorry that you're goddamn thirteen and have to suffer the indignity of being shipped off between this babysitter and that. I'm sorry I'm not around more, and that we don't get MTV up here. I'm real sorry Mom and Dad aren't around, and I dearly wish you wouldn't take it so personally when people die on you. It's no reflection on you. There's something willful in us that deifies pain, something that actually expects it. It is very prevalent in the two of us, and I wish you'd cut it out." Fenberg wanted to say more, but something familiar was rising that he expertly knew how to squelch.

"C'mon," said Fenberg, "let's get something to eat." He grabbed his coat and wrapped an arm around Joe's shoulder, crushing him with a hug. "Us against the nuts?"

"Us against the nuts," said Joe, nodding his head.

* * * * *

Bill and Emma's Mostly Fish was the closest thing in Basin Valley to a nice restaurant. It was eleven doors down from *The Bugle*. Generally, it was dark in Bill and Emma's. They had red tablecloths and matching naugahyde booths, and tonight Patsy Cline harmoniously lamented lost love on the jukebox. Fenberg toyed with the label on his beer bottle, ignoring Clifford. His youngest brother was hanging on Mike's arm, staring at nothing in particular, kicking the booth with his scuffed heels. Joe was going over the packet of information Fenberg had left with him. Tuberski was still out with Michael's truck, gathering supplies. The sheriff had sent two deputies and three volunteer posse members, all armed to the teeth, to keep John company.

The Fenbergs finished eating, and it was around six, still too early for the regular dinner crowd. There were a few reporters at the bar, glancing over and probably talking about them, Fenberg figured. The deputy who had been assigned to watch Fenberg sat at a small table across the restaurant, sipping coffee. At the end of Bill & Emma's bar sat a woman, smoking a cigarette and hunched over a martini. She looked familiar, but in the dim light Fenberg couldn't place her. Maybe she was a reporter. Or a tourist. She was a blonde though, like Tracy.

Fenberg smiled. He folded his arms, so his right hand could cup over the photo in his pocket. He was beginning to run out of hours in the day to worry about both Tracy and Mitikitski.

Perhaps he could arrange a timetable. Worry about Tracy from eight to noon, take a lunch. Fret over Elaine from two-to-six, dinner. Worry about miscellaneous items until bed, then have nightmares.

Clifford tugged on Mike's sleeve, pulling him down to table level so he could whisper in his ear. "Do you love McKitsky?" asked Clifford, unable to handle the complete Polish pronunciation. Fenberg looked at his brother. Cliff was blushing. One has to be very careful in talking with children, he always noted. Fenberg didn't want any latent male asshole insensitivities to be inadvertently transmuted to the next generation.

"She's a very lovable person," said Fenberg. It was a rather pertinent question, especially because if he ever did get her back from his brother's giant cannibal attraction, they would probably be married, have the baby, and live at the ranch. It would be nice, though not necessary, to be in love with her.

Was he?

"Simply, love is a behavior," Tuberski had once said. "Not an emotion, not a feeling." Fenberg wondered where his brother came up with these things. The aggravating part was that Tuberski was always right.

"To further our definition, it is putting another's needs ahead of your own," Tuberski had waxed on. "It's all quite practical."

But what about those goosey feelings one gets? The fondness? The memories?

"Mental images, chemical charges. We create a gilded image in our mind and worship it, forcing the poor jerk we're with to bend to that image. Sadly, our god or goddess ends up becoming our monster. We are terrorized by what we've created. Don't confuse sex, baby talk, and romance with love. I don't think we can love as human beings. I've got a feeling that what love does come through is from some other place within us, somewhere invisible, the soul perhaps. I'd like to find out," Tuberski had said.

Fenberg had gone to first grade with Tracy. How long had he known Elaine? Three months? Mitikitski was pretty and funny. She was comfortable to be with, well versed in the practical and obscure. She had a nice butt. She was considerate, supportive, and a good kisser. She was mysterious, independent, and contrary enough to be entertaining long after the mush stage of the relationship had passed. He could make a long list of all the things they had in common, all the things he respected about her. But he couldn't love her. Not according to Tuberski's classic definition. He couldn't put Elaine's needs ahead of his own, because he couldn't let go of Tracy.

"But I love Tracy," Fenberg had said. He and John had had this conversation a long time before. Tuberski had been cleaning out a stall in the barn while Fenberg watched, which was in itself unusual.

"No," Tuberski had said, "You cannot *love* someone who has passed on. You can remember them fondly. Or miss them until you're sick, which is what you do. All that is is a morbid attachment. And true happiness comes from being free of attachments. *N'est-ce pas?*" Tuberski picked up a cast-iron stove, moving it from one end of the barn to the other. He reveled in labor involving the movement of objects two hundred pounds or heavier. All other forms of work he deemed unmanly.

Fenberg wanted to punch Tuberski in the nose. Not for his work ethic, but because he was right. All the great moments of joy in his life were when he was just beholding, in the act of. Not clinging fiercely with a falsely labeled fond memory. Those, in fact, made him miserable. Fenberg wanted to punch Tuberski in the nose even more for showing him clearly the difference between being miserable and being happy and leaving the burden of that awful choice on Fenberg's shoulders.

It wasn't that simple, Fenberg thought. It wasn't as simple as saying, "I'll never think about the wonderful life I had with Tracy." There were other forces at play. Elaine scared the hell out of him because when Fenberg laughed too hard, or dug too deep, well, there was that old familiar plug loosening, and once undone, everything would spill out of Michael, and spill out and spill out and spill out until there was nothing left.

Angry Joe returned to the table from video wars on the lounge machine, defeated but confident of success if only he could appropriate more funding. "Can I have some more quarters?"

Fenberg dug into his pockets. He started to tell Joe, " . . . just one more game," but was interrupted by shouting.

"He's a son of a bitch!" yelled the woman from the shadowy end of the bar.

"She's talking about you," Joe told Clifford. Cliff raised a tiny middle finger, but he scampered out of the booth to follow his brother to the video machines.

Fenberg squinted through the red plastic naugahyde gloom. The woman was Linda Behan, M. J. Behan's wife. She was plastered. Fenberg tossed a few bills on the table and slid out of the booth. "C'mon. Time to go."

Oblivious to Fenberg, the boys were narcotized by the red and green laser lights and explosions. Valuable points were being scored.

"Let's go. . . ."

Mrs. Behan had turned awkwardly around and was watching them. The machine was only a few stools away.

"Let 'em stay," said Mrs. Behan, holding on to the bar to steady her balance.

Fenberg smiled and nodded a polite hello, then turned back to the boys.

"Someone ought to have a little fun around here," she said, casting an evil, bleary eye at the bartender. He wouldn't serve her anymore. "No one wants to let people have fun anymore. You know what the problem with the world is right now?" She divided the question and her attention between Fenberg and the bartender. "Everybody . . . goes around killing everybody."

"It gets unforgiving out there from time to time," Fenberg admitted. "Last . . ." Fenberg wanted to say 'ball' but they didn't have balls in videos. He ended up saying 'thing' and told the boys they'd have to quit.

"Barkeep! Set up another one!" she yelled.

The bartender just dried off a glass and shook his head.

"I've got money! I've got lots of money!" She fumbled through her purse and pulled out a wrinkled ball of twenties and fifties. A few fell on the floor. She bent awkwardly, trying to pick them up. Fenberg steadied her back on her perch, then picked up the money. "You're a very good boy. I will give you a tip," she said, gingerly holding out a crumpled twenty.

"She comes in several nights a week, Mike," said the bartender. "Hey, she's great for business. I could open up another bar with what she packs away, but she's about a quart over her limit."

Her eyes lazily drifted back and forth from Fenberg to several horizons. Fenberg hadn't thought about it before, but whenever he ran into Mrs. Behan in town during the day, she did look a little ill. The red nose. The ever-present sunglasses that hid watery eyes and a frail, anemic appearance. Fenberg had dismissed it as a result of living with Behan. She craftily snapped the money back away from Fenberg.

"You're not the type to accept money from a woman," she said, laughing. "No. I will give you a more fitting reward. You're a newspaperman," she said, slurring the word, "like my husband. Hah!" She laughed at her joke.

"My husband's not a very good newspaperman. My husband's not a very good anything. You're a good newspaperman. Can you keep a secret?" She put her arm on Fenberg's shoulder, and Michael saw Joe making a sour face behind her. "I read your newspaper," she said, whispering. "Hah!"

Nice breath, thought Fenberg.

"That's not the secret," she said. "This is a very good secret, so you must promise not to print it in your newspaper. At least not on the front page. D'you promise?"

Fenberg's curiosity was piqued, he had to admit.

"Scout's honor," he said, holding up his hand. He turned partially away, searching for unpolluted air.

"He's not what he seems to be," she said, her voice barely audible.

"Who is?" Fenberg asked, shrugging.

"You see, Martin is hard to live with."

"I'm not surprised." Fenberg noted the black and blue bruise under her sunglasses.

"He's killing me slowly. He kills everything, everywhere we live, he kills. The kids just hate him. He's the cause of my drinking, you know?"

"Have you thought of leaving him?" Fenberg asked, trying to be sympathetic.

Mrs. Behan shook her head fearfully. No. She put her hand over her mouth. "I can't. I'm a coward. I'm also a drunk. I used to leave. I used to take the kids and pack up and leave, but he'd always find us. And then there'd be hell to pay. Oh!" She giggled. "I made a joke."

Fenberg looked above his head, as if something had flown over.

"You see, Martin's a devil. Which is funny, because Martin is a devil hiding behind a Bible."

"Well, not to be judgmental, but he *does* seem a little hard to be around for extended periods of time," agreed Fenberg.

"No, no, no no no *no*." She tugged on Fenberg's shirtfront.

"Easy. All cotton," said Fenberg, dislodging her.

"You don't understand. I mean, he really *is* a devil," she said, holding her fingers over her head to make two little horns.

"Come home, woman. You've had enough."

Linda Behan turned china-white. Her lower lip trembled. Fenberg turned to see M. J. Behan standing behind him. Behan looked terrible. His face was ashen, there was a marked loss of weight, clumps of hair were missing, and his eyes were runny. He looked like he had radiation poisoning.

"I didn't say anything. We were just having a little drink. I'll come home right now, okay? Have you had dinner yet? Can I fix you anything? I will." She stumbled off the stool and took short, concentrated I'm-not-drunk steps to the door. She muttered to herself as she walked, "I'll get some coffee and I'll be fine and I'll cook something for you and the kids as soon as we get home. I will."

The restaurant was silent.

"I'm sorry about the scene. I hope it didn't embarrass you, Michael," M. J. Behan said. The dark eyes blinked, preoccupied, troubled. "I'll see you in the morning then." He paused, thinking whether or not to remind Fenberg not to try to sneak off early, then disappeared.

"I guess dinner must be a very important meal at their house," Angry Joe finally said.

20

ON THE NATURE OF
MONSTERS AND WOMEN

(This editorial, penned by Michael Fenberg, the eleventh and final editor of *The Basin Valley Bugle*, was published March 12, right before he went looking for Mitikitski.)

The Fourth In A Series Of Public Apologies

by Michael Fenberg
Editor & Publisher

This is your basic bargain-basement editorial, three topics for the price of one column. First, I'd like to apologize. By the time this newsprint hits the streets, I will have skipped bail. Sorry. More than that, I'm sorry about my brother again.

For those of you who do not collect *Bugle* public apologies nor paste them in the family scrapbook, let it be officially recorded that I have made three other such apologies in years past for John. This is the fourth, and I hope, final one. We are all getting too old for this.

The first apology, if I remember correctly, was logged about ten years ago during my first few months as editor. I was young. I made a green decision to have Tuberski (at the time he went by the family moniker of Fenberg, Norwood Z.) collect a long past due account from Furgeson's Saw Mill (now out of business). Words were exchanged, and this is all secondhand, but Mr. Furgeson said something to the effect that he'd be struck blind and impotent before paying *The Bugle* one red cent of the fourteen hundred dollars he owed us. The rotter. Anyway, Furgeson sicced a good portion of his day crew on this paper's agent of collection, and after John waded through the horde of misguided lumberjacks (who I'm sure were just trying to save their jobs), John force-fed several complimentary issues of *The Bugle* to the toothpick mogul.

We assured all Basin Valley businessmen that it was not official policy to collect delinquent accounts in such a fashion. At the time, we said it would never happen again, and to our credit, it hasn't.

I also seem to remember apologizing for John's unsuccessful promotion of the Iron Butterfly reunion concert at Sage Hall Park a few Fourth of Julys ago (all moneys were cheerfully refunded) and, of course, public regrets were printed on page one recently for the unfortunate remarks and subsequent treeing of the Indian Grin President of the PTA by this reporter's brother, who was employed with the district for a short time as a noon aide.

We were sorry then, and we're sorry now.

To bring you up to date, my brother has now been implicated in a series of particularly grisly murders the only consolation of which is that most of the victims were from out of town.

Well last night, my brother came home. And he wasn't alone.

For the past several months, we've all been hiding and shivering behind bolted doors, speculating on the nature of the mysterious killer who has been haunting our fair valley and digesting good people, natives and tourists alike. I thought it was the work of a maniac. It's not. It's a monster.

I know it's a monster because I saw it myself.

Now this is where it gets confusing.

My brother, John, said that he has spent the better part of the last fiscal quarter living in a cave with this hairy missing link. John has given me his personal assurance that neither he nor his hominid friend have killed or eaten anyone in recent memory.

I hope he's right.

Last night, John Tuberski's monster carried off the adept managing editor of this paper, Miss Elaine Mitikitski. Good editors are hard, but not impossible, to replace. The big problem here is that I'm in love with Mitikitski.

I just haven't told anyone yet.

I guess I've got it bad. She breaks my heart in twelve places, and there are so many things I'd like to tell her, right down to the proposition that the two of us go through life together, with kids, IRA's, the whole marianna. I guess I care for her so much that even that isn't enough, and I'd like to ask that if she were willing, we could march through time together as two happy molecules, wearing white gloves and round shoes, holding hands.

It's terrible what love does to a guy.

If *The Bugle* is delivered to whatever cave you happen to be in right now, Elaine, I'd like to ask you to marry me. I'm on my way to find you.

And to you, faithful subscribers, I hope to see you all soon. Thanks for reading, and please buy ads.

It was nice owning your own newspaper. You didn't have to cut any of your own copy.

21

THE SEARCH FOR THE ELUSIVE
ELAINE MITIKITSKI

It was well past eleven, and Fenberg and Sheriff Bubba took turns casting worried glances toward the road. Tuberski had been given the relatively easy task of driving into town to fill up Michael's pickup with sixty gallons of gas and bring back the equipment. Three of Bubba's deputies went with him to make sure he returned. That was over four hours ago.

The ranch was bathed in light, a suddenly popular pastime, Fenberg noted. Let's go out to Mike's and light up the place like a supermarket grand opening. Besides the standard anti-Tuberski brigade of sheriffs, state police, and volunteer deputies, countless members of the press scampered about, jotting notes and sticking microphones into people's faces. The lights for the TV cameras created an artificial atmosphere, like a movie set, and Fenberg had given Clifford and Angry Joe the task of making sure none of the news crews used Fenberg's electrical outlets.

The sheriff paced in front of Fenberg and angrily rubbed his salt-and-pepper flattop. "If he's harmed one hair on my men, I swear to you, Michael . . ." Bubba said, stopping to point a stubby finger at Fenberg's nose.

To hell with your men, thought Fenberg. What about my truck?

There were several historical precedents of Tuberski being a car abuser.

It was no secret John had always coveted Michael's pickup.
The truck was rather impressive, rumbling a full yard above
ground on four tractoresque, gnarly, oversized Kelly-Springfield tires. It was painted with sixteen coats of gloss black,
including the bumpers. The only detail was the hand lettering
in white on the front fenders: *Fate Is The Hunter.*

Fenberg's pride and joy had four-wheel drive and a beefed-
up engine with so much horsepower that, given the chance,
it could drive up the side of a building. When Michael had
brought it home nearly six years ago, Tuberski was driven to
tears at the spiritual beauty of the big V-8. He lovingly
caressed the hood and bent down to kiss the bumper. He
was shocked when he saw a smudge on the onyx paint job,
and, like a doting Spanish madonna, quickly rubbed it out
with his T-shirt. He cooed and oohed and aahed around it for
a full fifteen minutes, complimenting and caressing. "Do you
think I could drive it?" he finally asked. Fenberg pursed his
lips and folded his arms. Tuberski was a higher insurance risk
than Ted Kennedy. "Maybe some other time," Fenberg said.
Tuberski's face sagged. His lower lip crept out in a pout.
"Please?" John asked.

Fenberg relented, halfway. His brother could sit in the
truck. But first, he had to change into some clean clothes.
Tuberski was already wearing clean clothes, but he sprinted
into the house and returned in freshly laundered Levi's, a
white dress shirt, sports coat, and tie. "The tie wasn't necessary," said Fenberg, "but go ahead." Tuberski gingerly kicked
the dust off his penny loafers and lowered himself gently
behind the wheel. Tuberski stared at the interior as if it were
a museum. He asked Fenberg, for the second time, please, oh
pretty please, Mikey, could he just start up the truck, please?
Fenberg smirked. You? A *car abuser*, drive my new $24,500
pickup? No. Never.

Tuberski begged and pleaded. He whined. He promised
things he couldn't possibly deliver, if only Fenberg would
find it in his heart to let him just turn the engine over. Fenberg stared malevolently at his brother, then daintily produced the keys. "For God's sake, please be careful. Don't

accidentally hit the stick and grind the gears. Just let it idle for a few seconds, then turn it off." Tuberski mouthed a silent thank-you and reverently inserted key into ignition.

Tuberski smiled warmly at Michael. Michael smiled warmly back. A wave of nausea crawled into Fenberg's stomach when he heard the whir of the electric windows ascending and the click of all four electric door locks. Tuberski was still smiling sweetly as he gunned the turbo-charged engine to nine thousand rpm's. The truck rocked back and forth violently. Great clouds of dust billowed out from underneath the chassis. John Tuberski popped the clutch and did a wheel stand, and the great black Ford screeched a hundred yards to the Fenberg front gate. Tuberski ground the stick into a vicious downshift, slamming on the brakes at the same time. Before he took off for three hours, after which he left the pickup in town, out of gas, Tuberski made a beeline for Fenberg, turning at the last moment so he could drive a half-dozen tight circles around Mikey. Fenberg stood in the dust, his shoulders rounded. Above the roar of the engine, all Fenberg could hear was Tuberski's maniacal graveyard laugh. Fenberg sighed. He would get even. Tuberski knew he would get even. It was the rules of the game.

"Here he comes!" someone in the press yelled.

"Thank God," said Fenberg.

Tuberski bounced in through the front gate. He was wearing a sheriff's hat, and a set of handcuffs dangled from around his ear. The three deputies were laughing uproariously in the front and back seats. Fenberg winced at the sound of the parking break being yanked a little too fervently. He walked full circle around the truck, inspecting for dings before asking for the keys.

"We stopped off on the way back for a soda," said Tuberski, grinning. Bubba looked angrily back and forth between John and Mike, suspicious they were passing some message. John formally returned the sheriff's hat and handcuffs. All three of the deputies were slightly askew; two were yawning. Bubba considered giving them a tongue-lashing, but he had other things on his mind.

"A word with you, Michael?" asked Bubba, staring narrowly at his three men. Bubba walked out of earshot. He and Mike stood on the fringe of the lights, vapors of breath puffing skyward. "I put myself in your shoes. I thought, what would I do if my Mary had been kidnapped by something, man or beast. I know I wouldn't wait around to find her. I also know you're the kind of man who does things his own way, Michael."

"So what are you getting at?"

Bubba laced his fingers into his gunbelt and kicked at a clump of weeds. "I wouldn't wait till morning, I'd figure out a way to escape. Take out on my own. I know I'd move faster that way."

"Well, Cousin, look over there," said Fenberg, nodding toward twoscore well-dressed anchorpeople, solemnly holding microphones. They had beseeching puppy eyes, hopeful Fenberg would toss out some statement, however insignificant. Or maybe he could clear up his only statement, the obscure and dated reference to ex-Beatle Paul McCartney being a walrus. "There are easily a hundred media people here and half-again as many cops. I don't think I'd get very far with a tail like that."

"You're a resourceful guy, Mike," said Bubba, smiling. "You'd find a way. But don't."

"I hear you," said Fenberg. They watched Charlie Two Eagles hand a leather rifle case to Bean Breath Brown, who was scampering about in the bed of the truck, loading gear.

"Ah, hell. I don't know," said Bubba, tucking his hands into his green sheriff's-issue ski parka. "There's just so many things here that don't make sense."

"Behan for one?"

"Behan for one."

"Yeah," said Fenberg. "That's been plaguing me too."

"I remember earlier today, back at the jail." Bubba looked away, almost embarrassed. "Behan was almost in a panic. He was frantic that we get the girl back. You don't act that desperate when you're out to do a Sunday-good deed."

Bubba watched the proceedings, taking in everything

peripherally, like a lifeguard on a tower. "I haven't told any-one this, not even my wife. But that guy Behan gives me the creeps, and I don't know what it is. Did you notice how sick he is?"

Decomposing seemed more appropriate, thought Fenberg.

"Why is he so all hot about coming with us? Why would a man in his condition want to go traipsing off into some of the roughest country in the state? Why would a man of his stand-ing hook up with such scum as the Magonogonovitch broth-ers?"

"Maybe you can ask him," said Fenberg, looking past the sheriff's crew cut. Car lights. A cream-colored Corniche drove slowly under the log gateway. Almost automatically, TV cam-eras whirred, transferring this new element—wealth—to videotape.

M. J. Behan slammed the door with authority, and his wife flinched at the sound. She stayed in the car, pulling her face back from the inquisitive lights. She had been beaten.

"I had a call. They informed me you were attempting to leave early," said Behan, squaring up against Fenberg.

"You're up rather late," said Michael.

"I don't sleep much at night," said Behan. He looked gaunt and ragged, but somehow stronger. Fenberg felt a repulsion and anger beyond reason. He caught himself measuring, mentally calculating the steps it would take for the pounce. There was a pull Fenberg couldn't explain, something that stirred deep, primitive feelings. Ridiculous. I *am* going crazy, thought Fenberg, shaking himself free from the gravitational field.

"We're just loading up for morning," Bubba answered for Fenberg. The answer seemed to satisfy Behan, who inspected the truck. "Do you think you'll really need all this?"

"Tough country up there. You never know what you might run into," said Fenberg.

Behan seemed to relish the last remark. He smiled slightly. "No. You never do."

Bean Breath scampered delicately around the gear. The truck was loaded, and Brown covered everything with a heavy tarp. Tuberski tugged hard on a nylon rope, crisscrossing it through one of the four chrome hitches on each side of the bed like shoestrings.

"It's midnight," said Fenberg. "The witching hour." He didn't know why he said it. "Make yourself comfortable, somewhere off my property. I'm going to catch a little sleep." Fenberg looked at Behan, evaluating the man as if he were a painting. Martin wore a full houndstooth overcoat, and his once-thick black hair was long and stringy. He'd become pale and thin since his arrival in Basin Valley just three months ago.

"Why is it I dislike you so much?" Fenberg asked him.

Behan's eyes. They were old and radiated a cold, confident power. "Maybe we share a common destiny."

Fenberg didn't look away this time. The answer seemed to satisfy him.

* * * * *

1:30 A.M. Bean Breath Brown slid out a ranch window and stealthily crawled past the sentries to the forest beyond. He silently but laboriously dragged with him a McCulloch chain saw, five wedges, an axe, and three boxes of Milk Duds.

2:30 A.M. The nearly full moon rose, and John Tuberski sat up abruptly from his sleep. The three deputies assigned to guard him were passed out, victims of trace dosages of tranquilizers with which Tuberski had earlier spiked their beers.

Tuberski tiptoed down the dark wood-paneled hallway and quietly opened Fenberg's bedroom door. The guard inside was awake and went for his pistol. Tuberski shook his head no and put a finger to his lips, then pointed to Fenberg. The naiveté and openness of the move immobilized the guard, giving Tuberski time to take three steps closer.

"Bad tactical error," whispered Tuberski, bending over with his hands on his knees and eye-level to the sitting deputy. "If you yell or make a move for that gun, I'll literally pull your head off your body. You see, I'm the one who killed and ate those ten people."

The guard froze in terror.

Tuberski weaved back and forth, his eyes widening to show the whites, and clicked his teeth together. The deputy sheriff gave no resistance as Tuberski handcuffed and gagged him. Teeth clenched, eyes trancelike, Tuberski slowly crossed the room, his hands outstretched for Fenberg. Fully dressed, Fenberg slapped the hands away and whispered for Tuberski to quit clowning around.

"That part about being a homicidal cannibal," Tuberski said, bending over again to the wide-eyed guard, "I was just sort of kidding. Say 'kay." He deftly jabbed the deputy with the tip of a small, feathered hypodermic dart. "Sweet dreams."

It took less than three minutes for the two Fenberg brothers and Charlie Two Eagles to sneak past Bubba's perimeter of security and overpower the guard sleeping in Michael's truck. Shots were fired, and the pickup had just a thirty-second head start on the high-powered interstate CHP cruisers and the armada of newsmen and sheriffs that followed.

Around the horseshoe bends and ice-slick hairpin turns, five screaming patrol cars lessened the gap. The lead driver wasn't state police or a member of the sheriff's department. He was Ranger Granger, the tall-haired national park supervisor who had a personal vendetta against the Fenbergs. Buckled in and smiling with perfect teeth, Ranger Granger watched the black truck's gruff acceleration, and he wondered just what in the hell Fenberg thought he was doing. On these narrow mountain roads, even Mario Andretti in a Ferrari couldn't gain that much distance in an out-an-out run for it, let alone Fenberg in a top-heavy pickup geared more for tractor pulling. And then it all became perfectly clear.

"Ah, shit!" The sound was distant, but familiar and quite unmistakable in this part of the country—the psychotic electric guitar whining of a chain saw. Granger gunned his Chrysler into overdrive and put down a quick few hundred yards. He didn't hear the crash of the timber over the noise from his engine, but he felt it. Like driving into an explosion or hurricane, Granger locked the brakes as pine needles, dust, dirt, and small rocks sneezed on his windshield. His car slid sideways into the obese oak lying perpendicular across the mountain road.

On the other side of the tree, Bean Breath Brown stood on the soft shoulder, examining his work. The tree was old and rotten, tagged by the road department for felling in the early spring. Tuberski jumped out of the passenger side, yelling for Bean to stop gawking and get in. Ranger Ray Granger stumbled from his car, blood trickling from a minor bump. He climbed the tree, pistol drawn. Tuberski grabbed Bean Breath in one hand and the chain saw in the other, swinging both into the bed of the truck. By the time the national park cop reached the top of the tree, all he saw was a wide row of red and yellow lights blink and disappear around a bend in the distance. It took CalTrans forty-five minutes to get there with all the right equipment, and another two hours to cut and bulldoze a lane through. But by that time, Fenberg's one-truck safari had long ago turned off onto an old logging road and disappeared into the forest, a black pebble swallowed by a green, leafy ocean.

* * * * *

In town, Martin Behan freely wandered around in the darkened offices of *The Basin Valley Bugle*. He sat in Fenberg's chair, the one Michael's grandfather had crafted. Behan regarded the silver-framed picture of Tracy and her son, with a lazy finger casually knocking it to the floor. The glass shattered. Behan picked up another photo, this one of Elaine. He rubbed the front of the glass down to the bottom of the frame, as if he could slip his fingers through and caress her breasts. Behan let that picture drop, too.

He walked out the back and took the long way around to his own office across the street. He stood at parade rest, head tilted slightly, watching *The Bugle*. There was a lot of history to the building. As a saloon nearly a century earlier, it had also served as an impromptu courtroom and meeting hall. A couple of surgeries had been performed on poker tables, and a few people had even been married there. Five generations of Fenbergs had sold real estate ads and logged the history of their community. There was a flicker of orange through the front window that danced here and there, growing to reds and yellows, licking out through the roof.

The Magonogonovitch brothers joined Behan. They carried rusty red, empty gas cans. The three men watched the blaze engulf the building before hearing the fire engines' wail from a half town away. "Get rid of those," Behan instructed, referring to the cans. The trio went their separate ways.

* * * * *

The sun made a halfhearted attempt to break through the gloomy netherworld that was the Orion National Forest at the tail end of winter. It was an unspectacular dawn, more of an ooze, and even though the truck was comfortably warm, Fenberg had the chills. They were lost, and Tuberski was annoying him.

"Buddy, I'm just trying to cheer you up," said Tuberski.

"I'd rather not be cheered up, thank you," said Fenberg.

"Can I cheer you up a little?"

"No."

Tuberski slowly raised the disconnected CB microphone to his mouth, staring at Fenberg for possible disciplinary action.

"Sky King to Penny. Sky to Penny. One Adam-Twelve, Kirk to *Enterprise*," spoke Tuberski.

"May I have some directions, please?" asked Fenberg.

"Matthews. 2150 to headquarters. . . ." Tuberski grinned.

"Look. John . . . *Shit!*" Fenberg screamed, a little high-pitched for a man his age. He swerved to miss a boulder. The move slid the old sleeping Indian off the back seat and onto the floor. He didn't wake. Bean squinched his nose and picked up his glasses.

"Smokies at the grapevine."

The big four-door pickup with *Fate Is The Hunter* painted on the side bounced roughly along, dipping across a brook, then underneath a car wash of low-hanging branches. Fenberg winced as they scraped along the paint job. There probably hadn't been another vehicle on this road in years, if you could call this a road. The truck rumbled, lurched forward and bounced through the resistance of underbrush, crushing small branches and spitting out rocks like an icebreaker in the North Atlantic. Fenberg reached another high point of some nameless topography, slammed on the brakes, and announced he wasn't going any farther.

Tuberski squinted into the sunrise. Several mountain ranges away was Basin Valley. And rising from Basin Valley was a narrow column of black smoke. It was too early in the season for a natural fire of that magnitude.

"Probably some poor soul left some newspapers by the pilot light or something," said Tuberski.

"Yeah. Poor guy," agreed Fenberg.

Fenberg asked again just where were they, and John chattered more banalities into the CB. Fenberg chewed on the inside of his cheek. "Where, I repeat, are we?"

"Here," said Tuberski, shrugging as if it were obvious. He reached to the floor of the back seat and roughly shook the old medicine man. "Hey! Wake up!"

Charlie Two Eagles groaned.

"Nice," said Fenberg, looking around. Mars in winter.

"We ought to be grateful for the weather," said Tuberski, unbuckling. "The sheriff won't be able to follow us in a helicopter with all this cloud cover."

"If we're here, then where's Elaine, and where's the monster?" Fenberg wanted to know.

"This isn't Versateller. You just don't drive up to a Sasquatch. You've got to sneak up on it. We'll hide the truck in some brush and go the rest of the way on foot." Tuberski pointed to their destination, a forbidding peak a half-day away. It looked like the Matterhorn at Disneyland, without the tracks. "Two to beam aboard, Scotty," said Tuberski, making radio static noises into the dead microphone.

"John, stop playing with the radio," said Fenberg.

"Spock . . . Bones . . . tricorders on. Wide beam to check for a large, hairy, Muppetlike life-form and a raven-haired beauty with a nice butt who doesn't practice birth control."

"That's pretty funny, John."

"Kirk to Elaine! Kirk to Elaine!" said Tuberski, leaning forward and feigning urgency. "Lieutenant Mitikitski . . . this is Kirk . . . Lieutenant . . . how do you like it like *this*?" asked John, accentuating the *this*.

The two brothers stared poker-faced at one another, Fenberg silently communicating his don't-you-think-it's-about-time-to-grow-up speech, Tuberski bouncing back with it's-going-to-be-a-long-expedition-if-you're-going-to-have-such-a-stuffy-attitude. They parked the truck under a tree, hiding it from prying eyes from the road or air with a camouflage of shrubs and brush.

"Cold this morning," said Fenberg, rubbing his hands together.

Tuberski drew a furnaceful of air through his nostrils and exhaled. "Thirty-six degrees, quite warm for this time of year, actually. No windchill factor. I'm quite happy."

"Hmmmmph," said Fenberg, pulling up the collar to his sheepskin jacket. The Indian and Bean climbed out of the back seat. Fenberg stuck his hands in his pockets and took in the horizon. White, green, and gray, nothing but miles of it. "I think it's going to rain."

"Nah," said Tuberski, hands on hips and looking at the sky. He wore a skintight white T-shirt. "Those aren't rain clouds. I can smell rain. We might get a light sprinkle of snow though. Just enough to cover our tracks."

"It's going to rain like hell," said Charlie, walking between the two brothers.

"So what makes you think Elaine and the creature are up there?" asked Fenberg, staring off toward the towering, treacherous mountain half covered in mist.

"Actually, there're two schools of thought here," said Tuberski, easily hoisting a massive backpack to his shoulders. Bean was back in the bed, gleefully tossing down provisions to Charlie Eagles, who let most hit the ground. "The creature could be hiding up there in Blind Widow Dome," said John, pointing to the icy mountain, "or, he could be back at the cave by Webster's Leap." Tuberski pointed to a valley in the opposite direction.

Fenberg didn't care for either choice. He wished they were closer.

"The Blind Widow is a tough but not impossible climb. Sophisticated mountaineering gear is not required," said Tuberski, shifting the weight of his pack. "It's the secret habitat of the creature. I think."

"You think."

"He used to wander off from time to time. Once I followed him," Tuberski said, nodding toward the peak. "It's a home away from home, a tree house. He goes there when he's troubled."

Fenberg watched his brother reach into a shirt pocket and pull out the large vial of pills. Nitroglycerin.

"What's the other school of thought?" Fenberg asked.

"That he's at the original cave where we stayed."

"That has more wisdom to me," said the Indian. He morosely regarded the backpack lying inanimately at his feet. "Do I have to carry one of these things?"

"No," said Fenberg.

"But come sundown, you can sleep standing up and not have any dinner," added Tuberski.

"Why *wouldn't* he go back to the cave?" asked Fenberg.

"Too obvious."

"We're following something that's half animal," said Fenberg, "not a Soviet chess master. Why wouldn't he go back to the cave? And how far is it, by the way?"

"It's only about a twenty minute drive. About three hours hiking at a good pace," said Tuberski. "Only problem is, during times of stress, he heads for the higher elevations."

"But you're not sure."

Tuberski reached into his back pocket and pulled out a blue stocking cap. He tugged it over his ears. "Pretty sure. Or maybe it's bears I'm thinking about."

The debate raged for several minutes, with Bean Breath Brown looking back and forth between the two brothers. Tuberski reminded Fenberg the element of surprise was of paramount importance, because if the creature spotted them, he might take Mitikitski so far into the backcountry they'd need a visa just to follow. Fenberg told Tuberski never to mention Visa in front of him.

"Buddy. Trust me on this one. I lived with the thing. I know all its habits. Your bride is going to be just fine. And once I get the medicine to the creature, he'll be fine, too. Remember, I want to find her just as badly as you do. She's the mother of my nephew. We'll try the Blind Widow first, then, if they're not there, at least by the light of the full moon tonight, we'll be able to make our way over to Webster's Leap."

Against Michael's better judgment, they traipsed off toward the Blind Widow Dome.

The men hiked in silence for the first hour, the only sounds coming from the muffled crunching of boots on wet snow and gravel. They all sniffed constantly. Seven in the morning, Fenberg calculated. Get to the top of the Dome by noon. An hour or two to look. Five hours back made it seven that night. Seven, dark, and full moon.

Fenberg alternately checked the sky and his partners. It peeved Fenberg, ever so slightly, that out of an expedition that included all three of the premiere town characters, he was the one in the worst shape. The occasional friendly three-on-three at the Cougar gym or an afternoon living room workout on the VCR with aerobic queen Kathy Smith (who looked amazingly like Tracy) didn't prepare Fenberg for the punishing uphill climb. And those clouds. It felt like an ambush. The storm gods were hiding, collecting every spare drop of moisture from here to Canada and when they could hold no more, they'd dump the rain in one huge drop the size of Australia. By the third hour, the sky had blackened, and Fenberg trudged along, following the dull rhythm of his weary steps, entranced with the tops of his brown, round-toed boots with the red shoelaces. My boots are my friends, my boots are my friends. He slammed into Tuberski's back-pack.

"Excuse me," said Tuberski.

Fenberg bounced off him.

Tuberski turned and beamed inanely. "What'd I tell you?" Tuberski was holding a small, broken branch. Fenberg looked stupidly at the twig. So?

"Hair-us specimen-us Abominable Snowman-icus North American-us," grinned Fenberg's little brother, holding the stick. A long tuft of blackish hair was tangled in it. "We're on the right track."

And so, it seemed, they were.

A few feet ahead, they found the first spoor. Evidently, the creature made no attempt to hide his tracks. Even Fenberg marveled at the prints. They were spaced two yards apart for a normal stride and up to twelve feet where the creature jumped a log or small runoff.

"Must have gained some weight, or maybe it's just the soft soil," Tuberski bent over and commented, sticking his finger into the footprint as a measuring stick. "Look at this. Nearly three inches deep."

"It might be because he's carrying Elaine," said Fenberg, hands on knees. Tuberski looked up and nodded in agreement.

"I got a feeling," Tuberski said, rising. "I have this feeling that in less than twenty-four hours, we'll all be back in town, laughing it up, in the early stages of rolling in the chips."

"I hope he's not going to tell us about how Ringling Brothers started again," said Charlie.

Fenberg wasn't sold on this "bring 'em back alive" concept, either. He'd be much happier if they could just find Elaine and never see that hairy apparition again. Although . . . a wheel clicked onto a gear in Fenberg's brain. One real, live Bigfoot. Five dollars a head, times five billion people, less twenty percent for expenses and no-shows . . .

"We're still far away from Bigfoot terrain," said Tuberski, stretching stiffly. "I'd say we got another hour of climbing and I mean to tell you, I gotta sit down. I'm bushed."

Fenberg could have kissed him. "How about if we cross over to that clearing there and sit down for a few minutes."

The men shuffled to a fallen white birch. They fell out of their packs and shared what was left of a thermos of hot tea.

Their resting ground was a flat ledge, blending into a wide, rocky entrance that was the dumping ground for several smaller canyons. There was the insistent sound of cascading water, and the ground was cold and hard, but it felt like a mattress to Fenberg. He jerked his head up.

"Do you smell something funny?" asked Fenberg, sniffing.

Bean Breath wrinkled his nose and made a face. Or maybe he looked that way all the time.

"Dead animal," pronounced the Indian.

"Maybe a skunk," said Tuberski.

From an enclave just a few hundred yards away, a huge, hairy creature was oblivious to the world he ruled. He was gnawing on a leg bone. The wind shifted.

"I guess this is what they call rarefied air," added Fenberg, closing his eyes.

"It's pretty thin," agreed Tuberski, sliding down to the ground and resting against the tree trunk. He pulled the cap down over his eyes. "We're up over two miles, you know," he pointed out.

*　*　*　*　*

There were times when Tuberski couldn't sleep. He'd close his eyes and smack his lips in languid contentment. Then that something would happen. It was beyond a dream or fantasy, beyond the realm of mind and nothing psychic. Tuberski would slip into a world beyond words and thought, a meditative state. No humming, no chanting, no hey-batter-batter, a place beyond transcendentalism. He had the gift of vision, and through him, not by him, healings took place, silent and secret.

Tuberski's eyes were closed, and the peace settled. He could see Fenberg clearly. Not in any pose or situation, but as more of an essence—Fenberg past, present, and future. It was like being momentarily yanked upward, above the clouds. Sins weren't forgiven. They didn't exist. All the offenses and defenses were suddenly gone, and all that was left was this clarity. It moved him to action. *Help your brother,* the Voice said.

Tuberski sat up with a start. He pulled up the edge of his cap and peeked suspiciously at Fenberg. Bean and the Indian were collapsed against another section of the log.

"Mike, did you just say something?" Tuberski asked, leaning on one arm. Fenberg shuffled on his side, his back to his brother. He told Tuberski to go away. Tuberski looked perplexed, then made a face. Oh. It's you again. That darn entity. It had no form, but was there. It had no name, but seemed to know Tuberski intimately well. Invisible, wayward, it came and went as it pleased, and when it did speak, it was often cryptic. Tuberski wondered what Joan of Arc would have done in a situation like this.

Tuberski stood.

Help your brother in the silence.

Tuberski sat back down. All right. What do you want now? As usual, I don't get it.

You will.

Help him from what?

You'll see.

When?

Soon.

There you go. Cryptic. Tuberski strained harder to listen, but the essence faded. Disgruntled, he shook his head. I don't know why you pester me. And why do you have to always be so cryptic? Why can't you just speak plainly? Sometimes it spoke to John in Biblical verse, which Tuberski found even more cryptic as it was happening. But later, the meanings became crystal clear, and John would smile.

John . . . the voice came back.

"Yes!" Tuberski answered aloud.

Half the fun is in finding out for yourself. And relax. I'll tell you when it's time to help your brother. You are my beloved son in whom I am well pleased.

And then it was gone for good, at least until next time. As Tuberski strained to hear, Fenberg suddenly sat up and strained to smell.

"Do you smell something?" Fenberg asked, sniffing.

"No." Tuberski sat with his eyes closed, turning his head like radar, trying to pick up the Voice. "Did you hear anything?"

"No. But I smell something. Don't you smell something?"

Tuberski caught the odor and opened his eyes. "God, it is rather horrendous, isn't it?" John said. The four men looked at one another with wrinkled faces, like Our Gang after stumbling upon a long-forgotten barrel of Limburger. "Are you thinking what I'm thinking?"

Fenberg nodded yes. It was the same scent of that creature in Elaine's apartment, only stronger. Fenberg reached for his leather rifle case. He unzipped it and pulled out the carbine. He slid in the syringe missile with the tiny feathered bee-stinger tip.

Tuberski stared ahead at a rocky formation a football field away from where the wind was blowing the odor. There was something wrong, something different. Tuberski loaded his own rifle. Fenberg saw him click in live ammo and didn't say anything.

Fenberg ordered Bean and the Indian to wait, which Charlie found perfectly agreeable.

"I think we can swing around up there. See those boulders?" Fenberg pointed to a stack of huge rocks.

"Just what I was thinking," said Tuberski. "Let me show myself first. That way, he might not panic."

"I just want to get Elaine out of there."

"We will. We will."

The Fenberg brothers doubletimed their way to the rocks. Michael pointed to the highest boulder as their destination. It was only seventy-five feet up, but Fenberg gritted his teeth every time a boot slipped or a hand broke loose a chunk of sediment. The odor grew stronger with a strong wind kicking the scent in their faces like an exhaust fan in a slaughterhouse. Fenberg opened and closed his trigger finger, making sure circulation was there when he needed it. They were close enough to hear a random grunt and stirring. There was something very huge, and very smelly, behind the next boulder, below them, though, thank God, below them.

Nothing could prepare Fenberg for the scene below. Squatting down over the carcass, crunching bones with his molars, was a man. Sort of. Except this man was covered with black, shaggy hair and must have weighed a ton. He was oblivious to everything but his meal.

"Darn," said Tuberski.

Fenberg glanced over and did a double take. He had expected to see his brother's face. Instead, he saw his brother's kneecap. Which meant, John was standing.

"Will you get down! What are you doing?" Fenberg barked in a harsh whisper.

The creature spotted Tuberski and leaped to its feet. It was larger than Fenberg remembered, maybe eleven feet tall.

"Geez Louise," said Tuberski, shaking his head.

"Goddamn it, he's spotted us!" whispered Fenberg, although there was no need to whisper. The monster had an arm reach of six feet, tacked onto shoulders that were ten feet off the ground, which gave the creature a total reach of sixteen feet. Fenberg and Tuberski were seventeen feet off the ground. Fenberg hoped the monster couldn't jump. It could.

Tuberski picked up some baseball-sized rocks and laconically threw them down at the beast.

Fenberg wondered if Tuberski had lost his mind and the creature shared Fenberg's wonderment. In this part of the world, *he* ruled, he didn't like the idea of someone throwing rocks at him. The monster screamed, a high-pitched jagged screech that sounded as if it would burst all of Fenberg's internal organs. It clambered frantically around its rocky perch, searching for a boulder or tree or some such weapon. Fenberg raised his rifle and aimed.

"Get out of here, you hairy throw rug!" yelled Tuberski. He pelted the creature with another rock, and it raised an ineffectual, protective arm. Tuberski followed with a shower of fastballs, bonking the beast in the chest, head, and buttocks. "Go on! Get out of here. Scram!"

The giant black man-thing picked up a cantaloupe-sized rock and sailed it over Tuberski's head into the next time zone. The monster just didn't have the snap in his wrist to deliver an effective bean ball. Realizing he was overmatched, the creature snorted and whimpered before scampering sideways down another trail and out of sight.

Fenberg lowered his rifle. There was a request for an explanation etched on his face.

"Ah, hell, I'm sorry, Mike," said Tuberski, mustering disgust so he wouldn't have to look directly at Fenberg. He brushed past his brother, headed back the way they had come. "It's the wrong goddamn Bigfoot," he said, shrugging.

A crushing exasperation fell over Fenberg, leaving him without the will or strength to chastise or choke his Baby Huey brother.

22

THE FIRST NIGHT OF THE
FULL MOON

Sheriff Bubba Fenberg jumped off to a late start after his quarry. There were over a hundred men in cars and on horseback hunting for Fenberg and Tuberski. It was nearly noon before all the search parties dispersed to scour the dozens of minor arteries and capillaries that connected to the main highway. CB and police radio were virtually useless in most of the up-and-down terrain, which didn't matter. No one had anything to report anyway.

By four that afternoon, all units had covered the sixteen roads off State Highway 398, and even a few outlets that hardly qualified as deer paths.

"That damn Fenberg's truck is so beefed up, he could make his own road," one searcher complained, "and the problem is that we have to check the road a foot at a time to see where, if he did, leave the highway."

At 4:30, Deputy Juarez was about ready to call it quits. He had drawn the fun detail—chauffeur to both Magonogonovitches, Sheriff Bubba, and another deputy, Bill Doherty, who was down with the flu in the back seat, useless. Juarez inched the sheriff's wagon along at two miles an hour on the dirt road. Bubba sat on the hood of the big lime green Chevy Suburban, scanning the endless vistas with his binoculars. Lom and Luther walked ahead of the truck, stalking along the fire trail, their eyes sweeping the ground for that something peculiar. Juarez wanted to get home. They were maybe thirty miles from base camp, and he had a daughter at home running a temperature.

"Fuck it. Let's call it a day," said Bubba, dropping the binoculars to his lap. He waved to Lom and Luther. They ignored him. Lom had something in his fingers he was showing his brother.

Juarez gently accelerated.

"Pine needles," said Luther.

So? thought Bubba, rubbing the fat that wrapped his kidneys. The sheriff glanced at the filthy fingernails that held a single pine needle.

"It's broken in half, Sheriff," said Luther. His brother nodded and spit a stream of tobacco. "Pine needles don't break in half falling out of a tree." The two fireplugs in overalls lightly jogged up the trail. Two miles up the road, the path turned to an angled section of solid granite. Nothing, not even a tank, would register a mark. It was Lom who found a bouquet of long branches, freshly cut, discarded in a ditch.

"They drug 'em to throw us off," said Luther. "Figured they'd make it to the granite section and wouldn't need 'em anymore. Betcha tire tracks'll pick up around that bend."

Luther was right.

Dusk came as the five men carefully drove across the slick granite section. With high beams and a pair of spotlights, the wide tire tracks from Fenberg's truck weren't hard to follow. Bubba watched as his men and the Magonogonovitches quickly pulled the branches and brush from Fenberg's truck.

Luther surmised correctly: "They were here. They hid the truck so it couldn't be spotted by an airplane." He delicately tiptoed around, reading the ground. Finally, he pointed. "They went that way. Blind Widow Dome."

"Sixteen-forty to base camp," Bubba called in. He got back an earful of static. Bubba fiddled with the frequency knob, but nothing came in. "Goddamn mountains. Two of us will stay here. I want Juarez and . . ."

"Sheriff?" interrupted Luther.

"What is it?"

Luther nodded toward the sky. Clouds were racing over the peaks, and a strong wind blew the tops of the trees. Even Bubba could smell the moisture. A great bald dome peeked between the trees in the east, drawing courage. It slowly rose, higher and higher, swollen with radiation and hiding a smile. The full moon.

"Might get wet real quick around here," said Luther. The other men looked at the sky, entranced. "If you were to ask me, I'd forget about trying to get back. We'll get rain in two, three minutes. Best to set up camp on the high ground. We're stuck here for the night, Sheriff. Maybe longer."

"What do you mean, stuck?"

"Yeah," interjected Juarez. He had a smooth, baby face for being in his late thirties. He had seven kids. "Let's just get in the damn car and drive back."

Luther looked at his brother. They chuckled at the deputy's dumb remark. It irritated Juarez.

"You'll be seeing raindrops the size of buckets here in a few seconds," said the speaking half of the Magonogonovitch family. "Remember that granite section we passed? It's gonna be slick as glass turned sideways. Crossing it would be suicide. And by the time we even get back to it, there'll be a hundred sections of road washed out. Mighty far to fall. Five hundred, a thousand feet straight down in some spots. We're stuck here, Deputy, like it or not." He grinned; his brother spat.

Juarez walked off, cursing to himself in Spanish.

Bubba had long ago resigned himself to the fact he'd never be a handsome man. But Lom and Luther added new and unexplored frontiers to the concept of ugly. They both possessed a fawning depravity, a curiosity directed only toward cruelty. Bubba wasn't fond of the notion of spending the night in cramped quarters with the Magonogonovitch brothers. But he also wasn't callous enough to make them sleep under the car during a flash flood.

Deputy Juarez anxiously played with the radio, hoping to bounce a message through to his wife for her not to worry, that he'd be all right. The rain started. The clouds raced in front of the moon, in a hurry itself to climb to safety.

23

THE MONSTER GETS FRESH AND
ELAINE GETS A HEADACHE

The rain came in friendly, inquisitive droplets at first. Mitikitski sat cross-legged at the mouth of the cave and watched
the miniature explosions on the dirt and snow. The drops
were a decoy, the vanguard of a bloated storm that would
harangue the mountains and trees, lashing them with an
insistent and unforgiving beating. Power, but no fury, thought
Mitikitski, enthralled by Nature's flexing of muscle.

She was cozy, wrapped in an oversized red down parka
with a wool blanket covering her legs. The wind carried the
rain away from the cave entrance, and she could enjoy the
booming claps of thunder and stabs of lightning from the California monsoon without getting electrocuted or wet. If Elaine
had been told three months earlier that she'd be spending a
Friday night in a cave, pregnant, the kidnapee of an Abominable Snowman, she would have said oh-yeah-right-sure to
any of the three.

The cold rain caused the portals of the cave to steam. She
guessed the inside temperature to be in the high sixties,
heated by the underground spring. A long, narrow tunnel
connected her home to another, smaller rock apartment
where the spring bubbled to the surface and formed a hot-
but-not-scalding mineral bath. The bath and laundry room.
Maybe tomorrow she'd soak and wash out some clothes. But
for now, she had to consider present company.

Her captor.

Mitikitski turned and positioned herself so she could see both storm and beast. The shaggy creature huddled over the crackling orange fire in the center of the cave, engrossed with sticking yet another hot dog on the end of a twig. It quickly looked up.

"Well. Here we are. Me. My baby. My roomie." It was the first time Elaine had spoken all day. Her voice buoyed the creature.

"You're a jerk."

His posture straightened, and he offered Elaine his best show business smile.

"Roomie, you scare me," said Elaine, looking back out at the storm. "I don't know what you want from me. And to let you know the God's honest truth, I'm afraid you're going to be the death of me. And my baby."

The creature cocked his bullet head to the side and whined, picking up the despair in her voice.

"And I can't let that happen," Elaine continued. She shook her head. "I've got to keep calm. I'll have to be strong. I may have to kill you, roomie. Better you than my baby."

"Foof," said the creature. He sniffed the cooking food and shrugged. There was that tone again. The vibration. Fear. Hostility. All day, the creature had tried various forms of placation. Gags. Tricks. Funny faces. Presents. All failed miserably. Maybe she was just hungry. Food would make her happy. God, he hoped so. It had been a rough twenty-four hours, and the creature was beginning to form the opinion that these softer ones might be a little hard to live with. He stole a sideways glance, curling his upper lip slightly. Elaine was staring outside.

Elaine's dream had returned last night. She hadn't had the nightmare in months. But this time, a tiny version of herself joined her at a neighboring stake. Hairy monsters crouched and feigned lunges at the baby.

Elaine needed a plan. Escape. Either that, or kill the thing. But how? An out-and-out fistfight was out of the question. Poison? As Socrates once said, "I drank what?" How about stabbing him in his sleep? Yeah. Right. I'll get into a knife fight with a thousand pound monster in a pitch black cave. Good thinking, Mitikitski. She watched as little streams of water zigzagged down the mountain, joining other streams and rivers, eager to splash into the Pacific two hundred miles away, and wished she could leave as easily.

"You're still a jerk," said Mitikitski.

The creature smiled, aiming to please.

Mitikitski wondered if Fenberg would be coming after her. Probably not. Maybe he didn't even know she was missing and if he did, wouldn't know where to look. He probably just thought she'd left town in a huff. He didn't owe her anything, really. Just a few months of good times. It was the same pattern. Meet someone. Smiles and flirtation, everything so fresh and exciting. Great sex, at least in the beginning. Life stories exchanged, earnestly. God. How many times would she have to tell someone her life story?

A boy or a girl?

A girl. Little Katie Scarlett O. Fenberg. The jerk. Fenberg, not the baby. Mitikitski didn't know that Fenberg knew that she was pregnant, and, at that moment, was desperately combing the wilderness searching for her. From her viewpoint, Fenberg was a *man*, and being a man wouldn't give a hoot, anyway. Mitikitski pursed her lips. She could see it clearly. The color would leave his face. He'd clear his throat like a gangly Jimmy Stewart and say something stupid like, "Are you sure?" No. I'm just holding the ball bag for the Lakers under my skirt. He might even be noble enough to marry her out of guilt. "Oh, hell. All right. Gee whiz, if I gotta," he'd say, kicking an invisible can. "I'll marry you." Even though you're not my first wife with the big tits, little waist, sunny disposition, and long blond hair, who speaks forty-two languages, just invented the cure for the common cold, and whoops, will you look at my watch, I've gotta speak before the General Assembly in twenty minutes. Sure. I'll marry you, even though nothing you could ever do would measure up to that ephemeral blond goddess, P.T.—Perfect Tracy.

"Fuck him," said Mitikitski, arms folded.

"Foofem," said the creature, trying to mimic her.

"I just really hate the fact that I like him so much," said Mitikitski. "It's aggravating." She looked over at the beast. "So what's your story, roomie?"

The creature's mouth ovaled to the size of a tiny round vowel. His nose twitched. He frantically scratched at a flea. I'm a man of mystery, Elaine. I live in the shadows. A loner. I'm a guy with a past, and maybe it's best you don't ask. He evicted the bug from his leg, inspected it, gave it a small, quivering snarl, and dropped it into the fire.

Elaine looked around the cave and shook her head. Something funny had been going on around here.

The cavern was cozy, about the size of a two-car garage with a tall ceiling stained with smoke. It was the west wall that intrigued Mitikitski. Someone had chalked a large mural in full color. It couldn't have been an ancient civilization, because the theme seemed to be some sort of tribute to the entertainment industry. It involved a drive-in theater in the middle of the dense forest. There was one car larger than the others, a '36 Chrysler woodie convertible. In it sat the spitting image of her kidnapper. He seemed quite happy. In other, smaller cars, were raccoons, bears, deer, and other denizens of the woods. The title *Quest for Fire* emblazoned the screen and every twinkling star in the heavens framed the face of a celebrity—Stallone, Eastwood, Harrison Ford, Lithgow, Streep, Jessica Lange, Debra Winger, and many others.

And where did the creature get all these furnishings, she wanted to know.

As if they were moving into a new house, all day the creature kept coming in and out with boxes and ice chests. One ghetto blaster, no batteries. A poolside lounge chair, cot, air mattress, poolside rocking chair, card table, and yet more ice chests. All white-and-green Coleman's, all filled with snow and perishables.

Mitikitski didn't know, of course, that Tuberski had made this his winter home. She wouldn't have believed that Tuberski had spent all his waking hours, grooming the beast into the slick role of legend, last American, by teaching it many basic and useful graces, like how to swing a golf club, how to master the box step, how to wrestle, how to play the drum solo from the surf hit "Wipeout" on his stomach. He couldn't get the beast to form words, except for a bastardized, yawning version of his first name, which the creature made sound more like Don than John.

Mitikitski had no idea that Tuberski had given the creature his patented version of the Doggie IQ Test (perfect score) or that he had spent a month and a half inventing a rudimentary hand signal system he had stolen from a book on primate communication. She was unaware of Tuberski's role as mentor in teaching the thing to cook, open pop-top cans, or the exhaustive lesson on why you had to put snow in the ice coolers to keep drinks cold and food fresh. One boring afternoon, Tuberski had even coerced the rocket-headed creature into taking a bath and allowing John to mousse his hair into a fifties' Elvis coiffure, which the creature immediately spoiled by rolling around in the dirt. Elaine didn't know it could catch fish by flycasting now, or that it could make a broom of branches to sweep the cave clean.

A large hand lightly touched her shoulder, and Mitikitski jumped. Elaine recoiled from the hand, and she could sense her reaction bothered the monster.

Elaine pushed her back against the warm cave wall as the huge paw reached out again for her face. The beast grunted softly.

"I really wish you'd keep your mitts to yourself there, roomie," said Elaine, backing along the wall.

He followed. He tugged lightly on her jacket, a signal. Mitikitski was still scared to death around him. He tugged on her again. She made herself stand and follow. Elaine had learned that when she didn't, he would pick her up and carry her where he wanted.

It was suppertime.

The fire cast a strangely peaceful, whirling dervish of light and shadows on the cave walls, orange, red, and yellow. It made the beast seem larger. And orange. Elaine could see a reflection of the fire, herself, and the rest of the cave in the luminescent eyes, although he really wasn't watching her. He was preoccupied with pulling a hot dog off a long, charred twig and inserting the frankfurter into a bun.

Here.

The leathery hand, about the same size as a first baseman's glove, reached out with the dog. He offered it with a short, "woof."

They had argued earlier on this subject. Mitikitski could not communicate the concept of vegetarianism to the beast, with all its implications. Thank you, no. She accepted the food and was surprised that her mouth was watering.

Fenberg, she figured.

His genes in her, causing her baby to act in a non-vegetarian health-food-person type fashion.

The hot dog wasn't bad. And it beat squirrel hands down. The creature watched approvingly as Elaine chewed, his head cocking forward a little as if to make sure she swallowed. Yes. More, all of it. He watched for a while, apparently satisfied from Mitikitski's feigned TV commercial smiles and sparkling eyes that she was enjoying dinner. With seeming concentration, he skewered another wienie on a stick and stuck it into the flames. Soon, he was absorbed with the crackling of grease in the fire.

They ate in silence, Elaine afraid to look directly at the creature. The creature now afraid to look directly at Elaine. He had stolen glances throughout the day, captivated by the long black hair falling loosely on her shoulders in waves and curls, the soft skin, the delicate pink lips. It was like watching her on the screen at the drive-in, only she was here. Tuberski had told the beast many things, most of which he forgot, including that one of the worst curses that could be laid on a person is to give him his heart's desire.

"You know, I've sort of noticed this behavioral pattern in my life," said Mitikitski, staring into the fire. There was a pause in the storm. "I've noticed that, ultimately, I always get attracted to the wrong kind of guy. Present company included."

The creature paused between bites, then stuffed an entire hot dog into his mouth.

"I always started out with the best of intentions, too. And okay, so maybe I'm guilty of trying to build the better companion. Maybe I pick guys I could improve or control. I'm sorry I did. I'm sorry for them and for me, but you know, really, all I ever wanted was someone to love me to pieces and make me laugh and be my friend. I find this perfect guy and again, something goes wrong. Something always goes wrong."

The creature chewed and thoughtfully regarded what Mitikitski had just said, minus the subtleties. Tuberski had spoken to him on this very subject. It was Tuberski's premise that there was one fundamental thing wrong with life, peculiar to each individual, that causes him misery. One identifiable unit that if ever discovered . . .

"I don't think I'm a bad person, basically. I consider myself maybe a little quick on the trigger, but I'm romantic," she told the creature. "I like sending and getting cards. I like buying presents and candlelight dinners and just talking on the phone a few minutes in the middle of the day to that someone you love. When I was in second grade, I tackled a boy I had a crush on. I didn't have any front teeth. I wrestled him to the ground and kissed him and then stood on his chest and gave this Tarzan yell. I was sort of a tomboy."

The creature chewed and watched Mitikitski's lips move, his almost ears twitching, catching the sounds of her voice. "All my life, I've mimicked the men I'm with. Did you know I was married three times?"

The creature looked quizzically at her.

"My first husband was a bowler. I learned bowling. I hated bowling. Well, I hated it four nights a week. And for a while, I was a motorcycle tough cookie, which aggravated my parents and confused me, and then I was a Mormonette for a bit. I always thought if I could please a man, he'd like me. It never worked that way. Then I meet that damn Fenberg, and God how I love him. He's been dancing twice in his life and volunteers to take lessons sixty miles away just to please me. And he holds me and makes me laugh and listens, and he's still so much in love with his wife."

The creature lowered his eyebrows, trying to stare at his lower lip. What could he say? His own story was that he was unacceptable. By his own kind. By the humans. Only Tuberski liked him.

"There's something wrong with a system like that."

Mitikitski's sister, Kamali Molly, and Tuberski shared similar opinions on the nature of the opposite sex:

POINT: Tuberski believed that having a relationship, especially a marriage, was like a land war in Asia. "Ike was right," Tuberski had said. "You can never win a land war in Asia. Your adversary is someone you'll never understand nor want to. And after the last shot is fired, you still end up paying massive reparations. Same thing with getting involved with a chick."

COUNTERPOINT: "A woman without a man is like a fish without a bicycle," quoth Kamali Molly, stealing the line from the T-shirt.

Both platforms seemed a little strict to Elaine. She half-heartedly tossed the remains of her dinner outside into the rain. She had a craving for dairy products.

"Do you have any ice cream?" Mitikitski asked. She started to stand but was stopped by a baleful glance. "Maybe later on."

Men.

Mitikitski remembered reading Indian and aboriginal lore which abounded with tales of hairy hominids lurking on the fringe of civilization, rubbing devilish hands at the chance to carry off an unattended maiden dawdling at stream's edge. (Hell. What did I do wrong? I was walking through downtown.) Africa, South America, Asia—all continents had their mythology about inter-species mating. A rare occurrence, nonetheless.

Mitikitski found her legs involuntarily tightening.

She looked at the creature through the flames. If he made a pass, what would she do?

Fight?

Against an eight-hundred-pound fresh guy?

Faint? Say she's got a headache?

Shit. She'd kill herself. But now she had another life to care for. Fuck it. She'd still kill herself. No, she couldn't. It would be the classic dilemma, at any rate. More college class Bigfoot information rolled to mind. There was one particularly riveting story, which had held the students in the professor's palm. It was about an Indian woman who died in 1940 at the ripe age of eighty-six. She'd been abducted from the Port Arthur area near Harrison Lake in British Columbia in the year 1871, supposedly by one of these creatures. The names meant nothing to Mitikitski, nor the dates, but she remembered them. The Indian woman swore she'd been kidnapped by a Sasquatch and "kept" by it for over a year.

A year.

Mitikitski remembered the snickers from class.

The old Indian woman tried to escape, time and time again, and finally succeeded, returning to the village, pregnant.

Which meant . . .

Well. Pregnancy did imply sex.

Mitikitski didn't want to think about that.

The Indian woman supposedly gave birth to a hideous-looking package, half-beast, half-man. It was either stillborn or raised in secret and hidden from the eyes of white men, so the teacher had said.

Mitikitski had been unconsciously palming her stomach.

What if?

She looked at the beast. A distant relative to that mating? It would certainly account for the intelligence, the eyes, the features, and perhaps his good taste in the opposite sex. All that she'd read indicated that the creature by nature was docile and shy. The killings? Maybe it had inherited an aggressive streak from his *Homo sapiens* ancestor. Maybe some odd combination of genes in a blender resulted in a homicidal nature. A cannibalistic tendency brought on by . . . what? The moon?

Mitikitski jumped. The long arm of the creature reached across, touching her. The rain had stopped. It seemed so noisily quiet now, like waking in the middle of the night when the furnace shuts off. The storm had been a bluff, just a passing visitor bringing its cargo to lands farther east. Already the clouds were clearing, and Mitikitski could see the yellow reflection of the full moon on the damp ground outside. The creature was staring at Elaine. He looked troubled. His lips twitched.

Thin, rubbery lips, indicative of a lack of B vitamins. There were lots of B vitamins in Mitikitski. She caught herself staring, wide-eyed, wondering if that was the mouth through which portions of formerly living people were passed?

The creature looked outside, entranced by the wavy reflection of the moon in a puddle.

Past the tongue, past the gums, look out tummy, here Mitikitski comes?

The creature was restless. He made a vague, whining sound and reached again for Elaine, taking in the details of her face and long hair. He delicately played with a dangling lock. Casually, as he had seen them do in the drive-in, he pretended to yawn and stretch, following through by draping a massive arm the size of a log around Mitikitski's shoulder. She could feel the weight all the way down to her tailbone.

Elaine gingerly disengaged herself as she had learned to do at the drive-in.

He moved his bullet-shaped head close to her, and Elaine smoothly rolled away, clambering on her hands and knees to the opposite side of the cave, which may have been a mistake, because as she crawled her perfectly-shaped rear end wiggled back and forth in a most inviting manner. The beast crawled after her. With an effortless push of the hand, he bowled her over on her back, looming over her. Mitikitski looked at the greasy face. Her eyes drifted southward, below his waist. She could tell his intentions were clear, quite dishonorable, and probably most injurious to her plumbing. "Thank you for the wonderful evening and please don't spoil it" was not going to work here, and Mitikitski inadvertently ended up teaching the creature something Tuberski never could have about the mandatory rituals that all males must learn while dating.

She taught the beast shame and rejection.

Mitikitski screamed and sobbed hysterically.

Was she hurt? Sick? What was wrong? It never went like this in the movies. It confused the monster, who looked down at the small thing rolled up in a ball. He whimpered sympathetically and lightly touched her face to reassure her, which caused her to scream all the more.

Emotion stuck in his throat. Something unfamiliar. Mitikitski wouldn't stop crying. And every time he touched her, to comfort her, to make it better, she cried all the harder. It made him feel powerless, strangely sad and lonely, then confused, then angry. He picked up a log and pounded the fire, sending an explosion of sparks through the cave. He slapped the ground and pounded the walls, causing the very mountain to shake. The beast stood over the small woman with the soft skin, his great fur coat heaving in and out with rage and adrenalin. His fists opened and closed.

There was silence. After a long moment, when Elaine looked up, he was gone. She could hear his angry and frustrated roars fading in the distance.

24

VICTIMS 11 AND 12

It had been a cramped, uncomfortable night for Fenberg. That it had also been a cramped, uncomfortable night for Bean Breath Brown, Charlie Two Eagles, and John Tuberski, Fenberg didn't particularly care.

They never made it to the cave on the night of the first moon.

After making a beeline to the wrong Bigfoot, the safari nearly sprinted down Blind Widow Dome.

Tuberski had been bird-watching as he walked the narrow path to the truck, when he collided into Fenberg's backpack. In turn, Bean Breath and the Indian smashed into John.

"Will you watch *mmmmmmmmf*—" Tuberski's protest was stopped short as Fenberg cupped a hand over his mouth and pointed. Sheriff Bubba Fenberg, the Magonogonovitch brothers and two deputies were rifling through Fenberg's pickup.

The felons crouched.

"What do we do?" Tuberski asked, whispering.

"Hide," suggested Fenberg, pulling the grinning Bean Breath Brown down into the shrubbery.

Lom heard the crack of dry brush and jerked his head around, searching the rocks and trees for movement. He stared directly at their hiding place. Satisfied nothing was there, he turned his attention back to looting Fenberg's truck.

"You got any ideas?" Fenberg whispered.

"Detour," said Tuberski, pointing back in the direction from which they had marched. The plan was to circumnavigate. Wait for the moon and see if they could find the cave by lunar light.

But it rained. In buckets. Forty miles away, in a yellow rain coat and galoshes, Angry Joe Fenberg, the temporary teenage editor of *The Basin Valley Bugle*, was on hand to personally cover the senior citizens' mobile home park which was in the process of washing away during the flash flood. It was a banner day for news. Joe covered the arson at *The Bugle* and paid himself the fifty dollar bonus for sneaking "It was a dark and stormy night . . ." into the lead of the senior citizen flood story. *The Bugle* continued its streak of 141 years of never missing an issue. Joe had the paper printed in the neighboring county, seventy-five miles away.

Back in the hills, the four somber men cuddled under a leaky rock overhang, wrapped in a plastic tarp, like monkeys in a giant trash bag. The storm cleared early. The available moonlight was sporadic as large and small clouds sprinted past, trying to catch up with the rest of the weather front. Fenberg had wanted to go on. Tuberski pleaded no.

"We've got to find her tonight," Fenberg said. "I've just got a damn feeling she's in danger."

"Wait out the storm, Mike," Tuberski counseled. "We'll only end up getting lost or injured walking in the middle of a storm like this at night."

Charlie pursed his lips and said nothing.

The storm had left a twinkling clear sky by four that morning, and the moon had left long before. The blackness gave way to dark blue, then to a subtle lightening of grays before the pale blue and orange sky of pre-dawn. Frogs and crickets scratched a tremendous racket, and the birds sang spring songs. Fenberg dreamed.

He was in downtown Los Angeles, feverishly pedaling Bean Breath Brown's bicycle, which had two flat tires. The traffic was heavy. Fenberg had to pedal all the way from LA to Basin Valley in ninety minutes to make love to Mitikitski.

He kept hearing the words: "If you don't make love to me within the next hour and a half, I'm leaving you."

It was an unfair version of Elaine, but it was, after all, Fenberg's dream. He could feel the exhausting grind of the fat, flat tires on the wet pavement. Dogs ran out of doorways to nip at his legs, and he couldn't pedal above a crawl. And it was a seventeen-hour drive at least by car. Tracy pulled up in a car next to Fenberg. She was older, heavier. "Don't you dare touch that woman," she scolded. "Don't you dare forget me."

But that wasn't what woke Fenberg.

In Fenberg's ear, somebody was softly whistling Beethoven's Sixth Symphony, the little ditty they play to indicate dawn in the Warner Brothers' cartoons. Fenberg woke with a start, entangled in his sleeping bag and tarp. Tuberski grinned. Frost was on the ground.

Fenberg looked around stupidly. He grabbed a handful of snow and rubbed it on his face and the back of his neck. "We've got to get going," he said, throwing off the tarp and sleeping bag. The icy air slapped him. He quickly stuffed his gear into the backpack, hoisting it to his shoulders as he marched down the trail.

His group scurried to break camp and follow. There was something building in Fenberg, something in him that was changing. It made the rest of the expedition jumpy.

* * * * *

The hot dogs, the almost-too-warm confines of the cave, and emotional exhaustion gave Mitikitski a blessedly peaceful night's sleep. She had crawled down the narrow rock hallway leading to the mineral spring. She had dragged firewood and provisions for a week's hiding. Mitikitski made several trips during the monster's absence, tugging along her cot, blanket, and a few ice chests. She had thought about making a run for it that night, but gave up the idea as impractical. This was California, but it might as well be darkest Africa. Elaine had no idea where she was. At least if the creature returned he wouldn't be able to squeeze through the narrow, rocky crawlway to get at her. She would leave by dawn's first light and run, swim, or crawl back to somewhere. Or starve on the way.

While Elaine slept through the night, the *Mandrango* killed. Twice.

Mitikitski stirred, then opened her eyes wide. Her forehead was sweaty from the humidity. There was the sickening realization that she had overslept. Light poured through the cave, and the creature had to be back. Elaine grabbed food and stuffed it into the extra jacket. How long had she slept? Cautiously, she inched forward down the narrow hall. There was a no-man's land coming up—a section of main cave wall that the beast could be leaning against, hiding.

Elaine reached into her jeans and hunted for change. She threw a few coins against the wall. A dull ping, but no reaction sound. Elaine crawled forward, reaching out, hoping she wouldn't feel anything hairy.

All clear.

Maybe he was sunning himself outside. It was the middle of the morning; he had to be back by now.

It was a pretty morning outside. Elaine stood in the entrance of the cave and took a deep breath through her nose. Either he was out there, or he wasn't.

* * * * *

Of the three parties, Sheriff Bubba Fenberg's posse had the worst evening.

They had slept in a tree.

Bubba and the Magonogonovitch brothers waited until the sun was well up before they shimmied down from the pine.

It had been a simple choice of survival.

They had kept the car running the night before, as rain hammered against the windshield. At least the heater was working. The rain stopped, and the natural noises of the forest coyly spoke, quietly at first, then with rhythm and confidence. The sound of running water put all five men to sleep, cramped but secure in the sheriff's green Suburban.

Sleep was a blessed sanctuary for Deputy Juarez, who had worried since the storm started about his wife and kids. He smiled. They'd be safe. The children would be preoccupied with television, and Dolores was a trooper. She knew he might be in the brush for several days. She'd probably wait up for him and fall asleep on the sofa, as she had so many times before. Juarez slept with his head resting against the stiff back seat, the soft brown portion of his neck close to the cold glass window.

A shadow crossed over his face, blocking out the moonlight. Subconsciously, he knew it wasn't a cloud. Juarez opened his eyes quickly, and his features contorted in a silent scream. A few inches away was the face, hideous, sinewy, and hairy. The scream froze in Juarez's throat as he sat, enraptured in terror. The cycle of the beast. Saliva dripped off the mandibles in expectation, and the eyes glowed yellow through the window in unholy need.

Juarez was too petrified to move or reach for his service revolver. The shock and sound of glass shattering broke the trance. Then he did scream, a short, panicked cry of pain and finality. The beast angrily pulled him through the jagged hole. Juarez felt his soul leave, but the body resisted, holding on with arms, finally with legs, then feet. Death was sudden. The monster held Carlos Juarez and ripped into the jugular. The legs stopped kicking.

The moonlit scene of grisly terror froze the remaining men until the beast reached in for the other deputy, Wilbur Doherty. Bubba Fenberg was in the front and pounded at the hairy arm as it dragged the screaming deputy through the same jagged hole. Bubba fumbled for his revolver and shot point-blank through the driver's side window, exploding the glass. The creature hissed in surprise and responded by beating the roof of the car with Doherty as if he were a rag doll.

With the poor light and the monster angrily cavorting outside the truck, Bubba was not positive that he registered all of his bullets into the creature. He knew that he hit the thing point-blank at least three times before it galloped off with the still-screaming deputy sheriff.

25

THE FABULOUS FENBERGS
vs. BEAN BREATH BROWN

It had not been a good morning for Bean Breath Brown.

Fenberg had strangled him.

People and their monsters. It was Bean's opinion that monsters ruined a person's sense of humor.

"We need a rest, Michael. All of us are past exhaustion," said Tuberski, pulling off a boot to examine a blister. "Especially you."

"I'm fine. You're fine. Get up, and let's go."

"Don't push it, Michael."

Fenberg kicked at Tuberski's boot. "Get up!" I'm not going to lose this woman. No. Not this time.

They had marched in silence since dawn, taking a long, laborious route back to the cave. They climbed up and down hills. They got dirty. They hacked their way at times to make a path where none existed, collecting small, irritating abrasions and cuts from sliding down embankments and grabbing jagged branches to keep from falling. Moisture clung to their hair and clothes and seeped into their lungs. One hill looked like the next, and the majestic scenery melted into monotony.

"What are you going to do, hit me?" asked Tuberski, looking up. It cut below the belt, and Fenberg blushed. He was dulled past exhaustion, in worse shape than any of them, but went on through will. Fenberg looked at Bean to see if the half-deaf/all-mute had heard his brother's remark. Bean had, but pretended he didn't.

"Fine. Stay here," said Fenberg, hefting the pack and marching off by himself.

"Ah, damn it to hell," said Tuberski.

Bean Breath Brown thoughtfully ran his nose down his sleeve and watched as Tuberski hurriedly put on his sock and boot. John called after Fenberg, who was getting smaller in the distance.

"Wait here!" snapped Tuberski, grabbing just a rifle and sprinting after Fenberg.

Yeah-yeah, sure-sure.

Fenberg blamed himself for arguing with Mitikitski. For Mitikitski leaving. For Mitikitski getting kidnapped. For committing the sin of coveting women, albeit a formerly living woman and albeit his wife, but a woman nonetheless. He blamed himself for letting Tracy drive in the snow. There was the ticket, thought Fenberg, not even aware of the pain in his legs, only their heaviness as he marched to the cave. Fenberg's attachment to the past was responsible for ruining a perfectly good relationship with a perfectly good Elaine Mitikitski. It was all taking its toll on Fenberg. There were cracks and bubbles wrinkling on the surface of Fenberg's well-constructed armor. Try as hard as he could to keep the whole package together, Fenberg was losing it. He feared he was going insane when actually, quite the opposite was occurring.

It worried Fenberg's fellow safari members.

"I'll tell you what it is," Tuberski had confided to Bean Breath Brown earlier on the trail. Tuberski looked around to see if Fenberg was in earshot. "Take me for instance. Me, I'm colorful. Mike, he's crazy."

Bean stared at the dark soil, not knowing what to say, or rather, gesture. It sounded like mutiny.

"Raymond, I'm telling you, don't ever fall in love. Or if you do, don't do it hard. It makes saps out of the best of us. You've got some crumbs on your cheek," said Tuberski, making a slight face as he flicked them off with a finger.

There were thin odds that Bean would ever fall in love, or that if he did, the favor would be returned. Bean Breath

Brown didn't have much in-the-field training with the opposite sex, and what little he did have came from getting beat up by the Basin Valley High School Pep Squad on a regular basis, an experience he sheepishly admitted was enjoyable. Bean had a vast library of black-and-white glossies that weren't quite pornography but weren't exactly fit for the front page of *The Bugle*'s sports section. Using a 78-135mm zoom lens and hiding under the bleachers, Bean Breath would snap several rolls of candids of the nubile Cougar cheerleaders in various unladylike positions. If you looked closely, you could generally spot, at worst, an artistic curve of the young feminine body and, at best, a nipple. When Raymond would gleefully show the spirit squad his latest batch of photos, the girls would crowd around, squeaking and bouncing on their tiptoes, eager to see what they imagined would be *Teen Beat*-type photos of attractive, wholesome coeds.

"Happiness is being free from expectations," Tuberski always said, paraphrasing the Buddha.

The cheerleaders' reactions were generally the same. The glee would melt from their faces, followed by shock, outrage, then anger. En masse, they'd shriek and scream and climb all over Bean Breath Brown, biting, pinching, grabbing, trying to tear the photographs to shreds and the grinning Bean Breath along with them. It wasn't a very adult approach to a relationship, but it was all that Raymond had.

* * * * *

Bean and the Indian were alone. It was about two in the afternoon. Bean disengaged himself from his pack and sat down on a fallen birch, first checking for jigger ants. He rifled through his backpack. A package of Twinkies. His last. Just as it had been when they were kids, Tuberski and Fenberg had gone ahead to scout, and Bean was left behind to not scout.

Raymond unwrapped the Twinkies and thought about throwing the wrapper over his shoulder or maybe just stuffing it in the end of the log. A baleful stare by Charlie Two Eagles stopped him in the act. Raymond sheepishly rolled up the cellophane and stuck it in his shirt pocket, which was already bulging from cupcake wrappers. Bean did not eat Twinkies like a normal human being. Charlie puffed on a cigarette, languidly watching the dirty little weasel of a man systematically peel off the thin golden top layer of the dessert cake with his yellow buck teeth. It was like watching an insect on educational TV.

Bean smiled lugubriously, offering bites to the Indian.

Charlie disinterestedly looked away and wished he had packed a bottle. Bean shrugged and nibbled. He had been the only one who would look at Fenberg after Michael went crazy.

That Fenberg was a cheapskate lower-rung capitalist didn't bother Bean Breath Brown. Bean worshiped the very typewriter keys with which Fenberg slandered people. Wasn't it Fenberg who had saved a then-fifty-four-pound Raymond (mostly teeth and glasses) from being pounded into a small wastebasket by the Magonogonovitch brothers for accidentally stepping on the corner of the Indian Grin Elementary sixth grade lawn when Bean was just a lowly fourth grader? Wasn't it Fenberg who had been the only person to visit Bean at his house during Christmas and who invariably dragged Raymond back to the ranch for dinner and presents? Wasn't it Fenberg who taught Bean how to take pictures and bought him a camera and made him the photography editor over all of Basin Valley? Wasn't it Fenberg who let Bean supplement his Egyptian slave wage at the paper by allowing him to pull weeds and do manly ranch work at four bucks an hour?

Wasn't it Fenberg who knocked Bean down in anger and held his throat in his hands?

Bean shrugged. He nibbled. He couldn't blame Fenberg.

Raymond didn't know anything about love, but he could tell by the way Fenberg looked at Mitikitski and vice versa, they were in love, the serious kind. Bean missed Elaine. She was one of the few people who was nice to him, and maybe when they found her Fenberg would stop choking people and find his sense of humor, which was one of Bean Breath's favorite things about his second family.

It seemed to be genetic, peculiar to all the Fenberg men.

Somewhere in the Fenberg gene pool swam a curly little molecule that was responsible for practical jokes. It was in all four brothers, but most pronounced in Michael.

It was rough growing up on the Fenberg ranch. Saran Wrap was tightly battened down over toilet seats. Alarm clocks went off regularly at three in the morning. Angry Joe and Clifford dragged out their departed mother's ancient Singer and sewed Tuberski's legholes closed on all his underwear and Tuberski responded, thematically, by welding shut their lunch pails.

All three reverently shied away from Fenberg.

Fenberg was the arms-folded, unblinking Zen master of practical jokes.

Once, after a particularly long lost weekend, Tuberski stumbled into Fenberg's room and ralphed on Fenberg's dresser. Fenberg dutifully cleaned up the discharge and mailed his unconscious brother in a crate to Walla Walla.

"Why?" Tuberski pleaded, coming back from Washington disheveled and dirty several days later.

"I always liked the name," Fenberg said, matter-of-factly.

Once, Fenberg placed the not-unhandsome photograph of a grinning John Tuberski in a gay lonely hearts magazine with the heading: DOMINANT CHAIN SAW GUY INTERESTED IN MATRIMONY.

For months, Tuberski received lots of interesting offers in the mail, all of which he returned with Fenberg's picture and private office telephone number.

When they were in high school, Michael stapled John to the garage door. Actually, he stapled Tuberski's football uniform to the garage door, with Tuberski still in it.

John had sinned grievously.

He had borrowed Michael's cherry '59 LeSabre "Buick Is A Beauty Too" convertible without telling Fenberg. In a foolish high school nocturnal stupor, he returned the next morning with a serious gash stretching from the right headlight several yards back to the dinosaurlike fin.

"I'm sorry, but I didn't do it, and I'm not paying to have it fixed."

"Oh, you'll pay," predicted Fenberg.

Fenberg borrowed a concoction from his father, the town publisher and veterinarian, and drugged Tuberski into puppy dreamland. John woke up several hours later to find himself as Basin Valley's own version of *The Man in the Iron Mask*. His tongue felt hairy. He felt light, and continuing the Gothic theme, someone had painted the letters C.A. in scarlet on his white practice football jersey.

Using nails, staples and strategically placed U-bolts, Fenberg had molded his brother into an O. J. Simpson-like pose, one knee bent in a high-stepping manner, an arm extended to straight-arm any incoming tacklers that Fenberg might later staple to the door to keep Tuberski company. A toddling Angry Joe in diapers stood off to the side, holding his bear, learning by example. Tuberski held onto a deflated football, which was crucified to the door by a large, rusty nail.

Tuberski strained his head and neck, trying to figure out what exactly had happened to him.

"I guess my first question would be, what do the letters 'C.A.' stand for," said Tuberski. Fenberg was wearing a black monk's robe, complete with hood.

"Car abuser," said Fenberg, half-smiling, half-smirking as he unwrapped a cat-o-nine-tails. "You've been a naughty defensive tackle, and I'm afraid we're going to have to punish you."

To Bean Breath Brown, those were the good old days.

But then came tragedy, followed closely by a crushing, aging responsibility. Fenberg was the man who changed Clifford's diapers after their parents sank into the North Pole. Fenberg was the man who ran the newspaper, paid people salaries, kept the ranch going, made sure plants were watered and animals fed. As he and Tuberski approached their thirties, Michael kept his wry comments to a minimum about John getting a "real job" and even offered encouragement and positive criticism on Tuberski's artwork. He still held Joe and rocked him in his lap in the dark hours when the boy cried from rage and loneliness. And Fenberg was the man who had knocked down Bean Breath Brown for offering him a cup of coffee.

* * * * *

It had happened two hours after breaking night camp, while they were resting. Tuberski, Bean, and the Indian were sprawled by a stream. Fenberg sat by himself, next to a nameless snow runoff. He carefully held the picture in both hands. Michael hadn't heard Raymond walk up behind him, and Bean didn't see the tears.

Brown stood behind Fenberg's left shoulder, the cup of coffee breathing steam into the cold air. He rubbed a runny nose on a sleeve before tapping Fenberg. Fenberg started, and the photo of Tracy flew from his hands into the dirt.

They both stared at the snapshot. Fenberg knocked the thermos cup from his friend's hand, then pushed him. Bean Breath Brown fell hard to the ground.

"Goddamn it, I'm tired of carrying you!" Fenberg snarled, holding Raymond by the throat and straddling him. His right fist was clenched, and Bean thought Fenberg would punch him. Fenberg looked dazed, vacant, staring not at, but through the smaller man. Michael shook his head slowly and turned away. He saw the picture, and the anger returned. Awkwardly, he kicked at the photo. Fenberg picked it up and gritted his teeth, ineffectually trying to tear it in half. The plastic sheath would bend but not tear, and Fenberg crushed it in half, back and forth, rolling it into a crude ball.

"You *asshole*! God how I hate you for leaving me! Do you fucking hear me!" He threw the crumpled snapshot in the air, and it fluttered to the ground harmlessly a few feet away, mocking him. Fenberg turned back around. John and the Indian quietly watched. Bean had crawled to safety, and Michael could find no words of apology.

* * * * *

The Twinkies were washed down by jelly-filled doughnuts and the last coffee from the thermos. The snack had done wonders for Bean. He smiled and patted his stomach. Sugar rush.

They were close to the cave, and, in fact, Fenberg was probably there right now, kissing Elaine's soft face and rounded cheeks, gently caressing her long hair, telling her he'd leave her never. Bean would even get to wear a tacky gray tuxedo in the wedding. Bean believed in happy endings.

The sun was in its nadir, and it was actually very warm for this high elevation, nearly sixty degrees.

"Wait here," Tuberski had instructed, but Raymond imagined the command was flexible enough for him to wander off into the brush to relieve himself.

Placing the remaining jelly-filled doughnut on the log, Bean tied his frayed, rapidly disintegrating shoelaces that held together an ancient pair of P F Flyers. The Indian was asleep, and Raymond Bean Breath Brown tiptoed away.

It was spring, and the woods would normally be noisy with the arguments of birds during nest-building season. The woods were quiet, but Bean was half-deaf. He didn't notice.

A monster waited for him.

One place was as good as the next, but Bean shopped for the right spot to relieve himself. A warm sensation trickling down his pant leg told a distant portion of Bean's brain that he hadn't quite made it. Brown had wet his pants.

Stepping from around a moss-covered formation, the beast crouched, ready to spring—the thin, livery lips bared back to show dark gums and yellowed tusks.

It was one of Tuberski's monster's favorite pastimes—sneaking up on dogs and hikers and scaring the bejesus out of them. Only this time, the trick backfired.

The snarl froze on the Bigfoot's face and slowly melted. The monster stood immobile, staring at the hideous apparition that crouched in front of him.

Yes, it was short, but it was obviously vicious. Bean Breath Brown's hands had involuntarily turned to claws—ragged, dirty fingers that flexed and unflexed, as if anticipating the feel of the creature's throat. Raspberry jelly oozed from between this hiker's teeth, mingling with the thick creamy filling from the Twinkies, forming a sickening blob that bubbled at the corners of Bean Breath's mouth. The eyes were menacing, oblate—magnified to obscene, deformed size through the cracked and pitted Coke-bottle lenses. One eye stared into the very soul of the Bigfoot, measuring him, the creature thought, for a place to sink his yellow teeth. The other eye operated spasmodically on its own, like a lighthouse beacon gone berserk. More horrible than anything the creature had seen at the drive-in, this small thing was *hissing* at him.

It was more than John Tuberski's monster's weak and broken heart could handle, and the messages of the body began their frightening sequence. The beast made an instinctual move to turn and flee, but was stopped by a curious tingling that ran up and down his arm. The sensation of being punched by a giant fist in the chest. No breath. Suffocation. The beast whined, hurt and confused. He looked up, and the branches of the forest roof seemed to spin and close in on him. He felt the tightening pain in the chest.

"Raymond! You back here?" Fenberg called out. Neither Bean nor the beast heard the thrashing of his heavy footsteps in the bush.

"Bean . . . Bean-o!" yelled Tuberski, stepping into the open in time to see his monster grab its heart, whirl in a 360-degree arc, and crash to the forest floor like a tall building in an earthquake.

"Oh, my God!" said Fenberg, standing next to his brother. "God have mercy, what happened!?"

Tuberski looked helplessly at the fallen creature, then at Bean Breath. John's eyes narrowed, and he set his jaw. "You goofy son of a bitch, you gave my monster a heart attack!"

Fenberg punched and pleaded as Tuberski choked Bean Breath Brown in an accusatory fashion. It was the second time that day Bean had been strangled by a member of the Fenberg family, and easygoing though he was, enough was enough.

* * * * *

"Do you miss her?"

"I seem to miss everyone."

"The melancholy editor." Tuberski poked at the campfire with a stick. "Fenberg as Hamlet."

"Pass the tights and codpiece," said Fenberg.

They had searched the woods all day and into the evening. There was no sign of Mitikitski. She had been at the cave, all right. They found traces of hair. Even the smell of her perfume lingered. Night covered the camp with a blanket of unhappiness. Separated from the rest of the men, the medicine man chanted his death song. Michael was only peripherally aware of the Indian and the surrounding woods. The strong odor of pine reminded Fenberg, somewhat backwardly, of Spic and Span.

"I miss the folks still," admitted Tuberski. "Although they were both certifiable, and Mom put everything in plastic bags. Sometimes I wonder if they're still alive."

"I seriously doubt that."

"You never know," said Tuberski, who sat in the cold air in his T-shirt.

"I guess they'll just join the mysterious ranks of all those other M.O.V.'s."

Tuberski raised his eyebrows quizzically.

"Missing On Vacation."

"Ah."

Fenberg smiled wearily into the flames. Fire. One of the more sensational phenomenons of nature—countless little explosions, one igniting the other, so fast and furious, so narcotizing. Fenberg found the campfire peaceful, a blissful retreat from thought, which was his ultimate monster.

"I thought about it myself," said Fenberg. "At least, I used to. The only two bodies the search parties never found were Mom's and Dad's. I used to think that maybe Eskimos rescued them, but where they crashed, well, I don't see how they could have survived for more than a few seconds."

"They could have been quickly frozen, and everything is intact," suggested Tuberski.

"You mean like Walt Disney?" asked Fenberg.

"Or a Swanson frozen entrée."

Tracy must have been cold too, thought Fenberg, lost in

the flames. Damn. I wasn't there to keep her warm. To keep either of them warm. "Could we change the subject of freeze-dried parents?"

Tuberski nodded and let it go. "I never met Mitikitski."

"You'd like her. She's really something."

"Is she crazy?"

"Not like Mom, or you, but she has tendencies. Who knows?" submitted Fenberg. "In years, with hard work and diligent practice, she could work up to it."

The creature snorted in his sleep and groaned painfully, then was silent. Michael and John watched expectantly for a moment before the breathing stabilized. It seemed so harmless in the firelight, like a shaggy, reconstructed museum exhibition. Michael watched the massive rib cage expand and contract. Fenberg shook his head. How could something the size of a small bedroom wander around so close to civilization for so many years without being captured?

Maybe it was just quiet.

It had looked at Fenberg.

Fenberg remembered an old Indian saying about the *Mandrango*: "If it even looks at you, your soul will be doomed to walk the twilight as a ghost, forever."

Unenlightened aboriginal nonsense, Fenberg hoped.

There were no spinning red eyes, no insane gleam, no special effects. But there had been something.

A monster with a weak heart. Not weak, but broken, Tuberski had pronounced. And now it lay there, sedated. All the shouting and gunshots hadn't produced an answering call from Mitikitski.

"I remember seeing her picture," said Tuberski.

"Huh?" Fenberg refocused on the here and now.

"Your girlfriend. I saw a picture of her on the mantel in the living room. She has a lot of character in that face."

"Yes, she does," Fenberg agreed reflectively.

"Vulnerability, and wildness."

"Yes. And a nice rear end," reminded Fenberg.

"How is she in bed?" asked Tuberski.

"A gentleman never tells," said Fenberg.

"You're right. How is she in bed?"

"Lurid, wicked," Fenberg revealed.

The brothers smiled. They breathed rhythmically. The Indian chanted, and Bean Breath smiled in his sleep, wrapped in his bag like a burrowing rodent.

"Do you love her?"

"Almost."

"Which means?"

"Almost all the way. Which means I don't."

"I see. The picture. You still love Tracy."

"No. And yes. Let's say I'm more attached. No. Let's say I'm very attached."

Tuberski nodded understandingly. He seemed to hear Charlie Two Eagles for the first time. *"Ni-yaw hi-yaw hi-yaw ho . . . ni-yaw hi-yaw hi-yaw ho . . ."* The Indian had been chanting nonstop for three hours. The monotonous drone helped Raymond and the creature sleep, but grated on Tuberski's nerves.

"You mind turning down the volume?" Tuberski called out.

"It's all right," said Fenberg, slouching forward on a camp-stool, his shoulders rounded, as if weighted by heavy air.

There was something in the camp. The place seemed haunted, strangely familiar to Fenberg. The Indian shunned the company of the white men and the beast. He sat in a circle of stones, his back to the group, chanting in front of his own small fire. Occasionally, he would offer a tiny bone or some fizzling powder to the flames.

"Something terrible will happen here. Soon," the Indian had said earlier.

"The girl?" Fenberg had to ask.

"Yes. And you. And me. And your brother. One will die. And the girl will be the bride of the beast," Charlie had predicted.

"I'm going to throw something at him," warned Tuberski, reaching for a log.

"Ni-yaw hi-yaw hi-yaw ho-nah . . ."

"I really ought to love Mitikitski," said Fenberg. "I really ought to just get on my darn knees and be thankful for her. I just can't forget my dead wife."

"Tracy?"

"That's the one."

"Is Elaine like her?"

"Taller. And crazier."

"Colorful," corrected Tuberski.

What you hide you keep.

"You wouldn't know another tune from the aboriginal hit parade, would you there, partner?" Tuberski called to the Indian.

The chant continued.

Tuberski raised his voice a few decibels. "Is that something you feel you must do?"

And continued.

"What's he saying?" Fenberg asked, still lost in the flames.

Tuberski took a good, long look around camp—the Indian, the monster, Bean Breath, his brother as Hamlet. Nuts in the woods. "He tells of a little island paradise," Tuberski began, "where topless brown girls dance the hula in grass skirts and play in the ocean all day. And one morning, the little princess, Ka-monia Ka-monia, was sad because her true love . . ."

Tuberski stopped.

He saw that his brother wasn't in the mood.

"He's getting to the part where her brother gets eaten by a shark, and she's chosen as a virgin sacrifice to appease the volcano gods, but I guess you don't want to hear that."

Fenberg smiled. "No. I guess not."

And the Indian chanted. "*Ni-yaw hi-yaw hi-yaw . . .*"

Tuberski picked up a small log and tossed it against a tree close to the Indian. *Thwock!*

Charlie jumped.

"Please. Take a commercial," suggested Tuberski.

Charlie Two Eagles straightened, mustering dignity and his belongings. He mumbled something out of earshot, something indelicate about Caucasians in his Alliklik mother tongue. John and Mike watched him drag his bedroll into the cave.

"It's like listening to an Indian telethon," said Tuberski,

brushing off his hands.

They sat in silence.

"I wake up every morning," Fenberg finally said. "Sometimes it seems so real, like she's lying there next to me. In those early moments before the light hits the room, I'll open my eyes halfway, and I can see the back of her head on the pillow next to me. Her blond hair is all mussed, and I see her shoulder blades. They reminded me of angel wings." Fenberg smiled at the recollection. "When we first slept together, the first time for a whole night, you know I didn't go to sleep? I watched her, all night. I remember then, looking at her back, thinking an angel had flown into my room, too tired to make it all the way to heaven."

Fenberg never cried, not at the funeral, not even alone. His eyes were moist and he wore a distant smile.

"It's actually quite pleasant, sometimes. I'll remember a lot of the laughs and those solid times. I remember bringing the baby home from the hospital and seeing Tracy rocking the little thing on the front porch. She looked up at me and we didn't have to say anything. I get fooled, mostly in the morning, when my defenses are down. I'll catch myself saving hot water for her in the shower, or I'll pour an extra cup of tea. And you know what's funny? I catch myself and I won't pour out the damn stuff. It'll just sit there, and I won't pour it out. It makes you wonder. How things can be so good one day and so lousy the next."

It was the nature of the three-dimensional man, thought Tuberski. The Adamic dream, good and evil, back and forth. John said nothing.

"We had a big argument, you know, that last day."

"No, I didn't."

Fenberg straightened and nodded his head yes. "I never got a chance to say good-bye." Fenberg thoughtfully chewed on the inside of his cheek and pondered that. John sat quietly, not able to look directly at his older brother. Strong Michael. Unflappable. Dependable. Responsible. A great ache lodged in his throat. Tuberski felt his own eyes moisten with a wave of compassion.

"God. How can you love someone so much and say such terrible things?" Fenberg wanted to know.

Human beings couldn't love, not for extended periods of time. It's a faculty that comes from someplace else. But Tuberski couldn't tell his brother that.

"She wanted to make up with me, and I just walked out. People should be horsewhipped for their pride," said Fenberg. He shook his head. "What's happening to me?"

"You're going batty. It's perfectly normal, all things considered."

"I used to have everything under control."

"That's batty."

"And I choked Bean."

"That's antisocial, yet correctable. You apologized."

"It frightened me. I've never been that mad at anyone before. Never. God, it scared me. I was mad enough to kill."

Tuberski tossed another log into the fire and stoked the embers. They wanted to keep the flames going as a beacon for Mitikitski. Tuberski shrugged and leaned back. "You weren't mad at Bean. You were mad at Tracy. You tried to tear up her picture."

Fenberg couldn't answer.

"She runs my life," Fenberg finally said, with a great weariness. "There isn't a day that goes by I don't think of her. Not a day." Fenberg laughed. "I live with a pain so great that I'm afraid I'm going to die. And then I'm afraid I won't. I meet a genuinely terrific girl, and I'm helpless. God help me."

Please.

"Mitikitski is going to have my kid, and I don't love her, and if there ever was a person to love, a person who deserves it, it's Mitikitski. Instead, I drive her away. And I nearly knock my friend's block off." Fenberg looked over at Bean. He was wrapped in his bag, asleep, still with the inane grin on his face. "I act like a monster, and I don't want to."

The monster in us never does, thought Tuberski.

"But I can't help myself. I can't face the fact that I'm so goddamn mad at her."

"Tracy?"

"Yeah." Fenberg felt dizzy. The control. Keeping the emotions in check. It was all swirling inside. "I can't face the fact that I'm so goddamn mad at her. What is a respectable time to mourn? A year? Two? I mourn every day, and I am very, very tired."

"Do you want to talk about that night?"

"Can't. Too painful."

Tuberski could understand.

Fenberg stared into the fire. His face was hot, his back cold. Nothing, it seems, is perfect.

"It was a textbook bad Christmas," Fenberg said, entranced by the firelight. "Lord, what a day. I had been working too much. I don't know. I don't know honestly what choice I had. The folks were off on vacation. Half the staff at the paper was out sick, and you know how it is at Christmas. It's our biggest revenue time, and the paper's three times larger than the rest of the year. I was practically living on that green couch in my office, eating doughnuts and drinking coffee. I was pretty tough to live with."

Tuberski remembered.

"I'd come home for a few hours rest, and the baby'd start crying, and I was a raw nerve." Fenberg rested his chin on his knee. "And we got into it again about Tracy and her job. I was defending the basic male asshole position of 'no wife of mine is ever going to . . .' you know, fill in the rest. I didn't mind her working, it was where she was working."

Tuberski smiled with recollection. "That's right. She was at the old A & W drive-through."

Fenberg nodded.

"She carried the baby strapped to her chest and waited on cars." Fenberg could see her clearly, the brown and orange uniform, the long blond hair tucked under a cap. Her nose was red from the cold, and she wore heavy mittens. The baby didn't seem to mind. "I guess she made good money on the tips. She said she could have left the baby with her folks, but she liked the company, and she said the kid helped triple her tips. Con woman."

Fenberg shook his head. The fire was blurring.

"It just irked me. That guy who managed the A & W, I can't even remember his name. Some town wag told me he'd pinched Tracy and would make it a point to grind up against her in the kitchen, and her carrying a damn little baby around. Son of a bitch. Damn it. It was like some sort of god-damn Charles Dickens story gone rotten. She wanted that first Christmas for us as a family to be special." Fenberg laughed. "You remember those crazy discussions you two would have about reincarnation and life going on?"

Tuberski fidgeted.

"Tracy said we'd still be friends ten thousand years from now. In the meantime, we'd need something of substance to mark that first Christmas. She was very secretive." Fenberg took a deep breath and went on. "We had an argument that morning before I went to work. About her job and this and that. It wasn't about anything, really, just a stupid argument. The baby started crying. Tracy started yelling back. I stormed out of the house and slammed the porch door behind me, jerk that I was.

"We had made this deal when we were married, starry-eyed newlyweds that we were. If ever we got in a fight or argument, we'd settle it right there, no matter what, no matter where we had to go, no matter if we were late. We'd settle it and end it with a kiss. We had had a few arguments by that time, and usually after the yelling and hurt feelings and mis-understandings were cleared away, we'd end up in bed. We didn't this time. Tracy stood in the doorway." Fenberg felt the lump burn in his throat. The vision of his wife was fading, and Fenberg squinted to bring it back. "She watched me walk to the truck, then called after me. 'Don't you want a kiss?' she said. I didn't stop. Didn't give her the goddamn courtesy of turning around. I said, 'Later.' Only there was no later."

Fenberg fought off the first wave and sucked in a deep breath. The flames had split in halves, then quarters, then eighths, dancing distortedly in Michael's eyes.

"She drove all the way down to San Francisco that day. All the way into San Francisco to go to a goddamn foundry. She had ordered bronze end-pieces to a bench. Our family bench. We were supposed to take pictures on that bench every Christmas as our family grew. I guess you know the rest. The storm. The road conditions. The drunk that side-swiped her and ran her off the road into the gully, and how that goddamn bronze bench slid from the back and pinned her against the wheel."

Fenberg hadn't identified the bodies. He didn't go to the funeral, but watched from a distant hill, and afterwards he threw away the Christmas card Tracy had written to go with the bench: "Solid, like us." Only life wasn't very solid. Fenberg hadn't cried since he was eight.

"John, I never got a chance to say good-bye to her. . . ."

Tuberski reached out and handed Fenberg the crumpled, plastic-covered snapshot of Tracy and Jack. "I think you dropped this earlier. I sort of tried to straighten it out," said John, holding the picture in front of Fenberg. "Do you want to say good-bye now, Mikey?"

The pain and anguish that had been stored for so long engulfed Michael, overpowering him. The tears came in torrents. Fenberg gently took hold of the picture and clutched it to his chest. He bawled like a baby.

Tuberski lit a Hav-A-Tampa and quietly rubbed Michael's back, helping the monsters fly away. He watched his brother sob uncontrollably in a very undignified but healthy fashion, and John judged it as good. Well, not good, because Tuberski didn't believe in good or evil, but it was certainly therapeutic and would probably serve to cure Fenberg up to the ninety-nine percent mark.

It struck John that something was still missing. And then the Voice brought it to him.

When Fenberg fell asleep from exhaustion later that evening, Tuberski scrounged for some scratch paper and something to write with. He printed a sign and clipped it to Fenberg's backpack: How do you like it like *this?*

God, evidently, does have a sense of humor, Tuberski figured.

26

MUTUAL OF OMAH

The moon rose quietly, like an alien spaceship.

It hovered, behind a tree-lined mountain, then effortlessly rose for a full inspection of the planet below.

"Ten o'clock," said Fenberg, glancing at his watch.

Four sets of eyes stared heavenward. Another set was stubbornly closed. The medicine man rocked back and forth by his fire, quietly mumbling an ancient protective chant.

The creature stared, mesmerized by the shining orb. Flecks of chicken and noodles trickled down his hairy chin as he tried to chew the tiny morsels in the soup Tuberski had prepared. The beast was oblivious to the men staring at him, unaware of the high-powered rifle resting on Fenberg's leg, aimed in his direction.

Twelve people. Dead. Eaten. All during the full moon.

"He's moving!" Fenberg straightened; the rifle barrel zeroed in for the creature's heart.

"Wait!" snapped Tuberski, holding up his hand. "It's okay. He's just changing positions."

The creature sat cross-legged, head bowed back, enthralled by the swollen moon.

"Please point that thing away," pleaded Tuberski.

"Sorry," said Fenberg, shaking his head no. The rifle didn't move.

"Mike, I lived with it for three months. . . ."

"You said he was never around during the full moon."

Tuberski had no argument.

"While he may be perfectly tame most of the month, there might be some effect the moon has on him." There were already several dead and digested people, and Fenberg had no intention of being on anyone's menu.

For three hours the men watched the monster, who in turn watched the slow journey of the lunar satellite. A little after one, he drifted to sleep.

"Something doesn't make sense here," said Fenberg, slowly getting to his feet. He shook his legs to get the circulation going. They woke the Indian.

"Charlie!" whispered Fenberg, shaking the Indian by the shoulder. "Charlie, I want you to look at something."

The old man looked sleepily at Fenberg, then at the dying fire. He shook himself alert. "I have fallen asleep! The *Mandrango*, where is he?"

"Monster dreamland. Relax," said Tuberski, a rifle over his shoulder. "He's fast asleep."

"That can't be," said the medicine man. He studied the fire and charred trinkets in the ashes. "Something is wrong. On this night, before the moon passes a quarter of the sky, he must make his transformation and kill."

"The only thing he's killed is a half-case of chicken soup." Tuberski shook his head and smiled at Fenberg. "Where does he get all this baloney? Do you mind telling me how it was arbitrarily arrived at that the big Muppet goes berserk when the moon gets to a quarter of the sky? Why not three-eighths? How about fifteen-sixteenths? You got anything against metric? You're so full of it," said Tuberski, waving a disgusted hand at the sitting Indian.

"There are many things on this plane of existence that the white man—" Charlie began, defensively. Tuberski interrupted him.

"Yeah, yeah, yeah. Take a look at him yourself. He's asleep," said Tuberski, pointing his rifle at the snoozing beast. Charlie turned the other way.

"No. It is a curse to do so."

"Charlie, we've been staring at the thing's ugly mug all night, and I don't feel in the slightest cursed," said Fenberg.

"You will be," promised the Indian. He folded his arms across his chest.

"Lookit," said Fenberg, leaning on one leg and cradling his rifle. "I want you to take a peek at this thing. There's something fishy going on, and I can't put my finger on it. C'mon. I need your help. You know these woods and everything in them. I respect your opinion."

Tuberski made a face and looked away.

Charlie stubbornly shook his white head. No. The curse. His soul. The mark of the beast would be burned on it.

"Malarkey," said Tuberski, folding his arms. Bean Breath Brown looked up at the towering artist-mystic-warrior-entrepreneur and imitated his posture.

"How about if you don't look *directly* at it?" asked Fenberg. The Indian didn't understand.

Fenberg looked around for a mirror or shiny object.

"Here," he said, pulling the knife from Charlie's worn leather sheath. "Just walk over to it, turn your back, then look at it through the reflection of the knife." Fenberg held the knife to his eyes, demonstrating. "See?"

"Jason and the Medusa," recognized Tuberski. " 'Kay. Good hustle."

Charlie had reservations. Tuberski and Fenberg helped him to his feet. He closed his eyes as they guided him to the creature.

"Shhh," said Tuberski, turning the Indian around. "Now open your eyes and take a look." Fenberg handed him the knife.

Charlie Two Eagles twisted the blade and looked. He saw the reflection of a distorted flat face, two bowling ball holes for a nose, a wide, thin mouth, and no sharp teeth, apparently.

"I can't see his eyes," said Charlie.

"He's got two of them," said Tuberski.

"I need to know the color."

"Raspberry red and lemon yellow," said Tuberski.

"Brown," corrected Fenberg. "Just plain brown. Why do you ask?"

"You're sure they're not yellow?"

"Positive."

"They're supposed to be yellow, like a wild dog's," said Charlie, putting the reflecting knife to his eyes again. Something was wrong. "The ears. They're not right. And the nose, it should be more pointed, like a badger's." Before Tuberski could manage another bit of sarcasm, the old medicine man turned full around and looked at the beast. "Oh-oh . . ."

Fenberg looked back and forth between the Indian and the sleeping creature. "What do you mean, 'oh-oh'?"

"This is not the *Mandrango*," pronounced Charlie Two Eagles, refolding his arms judiciously.

"What do you mean, this isn't the *Mandrango*?" Fenberg wanted to know. "I'll tell you something. This sure isn't two guys asleep in a monster suit."

"Chuck, if I may intervene here," said Tuberski, ambling over and putting a hand on the Indian's shoulder. "For the past two days we have suffered through a long-playing album of yours, listening to aboriginal mumbo jumbo, watching you throw bones and lighter fluid into the fire, all the while half-believing your rascally antics. 'Bride of the beast. Hunger without end. Human blood cocktails,'" reminded Tuberski. "Now didn't you say that?"

"I said most. Yes. But as usual, you misquote me."

"Misquote, mis-shmote. You know what your problem is . . ."

Fenberg stepped between them. "Hold it. Just hold it. What's the problem here?"

"Here's the problem," said Charlie, lifting the sleeping giant's hairy foot. His tone indicated it should be painfully obvious to anyone except an ignorant white person. "You've got the wrong damn monster."

"Again?" asked Fenberg.

Charlie unceremoniously dropped the creature's foot. The monster grumbled and smacked his chops. He turned over on his side and curled into a ball.

"This is just a smelly old Omah," announced Charlie.

"A what?" Fenberg wanted clarification.

"An *Omah!*"

"As in '. . . my papa' or 'Mutual of?'" asked Tuberski.

"An Omah! An Omah! A Bigfoot, you stupid white man! They're as dangerous as a reservation dog. The woods are filled with them," said Charlie, gesturing magnanimously around at the surrounding foliage. "You've got the wrong monster!"

Tuberski automatically took two steps back, out of Fenberg's immediate reach, and stared dolefully at his boots.

MRS. BEHAN'S COMPLAINT

"I've come to lodge a complaint," said Mrs. Behan, her children lined up behind her like quail. "I also want protective custody guaranteed for myself and my children."

Deputy Diesel looked up from his paperwork. He had been with the Tulare County Sheriff's Department for thirty years and considered himself a pretty good judge of character. He theorized Mrs. Behan was a kook.

"What seems to be the problem, ma'am?"

"My husband isn't what he pretends to be," she said flatly.

"None of us are, ma'am," said Diesel, looking back down at his forms.

"He's a monster," she said. The children huddled closer to her. They had driven all morning to get out of Basin County. Tulare's county seat was the closest city of substance.

"Drinks?"

"Uh, no."

"Roughs you up?"

"Once."

"Is he one of these psychological types, masked threats and such?"

"You don't seem to understand, officer," said Mrs. Behan, putting her purse on his desk and pulling out an ancient, tattered diary. "He really *is* a monster."

WILL THE REAL MONSTER
(SLURP)
PLEASE REPLACE HIS TONGUE?

M. J. Behan sat at his desk at home and manually placed his tongue back into his mouth. He had been losing control of several normally automatic bodily functions lately and caught himself on several occasions with what could be construed as a toothy grin and lolling tongue.

Slurp. Replace tongue.

And there were the shoulders. For a bony man allegedly in his fifties, M. J. Behan had very wide shoulders. They were tight, as if some dollmaker had created Behan and substituted a million taut rubbers bands instead of muscle, and each rubber band had been tied into a dozen tight knots. Snap. Ping. Tension. Behan arched his neck first to the right, then twisted it quickly to the left. Some people crack their knuckles. Behan cracked his neck.

But this morning, his neck wouldn't crack, and it nearly drove Behan to tears of desperation. He loved the cracking sound.

Tension.

Pop.

Release.

Breathe.

For two nights running, he had galloped naked through the woods, hunting for Elaine. All he found was dinner—two screaming deputies the first morning, an unsuspecting

camper last night. Three days a month, the moon was full for
Behan. Three days a month, Behan turned into a monster.
The old Indian had been right. Behan would kill and kill with
increasing intensity, his hunger would grow geometrically,
until he found his bride—the assistant managing editor of *The
Basin Valley Bugle*.

He could fulfill his prophecy, his destiny, tonight. Or, he
could wait. One more month. Another full moon. Another
seventy-seven years, which was the exact length of the
Nagomo cycle. Another seventy-seven years until he could
find his bride. The pain, the gut-tearing emotions—Martin
James knew he couldn't go through it all again. As if he had a
choice. He had to laugh. The sighting of the Bigfoot at first
had been a blessing—a convenient scapegoat on which to
blame his murders. It had now turned into a curse. The Bigfoot had kidnapped his bride, and if Behan had a sense of
humor, he would have found the situation rather rich.

He'd nearly had her last night.

He had picked up the scent, that one-in-the-universe scent.
She was alone, asleep in a branch of a tree. He was only a
few agonizing steps from Elaine when the first rays of dawn
crippled him in stride, doubling him over.

So close.

Behan smiled.

He really couldn't lose. If the searchers found her during
the day, they'd bring her to town. No matter where she
stayed, no force on earth could keep her from him. And if
she stayed lost in the woods, so much the better. His powers
were greatest tonight. It would be a simple task to find her in
the dark.

And besides.

He had help.

Ever since Elaine Mitikitski had been a toddler, she had
been watched. Psychic forces whispered to her, followed her.
Hairy, cherubic dark angels perched in doorways, smiling
with curved teeth. Her destiny. They knew, and they told
Behan. They knew of her return to Basin Valley. She had
been the bride of the Indian torn from the cabin seventy-

seven years ago when Behan had carried her off. That time she had died. Now she had come back, reborn, to pay her debt all over again.

Behan sat in a maroon overstuffed leather chair in his unfinished library. Maybe it was the smell of the paint and sawdust that was irritating. He was a renifleur—someone with a superhuman sense of smell. Even the simplest odors overpowered him, made him dizzy, or sleepy, or sexually aroused, or ravenously hungry. The odors had been getting more and more intense, as he knew they would. His time was coming, and the whole process was making M. J. Behan a wreck.

His pulse hadn't dipped below one hundred fifteen the past two days. Not only had his sense of smell increased, but he found his hearing and eyesight had been heightened to psychedelic levels.

Prickly.

That's what he felt. Hypersensitive. He hadn't cried for over a hundred years, since he was a child, but Behan found himself breaking into hysterics for the most innocent of reasons. Linda had given M. J. his breakfast cereal in a plastic bowl and snap. Tears. "I wanted a *glass* bowl," he shrieked, backhanding his cornflakes against a cupboard.

He wasn't hungry anyway.

And then, there was the laughing, which was completely new to Behan seeing that he had no sense of humor and on his best days could only muster an ingratiating smile. Behan had developed a maniacal, bass, graveyard laugh, just like Tuberski's, except Behan wasn't kidding. He really was maniacal.

Mwa-ha. Mwa-ha-ha-ha. Slurp. Reinsert tongue.

Linda had taken the children to town this morning, and Behan sensed she wouldn't be back. Fine. Who needs her now? He'd soon have Elaine. He'd watched Linda hop around the kitchen like a stupid bird. She smiled too much at breakfast, a sure sign. Too cheery, too accommodating, too conversational.

"More bacon, honey? Warm up the coffee? Another dozen

eggs before you go back to bed? My, you certainly have been hungry," she said, smiling and wiping up the cereal off the floor. "You kids please hurry with your breakfast. I've got a million errands, and I want to take you all into town for shoes."

Shoes. Shoes indeed. She made it a point not to look at him.

There were times when Behan wished they all didn't fear him so much. Despite the fact he was a monster, deep down, M. J. liked the security of family life, although family life did not return the compliment. Why were they all so afraid of him?

Well, for starters, if you wouldn't pinch them . . .

Behan jerked in his chair. He scanned the study. That Voice again. It confused Behan. Sometimes, he thought it was God talking to him. At other times, he knew it to be the devil.

It had to be the devil, Behan resigned himself. For what he had done, even God would not talk to M. J. Behan. Or so he thought.

Everyone was uncomfortable around Behan.

Everyone feared him, or loathed him. It was the price he had paid so many years ago, and tonight there would be another price to pay. The wedding and entry of Elaine Mitikitski into the Brotherhood of Darkness. The deaths of Fenberg and Tuberski. A small price to pay.

It was quiet in the house with everyone gone. This was their eleventh home, and it seemed that every one, with the fresh paint and smell of new carpeting, had brought with it the hope that this time, somehow, things might be different.

Behan had tried to separate his private life from his family life this time around.

Sometimes, the family would forget. He would tickle or hug one of the kids or bump into Linda in a narrow hallway, her arms filled with linen. He'd look at her, and the eyes would be open, friendly, as if seeing him for the first time. Then she'd remember. She knew. The kids didn't, except for Darla. Like a steel door slamming, Linda's eyes would break contact, and the smile would turn to uncertainty, submissiveness, and his wife would turn away.

Didn't she think that vicious people have feelings too?

The kids snubbed him. When they were outside, playing, the children frolicked, unhindered and natural. Behan would peek from behind a curtain, stealing scenes of laughter and victory. There was even a time when he could join them, for a moment. Now it was uncomfortable for everyone, as if he were Richard Nixon stopping at the beach to throw the Frisbee around with some kids.

This time, Behan had thought, he might be able to make a marriage work. Except a man cannot serve two masters, and Behan's destiny came up, and his wife didn't understand.

"What would you think if I brought home another wife. A higher wife than you?" Behan had asked the missus.

A taller woman? What do you mean, a higher wife? What do you mean, *another* wife? They were Baptists, not Mormons, Linda thought, her eyes darting back and forth. She didn't say anything, being basically scared right down to her skeletal system of this strange man who crawled out windows and returned at dawn with his clothes torn and mud on his bare feet.

"You have served me well over the years," Behan had said. "You have a choice. I will, in a few days, be bringing home another woman. . . ."

Short SOB.

"It is something I know you don't understand, but let's just say it's in the cards for me. My destiny. You have been a good and fitting mother of my children, for which you have lived well. I am not without appreciation. I will pay . . ."

Oh, don't worry, you'll pay. Linda could only smile weakly.

"And I am offering you and the children the right to stay here for a while, so you can aid in the upkeep of the house."

Linda's eyes had widened.

"Or, you have the choice of taking the children and a comfortable monthly allowance. . . ."

Linda had taken curtain number two.

Behan figured it a relief to be rid of her. At least, with his new bride, he wouldn't have to keep up the charade he had created with Linda. At least, he and Mitikitski would both be monsters.

Behan jerked his neck quickly to the side. It didn't crack. Behan ground his teeth.

There was something in Behan's permanent life-file that kept him looking for a family. He had been married seventeen times before Linda, and each time tried not to let his personal life dribble into the parlor. But Behan wasn't a bigamist, or a thief, or a CIA double agent, all comparatively easy pastimes to conceal from one's spouse. Behan was a monster. He'd killed most of his wives. The other ones, the lucky ones, Behan just walked out on.

"What you hide, you keep," Tuberski would always say. Of course, Behan didn't know John was an up-and-coming great mystic, and even if he knew Tuberski was speaking the truth, the most polite response he'd give Fenberg's brother would be a sneer.

Mwa-ha. Mwa-ha-ha. Replace the tongue.

Ultimate bad behavior. It was a living.

Behan was attracted to a pile of boxes packed full of books. His aging, arthritic, spotted hands dug through a sealed crate and held a recent red leather photo album.

Family number eighteen.

Pictures of Behan and Linda, dating in college. They had gone to a Bible school. Behan had wanted a challenge this time around. And, subconsciously, a little fire insurance. He turned the pages. Wedding pictures, baby pictures, photos of children growing up. Of all the children he had sired in a century and a half, he both liked and disliked Darla the most. She had a mouth on her.

Christmas and holiday photos. Somehow, a family gave him a grip on mortality, a concept he missed. Behan stared at the latest family portrait, at himself in particular. He looked the same in all the pictures—tired, stern. That appearance would change soon. Tonight, in fact. The Dark Brotherhood had guaranteed him a young body, a handsome face for his bride to love and caress. Behan's eyes wandered to other members of his family. Deep down, very deep down, buried under the hate-without-end, the fear, the self-loathing, he did hold some minuscule amount of affection for the children. He wondered what he had looked like as a baby.

Round body, block head.

He had no childhood pictures of himself. The camera had not been invented when M. J. Behan entered the world.

Behan tossed the album on the desk and limped across the room to the huge antique safe. He bent, with difficulty, spinning the six-tumbler lock. Inside was a comfortable fortune in negotiable bonds, cash, jewelry, more photo albums. Different families, of course.

The Behans of the fifties. Her name was Emily. No children. She caught him on a bad night, hair bristling, blood on teeth and hands, crawling through a window. He killed her for it.

Three families during the forties and the great war, which he followed, trailing behind the lines, silently stealing a sentry in the dead of a fog-shrouded night, tiptoeing after the clicking of a high-heeled prostitute in a cobblestone alley. Families of the thirties and twenties, families at the turn of the century. Those were more his times.

1892. Chicago.

His hair was greased and parted down the middle. He sported a handlebar moustache and muttonchops. His derby posed in one hand, Behan stood with the other hand on the shoulder of yet another wife (number three) who had that look of knowing a terrible secret.

Mwa-ha. Mwa-ha-ha.

Martin James Behan had come to America on January 6, 1850. Zachary Taylor was president, and scores of Irish were fleeing the Emerald Isle and its great potato famine. He crossed the Atlantic alone, aboard a creaking ship overflowing with his impoverished Celtic countrymen. Behan was ten, a sickly unbaptized boy with a bad left leg and crumpled note to be delivered to a distant cousin in Philadelphia.

To his second cousin, Dorothy Irene, he was moody and sullen. To her husband, he was a burden and just another mouth to feed. Martin was constantly on the losing end of fights he had started, bullied those few who were smaller than he was, stole, made contrary remarks injurious to people's feelings, and bit Dorothy Irene's baby. Dorothy's husband wasn't Dr. Spock, frequently beating Martin like the proverbial redheaded stepchild. Martin stabbed him, severing several nerves in the man's right arm.

At thirteen, Martin ran away from home.

There was a blur of ill-paying, backbreaking jobs and runins with the law. Martin nurtured a hatred for his fellow man, born of fear and insecurity and confirmed by other people. He sought power. In the Bowie knife he cuddled. In his drunken fantasies of being better than he was. By seventeen, he found himself in voodoo country. New Orleans.

Behan became a clam sheller, a job that lacerated his hands with a thousand razor cuts. He reeked of the ocean's stench and was paid little. One moonlit evening, he found himself in a back alley behind a filthy salt-air bar, fighting with an enormous fellow sheller whom Behan had had the temerity to call a ". . . filthy black monkey-man."

"And so you will see I am," said his fellow clammer, smiling to expose a row of sharpened white incisors.

He was the first person Behan had ever killed. The man put an unreasoning terror in Behan, the animal-like way he crouched, the way he used his nails and teeth. This time, it was Behan who was the bitee. The huge black man lifted him high off the ground, gnawing his teeth deep into Martin's chest. As Behan slammed the knife into the dark rib cage, leveraging and shoving toward the heart, he felt the poisonous burning swim violently through his own body.

Was it rabies? A tropical fever? Behan didn't know at the time. He lay, alternately shivering and sweating, in a fly-infested lean-to, the humid Gulf winds adding to his delirium.

Then, Behan had a visitor.

An ancient, grinning Negress who called herself a sorceress parted the colorful beads that served as Behan's door. She reverently led a lady of means to Martin. The woman was an effortless beauty, European, old money, with silver blond hair tied back simply in a bun. She seemed to float into the room, wearing a long, cream-colored cape. Behan had taken the life of a member of the Dark Brotherhood. He must pay for that life with his. The woman caressed him fondly, wiping the salted sweat from his swollen, bug-bitten forehead with a cool, damp cloth. Service would not be without rewards— riches, travel, power, and the respect that he had never known. He would one day be handsome and have a beautiful bride to love and serve him.

The trade-off?

He would be a collector of souls.

The ritual was gruesome, gratuitously violent, and involved the moaning act of sex with, sadly, the aging black sorceress, the pulling of teeth and a rib without local or general anesthesia, and the consumption of unrecognizable Third World barnyard fare. As he lay there dying, on that filthy cot with the sand crabs laboriously crawling across his floor, he looked up at the regal blonde. She smiled so warmly, so understandingly, having, in her profession, the ability to take a pleasing shape and all. Really, all the muck-a-lucka and splattering of blood was unnecessary for the lending of one's soul. All the queen of darkness needed was his nodding consent. That's all anyone needs, really. Weakly, he smiled and moved his head. Yes.

And so, Behan became a member of that elite group, older than time, organized very much like Amway, the secret and most powerful organization on this plane of existence. Behan actually started quite high in the organization—a collector of souls, a position Tuberski would have considered ridiculous because souls can only be borrowed, never taken. But, where God is not realized, the devil rules and, of course, Tuberski wasn't in the neighborhood at the time to share his Zen cowboyisms with Behan anyway.

*　*　*　*　*

The phone rang in the study, and Behan closed the yellowed photo album. He shut the safe and spun the tumbler. "*Mwa-ha* . . ."

"I beg your pardon?" asked the caller.

Slurp. Behan manually put his tongue back in his mouth. "This is Mr. Behan."

"Tonight is your last night." The woman called from a palatial estate in Mexico. She thanked Behan for bringing many new devotees to the Brotherhood of Darkness, but added that it would be a good idea for Behan to add a Miss Mitikitski to the roster. And don't forget to kill Fenberg and Tuberski, she said matter-of-factly, like Catherine Deneuve ordering groceries. "Don't fail, Martin."

"I won't," Behan spoke to a dial tone. He recognized the voice. It was the woman who had indoctrinated him in that Louisiana shack nearly two centuries ago.

The sun was setting. It was time to go.

Behan hung up the phone and opened the top drawer to his desk. He pulled out an eight-by-ten glossy of a strikingly beautiful raven-haired editor and felt an involuntary stirring that wasn't his tongue. Behan dug deeper into a box and came up with another photo album, still in protective plastic. He unwrapped it and gently laid the photograph of Elaine Mitikitski on the first page.

29

BEHAN AND MITIKITSKI'S
INCORRECT CONCEPT OF
THE REPAYING OF KARMA

The bounce was gone from Mitikitski's step, but she was thankful to have finally found what looked to be an old fire trail. A possible road back to civilization. It had rained for most of the morning and afternoon. The storm pummeled the forest and forced Elaine to spend most of the day under a leaky tree. At best, she had covered only two miles before finding the trail, which was still treacherous and slippery.

She was hungry.

She had an intense craving for tomatoes, vinegar, and Spanish olives. Earlier it was a meatball sandwich, plenty of drippy sauce and grease, please. Her pants felt three sizes too small. Babies. At least the morning sickness was gone.

Mitikitski walked and considered things.

She was undecided about what to do about Fenberg, whom she partly blamed for her unscheduled camping trip. This was not the best way to spend a pregnancy. Mitikitski wanted to be pampered. She could not decide which fantasy she preferred. Being coddled by a doting Fenberg, which included having her back rubbed, being spoon-fed, not lifting anything over seven ounces, and making Mike her sex slave because now that she was pregnant, her hormones had gone tilt. Her other fantasy leaned more to the poor-pitiful-me Spanish nunnery side. Or, at least, to returning home. Her parents would be initially shocked, but supportive. She and Kamali Molly could shop for designer maternity wear. She'd have the baby herself, love it, educate it, go on with her career, and stick mom and dad with daytime babysitting, as they would love that anyway. After all, who was she trying to kid?

Mitikitski hit a slick spot and skidded a few feet on one foot before regaining her balance. She said "Shit!" and stared malevolently at her skid mark before resuming the march.

No. Fenberg didn't love her, she thought. He couldn't even frame the words. Once, in a playful battle, she'd laughed and told Fenberg for the first time, "I love you." He looked at her funny, as if she had called him a name in a foreign tongue. Say it, you donkey Boy Scout you. It's a myth, Elaine considered. A man is supposed to say, "I love you," and there's the tinkling of harps and xylophones, and suddenly the world's a better place for democracy. No. I am pretty sick of men. I hope this one's a girl. She patted her stomach. Just kidding. Then hugged it. Whether you're a boy or girl in there, you're going to have one person who'll love you to pieces. She looked heavenward. Whatever that means, you'll have to show me, 'cause I don't know.

Mitikitski marched in cadence. It was so pretty out here, high above the world, the sun going down.

Maybe, when the child was older, she'd take it back to see its father. He'd probably still be running that little paper. He'd be older, a little gray at the temples, a couple of laugh lines at the eyes. That's another damn thing about men. They age so gracefully. Elaine maliciously pictured him with a fat wife, just to spite the guy. Her daughter (okay—or son) would fall in love with him, handsome charmer the bastard was, and want to stay. He'd bribe her with horses and movies and fresh air. And then he'd look at Elaine, up over the head of the child, with that look of his. That look with those melting silver eyes that would silently say, "Gee, honey, I've been a jerk, let's get back together." And he'd break her heart all over again.

Geez. Knock it off, Mitikitski, Elaine chastised herself.

Elaine picked up the pace, now that the fire trail was slanting downhill. She had to be careful. It would be dark soon, and she noticed the road dropped off a few places to a rocky gorge maybe five hundred feet straight down.

She was sure there would be search parties. Well, maybe. Maybe even that Fenberg person would take a couple hours out of his schedule to search for her. On second thought, I doubt it. Self-centered . . .

Go sit on it, Fenberg.

She was nearing Webster's Leap, but didn't know it.

Mitikitski stopped. Her head craned forward. She heard a rumbling sound, she thought. Yes! A car engine. It was coming her way. Oh, God! Thank you, thank you, thank you, she said to herself. Maybe it was even Michael! Mitikitski wiggled out of the backpack she had commandeered from Camp Bigfoot. The car was getting closer. Elaine fumbled through the nylon pack, looking for a brush and mirror.

"Gag," she said, making a face at her reflection. What the hell are you doing? You're getting rescued, not going on a date. You're supposed to look disheveled.

Nonetheless, Mitikitski straightened and prepped, as best she could. She dusted off her clothes, sucked in her stomach, and stood—feet together, shoulders back—at attention.

It was a new Range Rover. Mitikitski held a hand to shield her eyes from the setting sun. Four men in it. On the passenger's side, she could make out a sheriff's uniform. It was Michael's cousin, Bubba. Mitikitski stood on her tiptoes and waved.

"Oh, *God* am I glad to see someone!" said Mitikitski as the Rover splashed though a puddle and bounced to a stop next to her. "Mr. Behan?"

"Hello, Elaine," said the werewolf.

Mitikitski took a step back. Something funny here. Both Magonogonovitch brothers were sitting in the back seat, staring straight ahead, as if entranced. The sheriff had been obviously beaten, and his hands were handcuffed behind his back.

"Going my way?" Behan asked, smiling.

*   *   *   *   *

Mitikitski was at the point of being fairly sick and tired of getting carted off by monsters and loonies. She was tired of camping out. Tired of the outdoors and none too fond anymore of campfires.

She wanted her apartment. She wanted her bathtub and robe.

"I don't think this is too damn funny," said Elaine loudly, ineffectually struggling as the dazed Magonogonovitch brothers tied her hands behind her back with leather straps. She looked at a carved-out stump, about six-feet tall, blackened by fire. The unusual grotesque curvature of the wood created a standing throne, with two roots as spread-apart stirrups. More leather harnesses dangled from the dead tree. It looked like a gynecologist's table for a druid. "It's getting old, real fast," she said, straightening with dignity and composure. "Would you mind telling me just what in the hell you are doing?"

The Magonogonovitches finished their task and sat down at Behan's feet like trained dogs.

"I've been searching for you for a hundred years," said Behan. His face seemed older, more wrinkled, yet stronger, Elaine thought.

"Well, I imagine it must *seem* like a hundred years," said Elaine.

"Once, long ago, I found you. Do you remember?" Behan asked.

Elaine didn't. She went on, explaining rapidly what she had been doing these past few days, and a joke's a joke, but could Mr. Behan please untie her now? Behan smiled, inhaling the smell of sulphur from the flames.

"It was up here, a century ago. Your hair was just as long and dark, only without the curl. You certainly came back prettier. Ironic. Your husband Michael left you. Alone. Of course, that wasn't his name then. It was all so perfect, except you were carrying his child, and I had to kill you for your infidelity and wait. Wait another hundred years. Do you remember?"

No. This all seemed like nonsense to Mitikitski. She looked at Bubba, then back at Behan, suspiciously.

"Why is the sheriff tied up?" she wanted to know.

"Dinner," said Behan.

Mwa-ha.

He looked at the sky. "Soon the moon will be full, and I will go through this charade a final time. I need my sleep. So do you."

Behan walked over to Elaine, gliding with an animal's grace. He studied her, gently rubbing her face, then placed two fingers on the artery in her neck. Her pulse. Elaine shivered and drew back. "Soon you will beg for my touch, little princess."

"Don't bet the rent money," said Mitikitski, involuntarily squeezing her legs together.

Behan smiled and ran his fingers roughly through Elaine's hair, pulling her head back. His tongue lolled out.

"I sleep," Behan said, standing suddenly. "Watch them," he instructed the brothers. They silently nodded. Elaine screamed.

"Help!"

Mitikitski took a deep breath and screamed again, her voice echoing off canyon walls.

"HEEEEEEEEEEEEEELLLLLLPPPPPPPPPPPPP!"

Behan turned. "No one can hear you. But if you scream again, I'll gag you. I prefer my women quiet."

Elaine glowered, but kept silent. Oh, we're going to get along just great. Elaine tugged at her bonds, looking around the area. Behan gave her the willies. The two stone-faced brothers gave her the willies. The woods gave her the willies. Everything was giving her the willies, and the first chance she had . . .

"I'm a dead man."

Mitikitski looked down at the sheriff, then at the brothers sitting impassively like gargoyles a few feet away.

"What?" she whispered. It was the first time the sheriff had spoken. Mitikitski inched closer. The brothers saw, but made no move to restrain her. She wiggled a few feet closer, and when they showed no interest she slid all the way on her rear end next to Bubba. "What did you say?"

Fenberg's cousin looked blankly at Mitikitski, as if it should be quite clear. "I'm a dead man," he repeated. There was dried blood at the corner of his mouth, and his left eye was blackened.

"Would you mind telling me what's going on here?" asked Elaine.

"The comment he made? About dinner? He wasn't kidding."

"What are you talking about? What happened here? Why are you tied up, and why are those goofs staring at us?" whispered Mitikitski.

"They're his slaves," said Bubba tiredly. "We had the killer living in town with us all along. It wasn't Mike's brother, and it wasn't the Bigfoot creature. It was Behan."

"What?" Mitikitski shook her head. The MO of the murders. Those people brutally torn to shreds? Behan was a frail man in his late fifties.

"He killed two of my deputies last night, although he was in a different form. He can change his body structure. Did you know that?"

Mitikitski nodded, unsure. She wanted to mentally add Bubba Fenberg to her list of loonies, but couldn't.

"He's a werewolf, and soon, when the moon comes over the ridge there, he'll change form, just like he did last night. I didn't know it was him. We were just trying to find our way back to town. Our radio was out, and I guess the road must be blocked. I don't know how he got through." With his head, Bubba motioned toward Behan. "But he did. Me and the two brothers were walking along the fire trail when he drove up behind us. I said I was mighty glad to see him, then these two clowns drop to their knees and start bowing in front of him. And Behan starts acting real crazy . . ."

Some part of Elaine recognized that, yes, dear God, he wasn't kidding.

". . . like he's having an epileptic attack or something, and he can't control his face. Suddenly, he knocks me down, and I mean, knocks me down. I outweigh him by a hundred pounds, and he pushed me a good twenty feet backwards. I pick myself up, and he's on me, hitting me, slapping me, all the while laughing. I draw my gun, and he knocks it out of my hand. Then he turns on these two. I've never seen a man move so fast. He pounces on that one," Bubba said, gesturing toward Lom. "He leaps on top of him and is biting him on the neck, and Lom is screaming for his brother to help him, get him off, and I can see Behan's bitten a huge chunk out of Lom's neck."

Mitikitski looked at Lom. There wasn't a mark on him.

"Then, the old man turns on Luther. He's making these weird noises, like an animal, like a mountain lion when it's real mad. Behan starts biting and scratching at Luther, and Luther is twice Behan's size, and he can't do a thing to defend himself."

No marks on Luther either, Elaine noticed.

"I couldn't run. It was like I was hypnotized. Behan's jumping up and down like a madman. There's blood all over his face. He keeps whirling above them, chanting something in, I don't know . . . it sounded like Spanish. . . ."

Latin.

"They stopped their screaming and just lay there on the ground, going through convulsions. After a few minutes, Behan gives them a signal, like he's calling them from the grave. They rise. There's not a scratch on them."

Elaine had a sickly feeling in her stomach. She looked at the post. The dream.

"I finally snapped out of it," Bubba said, entranced by his recollection. "I got up to run and Behan snaps his fingers. They ran after me and brought me back. They dragged me in front of him and I . . . his eyes. It was like all the evil in the world was coming out of his eyes, pulling on my . . ."

Soul?

"I think that will be enough," said Behan, not rising from his bedroll. As if from a silent command, Lom stood. He slapped Bubba, knocking him off-balance.

"If you have a say-so, make sure I die quick, Miss," Bubba Fenberg begged of Elaine. He read the puzzlement on her face. "Don't you see? You're going to be just like him. There's going to be sacrifices here tonight. I know I'm going to die. And maybe that's a better boat to be in than yours."

* * * * *

Except for the sleeping Behan, everyone at Webster's Leap stared.

The Magonogonovitch brothers stared blankly at Elaine. The sheriff stared blankly into space. Mitikitski stared into the woods, planning escape.

It didn't look good.

She had been quietly rubbing and twisting at the knots that held her wrists behind her back. At least they hadn't used handcuffs, as they had on the sheriff. Mitikitski worked one knot undone, gingerly urging and tugging on the next. Her fingers were sore and bleeding at the nails. Her plot was simple. Run like the dickens. She figured because of her smaller size, she might be able to outmaneuver the larger, chubbier guards once she made it to the bushes. From there, she'd simply put distance between them. It might be a ten mile run. It might be forty. She had no idea where she was, but Mitikitski knew anywhere was better than here.

God, it was dark out there.

From his deep sleep, Behan sat up quickly.

The transformation was beginning.

Behan stood and stretched. He snapped his fingers, and obediently the brothers rose and stood in the background. Mitikitski tried not to look at Behan. There were long tufts of hair that had grown from his ears while he slept, and not only had the nose imperceptibly inched out, but his entire face seemed to have been crushed thinner.

"There is always this period of the calm before the storm," he said. "It's a rather regular cycle, quite predictable. I suppose this is the time I enjoy the most, to be quite honest. It is the only time I am at peace."

"Mr. Behan, I'd like you to let me go."

"I can't do that, Elaine."

"If you're worried about me telling anyone about this, I

won't," promised Mitikitski. "I'm just afraid things will go too far, that something will happen here you won't be able to change. It's not too late."

Behan smiled reflectively. "Sometimes I tell myself that. Actually, it's quite out of my hands. It's been out of my hands for two centuries almost. I sold my soul, you see. Do you find that hard to believe?"

"I'm sorry," said Elaine. "I really don't understand."

"I'm a werewolf," admitted Behan simply. A spasm of pain jerked him forward. He winced, his face momentarily contorting from the pain. Mitikitski drew back, and Behan held out his darkening palm. "Nothing to worry about. Just a small tremor before the big quake."

"I don't want to die."

Bubba Fenberg gave Elaine a deeply concerned what-about-me look.

"I don't want the sheriff to die, either," said Mitikitski. "You do have a choice here."

"You really have nothing to worry about, Elaine," Behan said, almost tenderly. "Life? You will live forever. You will be rich, powerful, beautiful forever. You will have slaves. You will travel to exotic places no person has seen. Him?" Behan nodded toward the sheriff and shrugged. "His fate is already recorded. I will promise to end it quickly though. A wedding present, for you."

Bubba looked like he was going to be sick. Elaine wanted to know, why me? She was trying to buy time.

"I don't know exactly why you. It has something to do with your past. You were shown to me often over the years, promised to me as my bride. You and I are to learn the secrets. And I will get a new body, strong, young, handsome, not this crippled, apologetic form. She promised me this."

"She?" Elaine stopped tugging on the sweaty straps

"She is the leader of the Brotherhood of Darkness and is three thousand years old."

"I'll bet she doesn't look a day over twenty-nine," said Elaine.

"Forty, actually. She's in motion pictures," explained

Behan. "When you were a little girl, she would take me to you, and we would watch you play in the school yard, or watch you sleep from your window."

Elaine shivered with violation.

"I don't know why you, of all people," Behan went on. "It has something to do with your—I hate this word—karma. Evidently, you were a high sorceress in ancient Egypt many lifetimes ago, responsible for the deaths of thousands."

"I'm sorry."

Behan shrugged. "We all do the best we can. But now, the check's come. You must repay the karma."

Tuberski would have explained that the repaying of karma is just another erroneous concept, the equivalent to an Eastern old housewives' tale, given power only because of a false universal belief. But Tuberski was miles away.

"No offense, but I don't believe in all this stuff . . ."

"No matter. It's experiential, and we'll have many years together to talk of such interesting matters."

". . . and whether I did or not, I don't think I'd want to marry anyone who has murdered people in cold blood, and add to that the slight hitch that I'm already . . ."

"It's hot," Behan interrupted, "the blood, always hot." He shook his head violently, as if to shake out whispers of remorse. "I have killed hundreds with my bare hands. Hundreds. One more won't make much difference, will it? Or a hundred more? I'm a balancer of nature, even God could not . . ." Behan shuddered and doubled over. The pain. Mitikitski couldn't tell if Behan were groaning, or if his body, by itself, was creaking.

"Are you all right?" she asked, leaning forward.

"Yesss!" he hissed and straightened. A scream froze in Mitikitski's throat. The final metamorphosis of M. J. Behan—the voices, a cacophony of voices, as if a swarm of angry bees were buzzing inside his brain, each with an accusing voice. His heart rate rose, one-fifty, two hundred, three hundred, four hundred fifty beats per minute. Adrenalin. Exhaustion. Past exhaustion, his cells were on fire. His body underwent a burning, tearing sensation, and Behan was growing larger in front of Mitikitski's eyes. She watched, horrified, as his top palate extended another inch and his nose turned black, glistening. Hair, dark with silver tips, had grown out from under the eyes, and Behan's breath came in short, hungry stabs.

"Whoa, shit!" said Mitikitski, scooting backwards on her rear end. She bumped into Bubba and grabbed his leg. Bubba's eyes were closed. He was saying his Act of Contrition.

"Oooohhhhh, the pain!" groaned Behan. "I *like* it! It's okay now. It's okay," he said, taking his breath in deep draughts. "That part always makes me dizzy."

"Maybe if you tried to think of something pleasant," suggested Mitikitski.

"I am," said M. J. Behan, managing a contorted dog's smile. "I'm thinking of you." The moon slowly rose, creasing a serene grin of innocence and uninvolvement. Behan squatted on his haunches and turned his head at a severe angle to regard it.

"What's going to happen to me?" Mitikitski wanted to know. She worked feverishly. The knots were swelling tighter from her sweat.

Behan was rolling his head around in a slow arc.

"Do you want all the graphic details?"

She looked at the stake.

"Just the big picture."

"You will be tied to our wedding post. I will enter you. You will have my child, a gift to my master."

"We've got a problem," said Mitikitski.

"Silence."

"I'm already . . .

The word, "pregnant," was obliterated by a howl, half-demon, half-animal. Behan leaped from his crouching position, close to Mitikitski. She stopped fraying at the bindings. "When the moon is full in the sky, my transformation will be complete. No power on earth can stop me on this night, on this moon, when I am all-powerful. I will make my transformation from beast and will never crawl and hide in the bushes again!"

"How nice. A promotion." The knot was giving.

Behan was staring at the rising moon. He groaned and writhed on his feet, a drunken dancer, muscles bulging at a volcanic rate, cells mutating and multiplying at a frenzied pace, hair literally pouring out of his body. Behan tore at his clothes, ripping them off with huge, hooked talons. His voice was a vibrating, resonant growl.

"I will enter you soon, Bride. . . ."

Like hell you will, pooch, thought Elaine. The second knot, almost giving. I'll fucking die first.

"And then, dear one, we will feast together to sign our vows in blood!" Behan shrieked, pointing a claw at Bubba, who was trying to maintain a low profile.

Squirrels, hot dogs, sheriffs, Elaine's diet was going to hell. Literally.

"No, sorry. I don't eat people," said Mitikitski, "not even for special occasions."

"Oh, Elaine, everyone kills," said Behan, his chest, huge now, heaving in the moonlight. A short moment of calm overcame him. "I've got to sit down. This spell has been more severe than any, and the final thrust will be here shortly." Mitikitski didn't like the word, "thrust."

"Even my newfound servants, the noble brothers Magono-gonovitch, have killed. Did you know that?"

Elaine shook her head. No. Another knot free. One more to go. Her fingers were losing strength.

"They confessed their small crime to me. Such irony. Such a grand theme weaved through it all. Ahh. Your boyfriend, Michael. How we keep attracting the same people, through lifetime after lifetime. Michael was your husband a hundred years ago. Same essence. Different body. He left you, Elaine. I found you. You left me. And I killed you. Such a waste." Behan started, as if he had uttered some white curse. He stared hard at the ground for the longest minute. Memories flooded in, uncontrolled, of victims begging for mercy. Behan fought the softening with a snarl. "Your Michael died of a broken heart, fragile, weak, weak man he was. And in this little parenthesis, your Michael was married, as I'm sure you know. He had a small child. One cold winter night, these two lads, heads spinning from alcohol, were playing a dangerous game on the ice-covered highway. They ran a station wagon off the road."

"Oh, my God . . ." Elaine stopped her unraveling.

"Yes. Fenberg's wife and child. They could have stopped and saved the woman and baby. They didn't. They threw an empty whiskey bottle at the car instead. They laughed at the screams, mocking them, then drove off. Tonight, after our ceremony, you and I will run through the forest primeval. We will send Fenberg spinning into the void after his wife and child. And you will plead to do the killing. Which you may. I must have his brother though. Quite a . . . uhhh . . ."

Behan fell over backwards, spinning and rolling on the ground. He held his temples and screamed in the final metamorphosis. The canine incisors forced their way, pointed and deadly, to the surface. There was no semblance of a human face when he stood, only a monster, contorted with lust and hunger. Elaine pulled one hand free, then the other, quickly untying the bindings at her feet.

She ran nowhere.

They played with her for five minutes, tiring her out as she tried to find an opening in the circle they formed. Mitikitski kicked and screamed, hysterical, trying to force herself to black out and stay conscious at the same time. They strapped her to the stump, standing, her ankles wide apart. A talon reached out, popping Elaine's top blouse button, then the next, then the next. The hairy changeling put his face close to Elaine's. She thought of her baby, and strangely, that her dog back home had breath like this.

30

BRIDE OF THE BEAST

Whatever initial terror the Sasquatch held for Bean Breath Brown abated. They sat in the bed of Fenberg's pickup, bouncing along the fire road, occasionally thrown together when the truck hit a pothole. It was an exhilarating experience for the creature, the rush of cold air, a kaleidoscope of forest smells splashing against his nose. The troop had spent the entire day tracking Elaine Mitikitski, and it wasn't quite until nine that night they found the print of a tennis shoe on the trail. The truck rumbled slowly, picking up the tracks in the headlights.

"Don't you think we should be driving a little faster?" asked Tuberski. It was his turn to be worried.

"Yes. But I'm not going to risk smashing into her around a hairpin curve," said Fenberg. They came to a fork in the road and Fenberg hit the brakes.

"Do you see that?" asked Tuberski, pointing.

"Yeah. Tire tracks, coming from over there, it looks like." Fenberg pointed to the adjoining trail. They followed slowly the wide-profile tire treads and Mitikitski's shoe prints side by side. The road was treacherous. A mile down, they stopped the mud-splashed truck and climbed out.

"Stay back," said Fenberg, crouching down, silhouetted in the blinding lights blasting from six lights on the bumper, four on the roof, and the two regular high beams. The road was illuminated for two hundred yards. "Looks like she got in here. Her tracks stop. Oh geez, thank God," Fenberg said, taking a deep breath. "She's probably back in town by now."

"Well, let's call it a night then," said Tuberski, hands on hips. "I'd like to go home to a clean bed, even it is in a jailhouse."

Michael looked up at his brother. He could see John was concerned. Fenberg stood, putting the obligatory index finger on the front of Tuberski's chest.

"Do I have to?" asked John.

"Yes," said Fenberg.

Tuberski obediently looked down at his T-shirt, and Fenberg twitched him in the nose. "It's going to be fine, John," said Michael. "It's all going to be fine. They can't put you away for camping in the woods for three months, and even if they do, you'll have good company." Fenberg nodded toward Bean and the Indian. "We're all escaped jailbirds, too."

Tuberski chuckled.

"C'mon. Let's go home," said Fenberg.

The creature was leaning halfway out of the bed. He had been curiously watching the men crouch and point in the bright light. There was still the tightness in his chest. He felt tired, but better. Tuberski's neuro-dermal treatment and the medicine had helped. Imperceptibly, the wind changed. On the incoming breeze, the creature picked up a faint, pungent odor, something he had smelled a long time ago a great distance away. Something that made his skin crawl with uncertain challenge. His upper lip curled in an involuntary sneer. The creature stopped his cavernous guttural growl.

Something else rose in on the wind.

The creature twitched his head back and forth, as if trying to pull the smell out of the air. A new scent. Sweet, perfumey. Elaine Mitikitski. It was as clear as a telephone call to a human. The tangy, acidic spore was unfamiliar in total, confusing, but recognizable in part. It was a large predator, and the level of musk indicated it was about to attack. No. Mate. No. Attack and mate. The complex scent of Elaine's natural oils, her perfume, and most importantly, the smell of fear, told the beast Mitikitski was the victim.

"Wait," said Charlie, kneeling next to the print. "Something is not right."

"What do you mean?" asked Fenberg, coming back. Tuberski put his hands on his knees and bent over his brother's shoulder to look.

"She got in here," pointed Charlie.

"Yeah. So?" asked Tuberski.

"You are picking up a person to give him a ride. Do you let him crawl over your lap to get into your truck? See? She did not walk around to the other side. There are no footprints to show that the driver stepped out to let her in."

Fenberg shrugged. "Maybe she climbed into the bed."

"Or maybe it was a crewcab like Mike's, or a big Jeep with four doors, and she got into the back seat. Did you ever consider that, pathfinder?"

Charlie grunted and agreed.

Fenberg was eager to get back to town and see Elaine. Walking to the driver's side, he was bowled over by what felt like a runaway carpet truck. Fenberg got up on one elbow in time to see the Bigfoot sprint down the dirt road and disappear down an embankment.

Bean Breath Brown sprinted after the beast in hot pursuit.

"Damn it anyway," said Tuberski with mild disgust. He broke into a light jog. "Your sports editor must have scared him again. We better not let them get too far away, or we'll be up here for the rest of our lives." Tuberski stopped. He looked at Fenberg. "Would you mind getting up off your wallet and doing something useful?"

*　*　*　*　*

At first, the park superintendent with the big hair thought it was a UFO. In the distance, whatever it was seemed to be hovering about eight feet off the ground, with several white, yellow, and red lights. With an index finger raised slowly to his lips, Ranger Granger cautioned his deputy ranger, "Shhhhhh . . ."

Ranger Granger killed the ignition to the Ranger Granger-mobile and proceeded cautiously on foot. The UFO turned out to be Fenberg's truck, abandoned in the middle of nowhere, lights on and the engine running. Granger sent his assistant sprinting back to the park service vehicle to radio for help.

*   *   *   *   *

The angry sound of flash flood water pounding against great boulders was muffled, barely audible from the spot where Hiram Webster leapt 6,411 feet straight down to his death in 1926 over an unrequited love. They named the craggy plateau after his deed, and the Indians said the place was haunted. Mitikitski would concur.

The soft white flesh of her stomach excited the werewolf. The smell of her hair, her heavy breathing, the sensation of her small heart pounding—it was intoxicating to the beast. Elaine felt the hairy finger searching under the tooled leather belt Fenberg had given her. She wondered why she couldn't faint like women were supposed to. She writhed and struggled. She cried in anguish and terror, pain and revulsion. She heard her echo, bouncing off an impassive mountain in the distance. She stopped her screams. No. It wasn't an echo. The cry was high-pitched, like sheet metal tearing. It answered her in the forest a short distance away.

Behan as werewolf stood abruptly, straddling Mitikitski, frozen, his wet nose black, his eyes red. Only his ears flickered, trying to decipher the sound of something large, something heavy, something as dangerous as he crashing through the underbrush.

It was John Tuberski's Bigfoot.

The creature sprang into the clearing. He saw Elaine being held by the two yeomen. In the moonlight, the eight-hundred-pound hominid roared and pounded the ground with his fists.

And then he charged.

He bowled into the wolfman, driving him into a tree like a

linebacker ramming a quarterback. Eight hundred pounds accelerating to forty miles an hour. Saliva spewed from Behan's canine mouth as the wind was crushed from his lungs. The Sasquatch wasn't agile. He knew only brute strength. He backed and charged again, leveling the were-wolf in the ribs with a lowered shoulder, driving him hard again into the tree. Birds shrieked blindly into the night. For the first time in his transposed state, Behan felt pain. He screamed in rage and disbelief, clawing at the behemoth. The six-inch talons dug in and raked. The Bigfoot rolled off quickly, awkwardly trying to reach the burning cuts on his back, his screams tearing the air.

It was the ghoul's turn to attack.

The clumsy Bigfoot backed away as the wolfman stalked him. The werewolf that was Behan pounced on the slower beast, teeth and nails like razors. Tufts of hair and skin flew from the Sasquatch, and he helplessly swatted at his attacker. He whined in pain, powerless to stop his own murder.

"Keep him away from you!" shouted Mitikitski, trying to pull free from the black stump. "Grab onto him so he can't slash or bite you!"

The wolfman pounced again, and, this time, the Sasquatch met his charge by grabbing both wrists. Behan snarled and slashed with his open mouth, trying to sink his incisors into the vulnerable neck area, only inches away. Slowly, the creature squeezed Behan's wrists, harder, harder, forcing him to the ground.

"Break his arms!" cheered Mitikitski.

Disbelief filled the wolfman's eyes. It had never been like this. He tried to fall on his back, to kick the Sasquatch, but was pinned awkwardly, without leverage.

Mitikitski heard another crashing in the thicket. Bear Breath Brown and Tuberski bounced into camp with Fenberg and the Indian right behind. Fenberg had a rifle. The men were momentarily mesmerized by the two hairy, battling giants.

"Elaine!" Fenberg moved toward her. Tuberski put his hand on Fenberg's shoulder, stopping him.

On the windswept plateau, the full moon filling half the sky and lighting the conifer woods like a bristling foreign planet, the Bigfoot felt the familiar tightening pain in his chest. The left arm went numb, the strength quickly spilled. The teeth of the ancient beast slowly pulled toward Tuberski's creature.

"His heart!"

"John!"

Before Fenberg could stop him, Tuberski bounded into the melee, a split second too late. The teeth of the transformed M. J. Behan tore a gash in the creature's chest.

"Bastard!" yelled Tuberski, kicking the werewolf viciously in the small of the back. The blow would have paralyzed a normal man, but Behan in his madness was not normal. "Whoops," said Tuberski.

Behan rolled back to his feet, rubbing his kidneys. In great pain, the Bigfoot crawled off, out of the way.

"Get outta there!" screamed Fenberg, raising his rifle, trying to take a bead.

Tuberski bobbed and weaved, keeping out of the reach of the lunging talons. A wild swing by the monster, and Tuberski neatly dove under into a shoulder roll. "Shoot him!"

Fenberg pumped four quick rounds into the chest of the monster, but it seemed only to infuriate him. He stood straight up.

"The silver bullet!" shouted the Indian. "Use the silver bullet!"

Fenberg fumbled in his shirt pocket for the cartridge made of pure silver. He dropped it in the leaves with a half-dozen other bullets. The monster sprang.

All of six inches.

As Behan vaulted toward the unprotected Fenberg, Tuberski grabbed the werewolf's heel from behind. *Homo canis lupus* flew straight into the air and belly flopped hard on the ground. Tuberski clambered on top, sneaking an arm up and locking Behan around the neck in a full nelson.

In his transformed state, M. J. Behan weighed nearly three hundred fifty pounds. Tuberski held him off the ground and squeezed. The tendons in the back of the hairy neck were like steel fiber. They didn't bend. They didn't break.

"I can't fucking hold him!" said Tuberski, through gritted teeth. Beads of perspiration percolated at his forehead. "Find the fucking bullet, put it in the fucking gun, and blow his fucking head off! Please!" yelled Tuberski.

Fenberg fumbled in the damp mulch. "I can't fucking find it!"

"I'm losing it!" said Tuberski, straining. The werewolf flayed and screamed. It was like holding onto a giant, rabid bat.

"Got it!" Fenberg fumbled awkwardly, putting the silver bullet into the chamber. He had to take it out. A leaf was wrapped around it. "Fu-uck." He cleaned it off and quickly reloaded.

Stand up. Rifle to shoulder. "Christ, look out!"

Still holding the monster, Tuberski whirled to face the new challenge. His turn moved the werewolf out of Fenberg's line of fire. It also caused Luther Magonogonovitch to hit John Tuberski in the ear with a large branch. Luther clubbed him again, and Tuberski's grip slipped off. Behan whirled to roar in triumph.

"Yessss!" Behan screamed into the night.

The tables had turned. The werewolf was behind Tuberski, holding him as a shield, backing toward the edge of Webster's Leap. Tuberski's head weaved drunkenly. Behan held a curled talon by the throat of Fenberg's brother. "One swipe, and I will tear every vein and artery in his neck. Death will come in fifteen seconds, but it will seem much longer. Put the gun down."

"You touch him, I'll kill you," said Fenberg, evenly. He held the rifle steady, aiming straight for Tuberski's head. He would have to move the barrel quickly, right or left, when the moment opened.

"You already shot me. You see it has no effect," said Behan, his voice gravelly, teasing.

"I have a thirty-ought-six in the chamber. It's made of pure silver."

Behan laughed and adjusted the weight of his victim. "That, I'm afraid, is an old wives' tale."

"Then why are you holding my brother as a shield?"

Behan laughed again, throwing his head back. He howled. The sound even brought goose bumps to the Magonogonovitch brothers. "Damn nice to see you again, Mike!

"Interesting," said Behan. The voice was distorted, coming from the half-man, half-animal larynx. "I, who want my immortality, you who want your brother. No, Michael. I have come too far. I've waited too long." His head tilted curiously, looking over the precipice. He managed a toothy grin. "You might say this is my night to howl."

"What's he talking about, Charlie?" Fenberg asked. He couldn't afford to turn around. "Charlie? Charlie! Ray?"

Bean Breath Brown and the Indian had taken off for parts unknown.

"It seems we have a cozy little family get-together here," said the werewolf. "What do they call this, when everyone has a gun on the other and no one can move?"

"A Mexican standoff."

"Right," said Behan. He shifted Tuberski's great weight easily on one arm. "Shall we add another piece to the board to make it interesting? Lom!"

Elaine had a front row seat. Lom pulled a big buck knife and slit her straps. He held her by the arms.

"Lom," said M. J. in a voice that was almost singsong. "On my instruction, break the girl's neck."

Fenberg quickly aimed the gun at Behan's minion. The twin had Elaine's head secured in a viselike forearm. A pudgy hand was cupped at the side of Mitikitski's head. Pencil neck. That's what flashed through Elaine's mind. They used to call her "pencil neck" in school.

Fenberg quickly swiveled the rifle, pointing it first at Lom, then swinging it back at the werewolf.

"An interesting test of wills. An interesting menu of choices," laughed Behan. "One bullet that will kill me. One bullet that will save your girlfriend."

"Aim the rifle at him, Michael," said Mitikitski, standing up straight.

"God, thanks," said Tuberski, a little relieved. "What a gal."

"You've guessed wrong, Behan," Michael said. "I've got more than one silver bullet."

"I don't think so," said the monster with the mocking voice.

"I guess we'll find out real quick," said Fenberg, drawing a bead between Behan's eyes.

"Put your rifle down, and let me have the girl."

"No."

"I won't hurt her," Behan promised.

"I don't think so."

"Don't trust him, Michael," said Elaine, unable to budge under the calloused grip. "He's got some crazy idea that I'm destined to be his bride. He has to take me as his bride tonight, or he'll spend another hundred years in his present form."

The rifle went back on the wolfman.

"Quite true," said the werewolf. He started to inch sideways along the edge, kicking a few loose stones into the yawning, dark abyss.

"Don't move with him!" said Fenberg, taking a step forward.

The werewolf stopped.

"And that's another thing you can just get out of your head," said Mitikitski, squirming under Lom's muscled arm. "The joke's on you, no matter what happens tonight. I'll never have your child."

"What do you mean?" Behan loosened his grip.

"Because I'm pregnant already, you jerk," said Mitikitski, trying to swallow.

Tuberski felt a hot blast of putrid breath on the back of his neck. I wish you hadn't said that, he thought.

"I'm going to have a baby. Michael's baby. *Again*, Martin."

Fenberg and his brother looked at one another.

Again?

Tuberski had a slight smile wrinkling the corner of his mouth. He seemed at peace. M. J. Behan stared at Elaine for a long moment, and, in the silence, he knew what she said was true.

"Again," Behan said, almost reflectively. He rocked back and forth, gently holding Tuberski, looking behind him and listening to the water which seemed almost gentle in the distance. He screamed, and the anguish reverberated off distant hills and bounced back to mock the unholy creature.

Fenberg saw it all too clearly before it happened. It felt like he was out-of-body, watching. As Behan screamed the command for Lom to break Elaine's neck, Fenberg was already moving the rifle. His target area was five inches by seven inches. He swung the rifle, sighted, and fired in one movement. The bullet took off a section of Mitikitski's hair and most of Lom Magonogonovitch's head.

Fenberg expelled the cartridge and swung the gun around on Behan, too late. Three things happened. Fenberg saw the hairy apparition rake Tuberski in the chest with both claws. Tuberski cried out in pain. The beast flung him over the cliff toward the black rocky depths a quarter-mile below. Fenberg instinctively aimed for the diving figure of the werewolf, but was distracted. Lom's brother charged Fenberg from the opposite side. Fenberg moved his rifle in one hand and fired, blasting Luther in the chest. The twin in bib overalls fell at Fenberg's feet, tried to get back up, and fell back down. Dead. Fenberg sprinted to the edge of the cliff. He held the gun aimed at the bushes behind where the monster had disappeared.

"Come closer," motioned Fenberg to Elaine. Mitikitski scrambled next to him. Fenberg forced himself to look over the edge. Deep shadows cut back and forth on the face of the cliff. He couldn't see the bottom, even in the bright moonlight. Fenberg clutched at Mitikitski's hand and shut his eyes tightly. "No. Please," he pleaded quietly. "No.

"John?" Michael called out.

A rush of cold, damp air sliced into Fenberg's face. He heard no answer, just the dim roar of water.

Fenberg's mourning was cut short by a howling in the woods.

"It worked out rather well, didn't it?" taunted Behan. Fenberg spun into a sitting position, rolling the gun in a sweeping

arc. The fire danced orange shadows on the dead Magonogonovitch brothers. Fenberg's back was to the cliff. "Two
pawns for one bishop. It's a long night, Michael. And I am
most strong on this night of nights. Do you remember,
Michael, so long ago? I took her from you then. You ran the
moonlit hills a hundred years ago, bleating like a sick goat,
calling out the name of your Indian bride. We all lost that
night, Michael. I killed her. You killed yourself, a drunk with a
broken heart. And I had to wait a century."

Fenberg fired into the dark.

"Not bad, Michael, but a miss. Silver bullet, Michael?"

Fenberg heard the gravelly laugh, from another part of the
woods.

"All I have to live for now is revenge. Revenge tonight.
Revenge some other night. Or maybe during the day. I have
another hundred years, and long before I've served my sentence in this wretched body, I swear I will rip that baby from
you, Elaine. Again!" He laughed. "And you, Michael, will be
there to watch."

Fenberg swung the rifle back and forth, feeling Elaine next
to him. He took a deep breath to hold back the grief.

Will this night ever end?

"Which bullet, Michael? Which one do you have left?"
Behan called in that strange, childish, mocking singsong. "Is it
the silver one?"

No. Fenberg had used his silver bullet.

* * * * *

They walked along the fire trail in silence, Fenberg on the
outside, Elaine in the middle, the sheriff nearest the embankment. Fenberg stopped frequently, thinking he heard a
rustling ahead, or behind, or above. The quick rush of
padded feet.

Bubba was nearly comatose, still in deep shock from the
ordeal. Funny what people are made of, Fenberg reflected.
Here was a man who had broken up countless arguments
and fights, had witnessed the seamier side of life for twenty

five years. Fenberg watched him mindlessly plod along, cata-
tonic. Michael thought of all the things Elaine had been
through, and he felt . . . what?

Admiration.

That was the word. Fenberg admired Mitikitski.

"I've missed you," Fenberg had said, after they had put
some distance between themselves and Webster's Leap. "And
I want you to know, as best as I can say under present circumstances, that I'm ever so glad you're having our baby. I'll
do my darndest to love and care for you, to make you a good
husband and the baby a good father. Okay?"

Hot tears streamed down Mitikitski's smudged face. What
could she tell him after all this? You don't go through a living
nightmare and listen to tales of hauntings and demons and
being alive five thousand years ago and expect to start an
Ozzie and Harriet romance. Too much pain. Too many questions. I can never make this relationship work, she thought.
Maybe I can't make any relationship work.

Fenberg marched diligently along, fighting the melancholy.
He knew it would dull his senses if he let it in. Keep sharp.
Concentrate. Listen beyond what you are capable of hearing,
Tuberski had always said.

Norwood. Also known as the great John Tuberski himself.
John picked up the showmanship of signing his name in the
air, like the late heavyweight champion, John L. Sullivan.
Michael would bury his brother next to the empty grave of
his parents, next to Tracy and the Baby.

Judge not, Fenberg would write on the tombstone, as John
had requested. *Judge not good, judge not evil.*

Fenberg walked. Maybe there is reincarnation, as Tuberski
had believed. Maybe he'll come back as some bright, fresh
face. Maybe as my son, thought Fenberg. He looked at
Elaine's stomach and wondered.

Clutching at straws. Ears open. Concentrate.

"Where are we going, Michael?" asked Elaine.

"Back to the truck, honey," said Fenberg softly. "It's parked
up ahead on the fire trail. We'll see if we can find Raymond
and Charlie and go back home."

All the stars were out, and the moon cast long shadows on the gutted dirt road. Fenberg thought of the monster. Revenge tonight. Revenge some other night. That's all he had to live for.

"Are you okay?" Elaine asked.

"I'd be better if . . ." Fenberg didn't say he'd be better if John were still alive. If he hadn't fired that silver bullet. Or at least, if he had another.

They walked. At this elevation, they could see the lights of Basin Valley and a few other small outposts twinkling hopefully in the distance.

"The truck should be up ahead," said Fenberg. "It's hard to tell, but I think we ran off the trail right around here when we were chasing the Bigfoot." Funny, he thought. No, sad. The creature probably crawled away to die. Fenberg's brow furrowed. Funny, also, they should have seen the lights from the truck by now.

As the trio marched, the dirt crunching under their soles was the only sound to be heard in the crisp March air. In his stupor, the sheriff stumbled a few steps ahead.

"Bub, you're getting too far in front," warned Fenberg.

Bubba didn't hear. He broke into a trot, then clumsily ran, following the profile of the mountain around a sharp switchback.

"Sheriff!" Elaine called, and jogged after Bubba.

Fenberg grabbed her by the jacket. "Wait," he said. "I don't want you running around any blind corners." They cautiously walked around the bend, inching away from the shadowed ledge that jutted out above them. Mitikitski saw the sheriff first and screamed.

He was dead, his head nearly severed from the body, half-submerged in his own blood.

It was a diversion, and with some deeper instinct Fenberg knew it. But he had taken just enough time to stare at the body, no more than a second. That's when the werewolf sprang.

The monster had killed Bubba quickly, vaulted back to the ledge, doubled back, and pounced on Fenberg. The rifle was slapped from Michael's hands, as if it would have done him any good anyway.

"Run, Elaine, run!" yelled Fenberg.

Behan, his yellow eyes glowing red, the fur around his mouth stained with blood, held forth a beckoning claw. "Stay. Please."

Mitikitski backed against the dirt wall, frozen as Behan lifted the father of her child high in the air. The wind was cold. The rapids were entrancing, calling to Fenberg.

"You and your brother ruined my life," the beast said, the words garbled as if vibrating from a deep pit. "You stole a century of my life, and now I must wait, enduring the agony and humiliation of this unholy form." The werewolf brought Fenberg's face close to his, as if he were holding a baby. "Shall I bite your face off?"

Fenberg squirmed, trying to pull back from the sickening halitosis that yawned from the black gums.

"Or perhaps it would be better that I just scratch you. Do you know what happens if I scratch you?"

For once, Fenberg did not have a snappy comeback.

"The mark of the beast. That was how I started. You would become as me, not as great, of course, but at least I'd have some company in the eons to come."

"Do I get a third choice?" asked Fenberg, twisting his face away.

"Come join me, Michael." Behan brought up his free hand, as if to drag his claws down across Fenberg's eyes and cheek. "We could hunt together, own the night. Perhaps some day you'd thank me."

"Goddamn it, no!" Fenberg screamed and writhed. He saw lights bounce in the monster's yellow eyes, then disappear, then dance erratically and be gone again. Behan's head snapped up. He stared beyond Fenberg, looking down the road, his pointed, hairy ears twitching from the advance roar.

Gunshots. Engines.

Swerving around the corner on two wheels was Fenberg's F-350, the lights illuminating the road, the hills, the trees, and half the forest. Behan was momentarily blinded and raised his free hand to shield his sensitive eyes from the stabbing light of the racing lamps.

" 'Kay," said John Tuberski, momentarily panicking as he leaned to force the truck back on all four wheels. This time he had a legitimate excuse for abusing Fenberg's pickup truck. He grinned viciously. Tuberski double-clutched and shifted down into second gear, and the truck snapped forward, picking up speed and power. Right behind him, emptying their rifles into Fenberg's tailgate, was most of Basin Valley's Sheriff's Department and half the state police. And Ranger Granger.

Fenberg used the distraction. He planted both feet on the monster's neck and kicked free from the grip.

The tall-haired forest ranger was in the lead chase vehicle. He leaned out the window, splattering Fenberg's $26,000 pickup with fat bullets. Granger leaned forward, seeing something ahead on the narrow road—Fenberg, Mitikitski, and a seven-and-a-half-foot-tall werewolf.

"Hold your fire!" Granger yelled to his assistant. "You'll hit the woman! My God . . . what the hell is that thing?"

Tuberski was in third gear when he barreled into M. J. Behan. It seemed the werewolf's face expanded like a balloon, filling the windshield. Tuberski threw open the door at the last minute and dove from the suicide truck. As if he were being gored by some rampaging modern-day metallic buffalo, the werewolf attached himself to the hood as he and the truck flew over the edge, suspended for a brief moment in time and space.

Elaine and Michael watched, mesmerized, as the lights illuminated the hypnotic scene: Behan literally biting and tearing strips of metal off the hood and grill of the truck. In the end, the monster was no match for gravity or the Ford Motor Company. Martin James Behan plunged sixty-four hundred feet to the rapids below, hitting the ground first, the truck adding insult to injury by landing on top of him. It burst into orange flames, crackling and sizzling the remains of Fenberg's truck and the body of Behan underneath.

Tuberski had waited until the absolute last nanosecond to

jump and had rolled, bounced, and finally skidded right to the edge of the precipice. In the spotlight of off-road lights and high beams of the sheriff's battalion, he lay on his back, grimacing and spitting in a cloud of dust.

"Ouch! Goddamn, goddamn it, painted whores along the Nile, I think I twisted my ankle!" he said, getting up and hopping around on one foot. Fenberg noted Tuberski's shirt was bloodied and shredded, but there was no wound underneath. "God. You won't catch me doing that again," Tuberski said, slapping the dust from his torn white T-shirt and faded jeans. He limped over to the edge of the cliff to inspect the flaming wreckage below. "See ya. Wouldn't want to be ya," he said to the flaming werewolf. And to Michael, "Hellew, buddy." A grin emerged from the dirty face.

Fenberg hooked his thumbs in his belt. He let out a long blast of air.

"I guess I must have fallen about a hundred feet when Behan threw me over the cliff," said Tuberski. "I guess I sort of landed in a tree and knocked myself out."

"Stop saying, 'sort of.' "

"Sorry. Who's the chick?"

Fenberg pursed his lips. He looked over the cliff at the smoldering remains of his truck, then looked back at his brother.

"I'm sorry," said Tuberski, shrugging sheepishly while standing on one foot.

"You could have just slammed on the brakes and knocked him over the cliff," Fenberg pointed out.

"I'm sorry," said Tuberski. "I guess I wasn't thinking."

"You didn't have to *throw* my truck over the cliff, you know," said Fenberg.

"I guess I sort of wasn't thinking," said Tuberski.

"Don't say 'sort of.' "

* * * * *

Webster's Leap was filled with cars and lit like an Alpha Beta parking lot. Radios squawked. Mitikitski had acquired another vice. Wrapped in a heavy blanket, she sipped coffee.

"It turned out that Bean and Charlie the Indian had run off to get help," explained Tuberski. "Unfortunately, they got arrested. They led the local *gendarmes* to the truck, and the SOB's moved it. Took me a half hour to find it. Hey!" Tuberski yelled at a couple of paramedics who were nervously working on the wounds of the Sasquatch. "Make sure he's secure. Yeah, go ahead, don't worry. He's as playful as a kitten. You might want to be careful if you put any astringent on those cuts. He bites, you know."

The paramedics took long, respectful steps back.

Tuberski limped over to personally oversee the care of the Sasquatch. Mike and Elaine followed. *"Bigfoot-us gigantus make-us a millionaire-us*. Hell of a specimen, isn't he?" Tuberski asked, beaming.

"Do you have any idea what the hell that other thing was you hit?" asked a highway patrolman. "We saw it before it went over the brink. God, what a face. I think I'll be having nightmares for a month."

You're not the only one, thought Mitikitski.

"They're saying it was a bona fide werewolf, just like in the scary pictures," said the patrolman.

"Only quite real," said Fenberg.

They watched the paramedics and a few deputies load the creature onto a large gurney. The antiseptic white bandages wrapped around his dark fur were an odd contrast. Tuberski's monster was heavily sedated.

"Do we take this thing to a vet or to a hospital?" asked one of the ambulance drivers.

"That's a good question. Mikey?"

"I understand his wounds aren't too serious," said Fenberg. "Right?"

"Yeah," said the paramedic. "He's got that big gash on his back, but it should heal okay." He shook his head. *As if I know how one of these things should or should not recuperate.* "I'd make sure he gets some monitoring, though, to make sure he doesn't tear out the stitches when he wakes up. Probably ought to heavily secure him."

Fenberg called his brother off to the side. Tuberski bent to listen. "I think it would be in your best interest, and probably the creature's, if you took it back to the ranch," said Fenberg.

" 'Kay. Why?"

"The press is going to get wind of this, and they'll be tearing down doors to get at him," Fenberg pointed out. "It might be more soothing, especially with his heart condition," Fenberg whispered, "if he were in a quiet place with just a couple of familiar faces around. Besides. You're the only one who can communicate with him."

There were six men around the gurney. They lifted, but the gurney didn't budge.

"Here. Let me help," said Tuberski, holding a finger in the air. He gingerly limped over and waved three men off to the other side. "On three, ready, go, three," he said, easily lifting his end. The other six men strained with their half.

"What a guy, my baby brother," said Fenberg, putting his arm around Elaine. Elaine smiled. She pulled away slightly from Fenberg's hug, and Michael sensed this wasn't just the action of a woman in shock. There was a finality. "I guess we've got a lot to talk about. . . ."

Elaine nodded.

"I have this terrible feeling in my gut you're going to tell me something I'm not going to want to hear."

"Oh, Michael . . ." Elaine pulled away and hid her face in her hands. Fenberg reached out to hold her again, but stopped. He felt awkward. The police and others looked away. Fenberg shrugged. There you go. He wondered why they always left him . . . and he wondered why there wasn't a scratch on his brother's chest where the werewolf had gouged that serious wound.

PART III:

31

JUST A SUCKER FOR CRAZY WOMEN

The creature lay on the floor, in the room where Dale Fenberg had given birth to four male children. He lay in the fetal position, staring vacantly at the uncountable curly brown heads of carpeting that he dreamed were tiny versions of himself, an army of miniature Bigfoots that would rescue him, carrying him away on innumerable little shoulders. He felt the shame of the clear tubes that violated his body, sending foreign liquid in and his lifeblood out. Wires and electrodes connected him to machines. Screens tattled to any passerby the secrets of his thoughts, how fast his heart was beating. Fat canvas and leather belts, matted with damp hair, anchored him to the floor.

He stared at the shoes.

They belonged to two MD's, a zoologist, anthropologist, psychiatrist, veterinarian, and a cardiologist. The doctors stood, dressed in white lab coats, solemnly clearing their throats. The creature felt them staring but didn't look up.

It had been two weeks since that night on Webster's Leap, and at first, the creature had taken well to the warm, soft floor and the visits from all four Fenberg boys. And Elaine, before she left. It had taken just five days for recovery and he asked, in that whining, barking fashion that only Tuberski could understand—could he go? There was foraging to do, and dogs to scare, and movies to watch, and he felt much better, thank you. Could he go?

Those people in the white coats. They argued with Tuberski. Words the creature couldn't understand. Tuberski stood with crossed arms and shook his head, no. No. You can't take him, not to a lab, hospital, or zoo. He stays here. My bedroom, my monster, Tuberski would say, and the doctors would ahem and huff, expounding such cliches as ". . . outrage to science," and ". . . duty to mankind," and ". . . think what we can learn," and Tuberski would say, ". . . cry me a river."

Can I go?

Those people in white coats. Tuberski had done nothing to stop them. The creature looked blankly at the sea of brown carpeting. He had whined and snarled back. That's when he felt that annoying bee-sting prick in his right hip and saw one of the White Coats holding a long needle in him, inside him. He had batted the technician with an annoyed backhand and caused quite a commotion. He had pulled the strange-looking silver-and-clear insect from his leg and curiously inspected it. They stood watching, out of reach, as he rolled in a small, uncertain arc. From that time on, his head felt heavy and dull. Time passed in thick, oozing clumps, sunrise to afternoon and the long, long nights. He was dimly aware of Tuberski, always there. He wouldn't look at Tuberski, choosing, for those brief moments of lucidity between injections, to look at the great trees outside the window, gently beckoning with waving arms.

"Is he going to be all right?" Tuberski asked. No one answered. They believed the creature was dying.

"Do you think it's his wounds?" Tuberski filled the doorway. He leaned against the frame, his hands hidden behind his back.

"Shouldn't be," said one of the physicians, crouching to examine the beast. "They've healed nicely, remarkably, in fact. And there's no sign of any apparent foreign toxin from whatever it was that scratched him."

John reflectively touched the invisible scar on his own chest. "His heart?" he asked.

"That might be," said the cardiologist sarcastically. "But under these conditions, we can hardly tell. He needs to be moved to a lab."

"He's getting worse though, isn't he?"

"Yes. He's getting worse."

The creature hadn't touched food or water for two days. Hair fell out in clumps, and his eyes were sallow and distant.

"If we could just transfer him to a decent . . ."

Tuberski didn't know that most of the professionals here had privately, and through their universities and hospitals, filed suit against him. They wanted the beast. Tuberski stared past the doctors, trying to catch the deep-set brown eyes that no longer looked back. Hell. I don't want to give him to them, he thought.

"Mr. Tuberski, if we don't move him from here, you're going to lose your monster."

"Would that be so terrible?" he asked.

"I don't get you." He was the MD, thick beard, pale.

"Just speaking out loud, metaphorically."

The group shuffled uneasily. They considered Tuberski odd, worse yet, frivolous.

"What, learned people of four-year colleges, *is* a monster?" Tuberski smiled guilelessly as the committee in white lab coats oozed a silent superiority. "A beast of hair and fang? A vaporous apparition of ectoplasm? Something in a cheap suit crawling from the grave? Whatdya think?"

The group wasn't in the mood for twenty questions.

Tuberski chuckled. "All right. You guys have been a laugh riot, and I'd love to wax poetic, but I've got a couple of pies in the oven, and I've got something especially unpleasant to do." Like grow up. "Everybody say 'kay."

No one said 'kay.

"Everybody say good-bye."

Tuberski herded the huffing scientists down the hallway, guiding them en masse through the living room out the front door. From the porch, the group sputtered terse umbrages, eager anyway for progress reports on their covert legal assaults.

As they drove away, kicking up dust and gravel, Tuberski peered over to the hill on the left boundary of the ranch, then surveyed the woods toward the right. Scanning for reporters. The hills had been crawling with photographers, newsmen, and the curious. John and Mike had been averaging six bum-throws an hour. It was fun the first day, but the novelty soon wore thin. Tuberski went back inside.

The house was a mess, littered with mail—offers, threats, pleas for money. John Tuberski had earned more money in the short span of two weeks than he had in his entire life. He sold an exclusive magazine interview for a cool six figures—enough to pay off the ranch, all his credit card sins, buy some presents for the boys and a new pickup for Michael. The phone had rung incessantly, and they had to have a special unlisted number installed. That number rang, catching Tuberski in midstride.

"Michael?"

"Nope. Me, John."

"Is Michael there?"

"Who is this?" asked Tuberski.

"Granger."

"Farley or Stewart?"

"Ranger Granger . . . don't clown."

"It's my phone. I'll do what I want."

Ranger Granger steamed, then simmered. "Lookit. As soon as Michael gets in, tell him we've had reports that that half-breed so-and-so Red Dog Rassmussen has been seen again around these parts, drunker than a skunk. We've got people out looking for him."

"What do you mean, 'we'?" asked Tuberski. "You're a park ranger."

"Just tell Fenberg that Red Dog's got a gun and has been making threats directed toward him."

Tuberski hung up and considered that Red Dog Rassmussen had never liked the media, especially print.

* * * * *

Tuberski sauntered back to the room and slouched in the stained leather chair in the corner. The afternoon light poured into the room, warming it. Tuberski looked at the monster. Its back was toward him. He thought of doting *Sports Illustrated* calendar girls and beach-front homes. Fast cars, unlimited art supplies, and designer big-guy clothes. The vision seemed to be fading.

"It's an awful thing when the Big G in H taps one on the shoulder," he said to the beast. "I guess you've never wondered what makes things tick. Why we live in what seems to be a perfectly balanced universe, yet our own lives are so imperfect and out of balance. You ever think about that?"

The creature ignored him. The once hamsterish-round face was gaunt. The breaths came slower, labored. The eyes grew heavier, struggling to follow the waving branches outside. He tried to lift his head one last time, but couldn't. He exhaled jerkily with finality and closed his eyes. John looked down at the creature's peaceful face.

His meditations were interrupted by the screen door slamming and the unmistakable sound of dragging feet on wooden floors. The room was the first place Clifford visited upon getting up in the morning or coming home from school. Clifford called Tuberski a name as he walked in and punched his big brother in the back. Clifford attempted to force-feed a stale cookie to the beast.

"Don't do that," said Tuberski.

"He's playing dead," said Clifford.

"I know he's playing dead," said Tuberski.

"I taught him."

"No you didn't."

The creature couldn't stand the pestering and spit the crumbs out. Clifford called it "stupid" and ate the rest of the cookie himself.

"He's not going to make it much longer, you know," said the pale-faced boy with the bright, curly red hair.

"What makes you say that?"

"Those scientist guys are bad. They're killing him with, like their tests and stuff. He belongs outside, in the forest where he can be free. He needs his friends and trees and rocks. He needs fresh air, and he's got to have his freedom or he'll die, and all you'll have left is hair." It wasn't much of a motivational speech, content-wise, but the point was made.

"So you think I should let him go, huh?"

Clifford nodded yes. Tuberski considered this. He sighed. "Well, hell. I guess I was going to let him go anyway."

Clifford petted the creature, who didn't respond. "Were not."

"Was-so, was-so, you midget."

"Were not. I've got to go to the bathroom." Clifford clogged past, his ill-fitting jacket half-on, half-off. He tried to slug Tuberski on the way out, but John stepped nimbly away.

Tuberski knelt beside the last American legend and tugged the canvas belt that held the main harness. The creature's head jerked up, and he coughed alertly. "Yeah, that's right. We're getting you out of here."

As Tuberski fiddled with the buckles, the creature alternated glances at the trees and the top of John's head. "Yeah-yeah, I know. Woods, the great outdoors, scenic splendor, while I go back to the poorhouse. You ingrate pelt. But first, you're going to have to eat some vegetables and get some strength back. I'm sure as hell not going to carry you."

The creature nipped at Tuberski's hand, and Tuberski lightly cuffed him.

*   *   *   *   *

Fenberg had spent a quiet evening at home, figuring out where the family stood and taking care of unfinished business. The photo of Tracy and Jack had been taken from the shirt pocket and installed into an album. Fenberg was playing solitaire when Tuberski returned home late that evening.

"I guess you heard," said Tuberski, tossing his keys on the counter.

"Clifford was rather excited. So was the press," said Fenberg, leaning back to see where he could play a black eight.

"Irate was more like it." Tuberski grinned "Boy, I feel great," he said, slapping his hands together and rubbing them. "Almost noble."

Angry Joe and Cliff sauntered into the living room.

"It's that feeling you get when you do something against the tide, that's against popular opinion, but that you know in your heart is right. It's damn invigorating."

Fenberg thanked Robespierre, informing him that the nation's media had been hounding him all evening. Red ten, black jack. Tuberski had led them a merry chase on some rutty, narrow logging road with the creature in the back of the truck. Then Tuberski had allegedly slammed on his brakes, got out, reached into the lead car, and pulled the steering wheel off the column, stranding a million-dollar payroll of electronic mediamen in the middle of nowhere.

"That's why I lift big weights," said Tuberski, walking toward the kitchen. "This has been a long vacation. I've got painting to do, and manly home improvement, and listen, pal . . ." Tuberski addressed Clifford, who stuck out the very tip of his tongue. ". . . I owe a lot to you. That little speech of yours this afternoon, you may not know it, but it helped open my eyes on a grand, thematic level. I can sleep again."

"Makes sense," said Fenberg, shaking his head. Black two on a red three. "I can see his line of thinking. . . ."

Tuberski raided the icebox, pulling out the meat tray and a gallon of milk. He drank directly from the bottle.

". . . especially considering Cliff has watched *E.T.* four times a day on the VCR for the past week," continued Fenberg.

Tuberski held the milk to his mouth again, but didn't drink. He suspiciously watched Fenberg from the corner of an eye.

"This may be the wrong time to bring it up, partner." Queen of diamonds to the king of clubs. "But did you ever consider that there might have been some alternative to your 'grand, thematic' gesture?"

"What do you mean?" Tuberski scowled.

Fenberg hit a snag. Nothing to play. "Darn." He collected the cards and reshuffled. "Well, did it ever occur to you that it might have been smarter to keep the creature for—say, even another eight hours? You could have arranged for exclusive film and interview rights. *Then* let the thing go. If I were a network president, I'd pay seven figures for the only tape of a real, live, nine-foot-tall monster. I mean, I appreciate your dilemma, but didn't you once say that being rich and spiritual weren't necessarily different sticks."

Tuberski slowly lowered the milk. Millions, billions. "I have a few color rolls of film left," he answered meekly.

"If you ask me, I think he was just lacking a little vitamin D," Fenberg theorized. "Not enough sunshine." Fenberg's first card on the new deal was an ace. He let out a satisfied ahhh. "Me, I don't think he was dying. Too resilient. I think he was just depressed and homesick. In fact, I remember telling you, 'John, he's depressed and homesick. Walk him. Take him outside.' But you didn't want reporters with telephoto lenses getting freebies. There's a fable there, somewhere. . . ." Fenberg paused. Whenever possible, he enjoyed dishing back form-for-form to Basin Valley's economy-sized Aesop.

"Is it the doggie who saw his reflection in the water and dropped the bone? I think that would work. No. I'd have taken better care of the thing. Maybe even buy some land up here and create a fenced-in sanctuary. Show the thing off for a month, make a few hundred million, and then let it go."

Reeling from good advice, Tuberski reached for the counter to steady himself. "I've been duped," he said dizzily. Tuberski focused on Clifford. Blame and accusation bubbled in John's eyes. "I shouldn't have listened to you."

"You said you were going to let him go. . . . " squeaked Clifford in that high, grating voice.

"Yeah. Fucking smart. Take advice from a six-year-old," said Angry Joe. Clifford wiggled lewdly and stuck out his tongue.

"I'll kill him," swore Tuberski, vaulting over the counter and charging the baby of the family. Cliff's eyes dilated. He screamed "*Help, murder, police!*" and ran for the nearest bathroom with a functioning lock. Joe calmly followed to show Tuberski how to unlock the door from the outside.

The cards showed promised, but it was another short game. Fenberg reshuffled, ignoring the bloodcurdling screams in the background. Tuberski stormed back into the room, his eyes wild. He grabbed keys and a jacket. "I'll kill him later. Maybe I can still find the creature. He's probably still weak from lying in bed."

The screen door slammed behind Tuberski.

Fenberg smiled and shook his head. Alone now, he put the cards down and reached into his back pocket. He had been carrying the envelope all day. He was afraid to open it.

It was from Elaine.

The letter had a sharp crease in it and was molded in the shape of his rear end.

Fenberg reached across the long oak table and pulled a Hav-A-Tampa from the yellow box. This time, he lit it. Michael spun the letter around a few times. He thought about making tea. No. Let's get it over with. The smoke from the little cigar made him blink as he tore open the letter.

Dear Mike,

I've started to write this letter a thousand times. Each draft has come out the same. I think of you and smile. It's been a few short months, and I feel I've known you a hundred lifetimes. I know, I know. Please don't say previous lifetimes. You're a heck of a guy, Fenberg. It's you who breaks my heart in twelve places.

The past few weeks being an exception, I've never laughed so much around a man before. I've never been so happy with anyone as with you. Starting the days with you, going to the office, just being with you—it's like being on vacation.

You're the treasure I've searched for, and yet, well, maybe some of us weren't meant to find treasure. You bring out something in me, but here I find myself writing you a good-bye letter.

"Oh Elaine, no, you jerk," said Fenberg softly.

I'm scared, tired, drained, confused. In the past days, I've been kidnapped by two exotic and rare varieties of monsters, both of whom seemed intent on making me their bride. I've got bruises all over my arms from being grabbed, and I bruise so easy. Peculiar men seem be a pattern in my life, present company excluded.

But I digress.

I know your heart is in the right place, but mine isn't. My short life's history has been falling in behind some guy and imitating his lifestyle, so that I never found out what I wanted or who I am. I don't know, I guess I sound selfish.

But I know you, Fenberg. You're a heck of a guy who deserves special. I'm not sure that I can give you that special. I think you'd be happy with a woman who'd have your children and bake you pies and sit next to you at the high school football games on Friday nights.

This was far from the truth. Fenberg needed crazy.

I don't think I'm that woman.

I want to be somebody. To travel. To write. Live in a city. I'm twenty-five, and I don't know what makes me tick. I guess I better find out pretty quick, huh? Don't worry about the baby. I'll keep you posted, and when the time comes closer, I'll be in touch. I certainly don't want to keep you from your child. But please, Michael, don't try to call. I know you mean well, but I have good reasons for staying away. For good.

God.

I'm sorry for hurting you, Michael. Please find it in your heart to forgive me some day.

> *I love you so. . . .*
> *Elaine*

Fenberg pulled the phone toward him.

Then he slid it back, shaking his head. No. No more. No more chasing after ghosts and carting around photographic mausoleums. Fenberg had long ago resigned himself to the fact that those closest to him were either dearly departed or crazy. Elaine Mitikitski, while not being dearly departed, was

at least departed. And she certainly was crazy. Fenberg liked
that in a woman.

* * * * *

The next morning was beautiful, all-in-all. The snow was
receding to the tops of the Sierras, and the birds and squirrels, as they do in springtime, were making a happy racket.
Fenberg was taking a long, aimless walk through downtown
Basin Valley. Hands in his pockets, he walked through the
town square, carefully avoiding stepping on any lines or
cracks in the sidewalk. Fenberg was preoccupied. There were
a million things to do.

Mrs. Behan had graciously mailed Fenberg a handsome
check to make up for any hardship and damage her husband
had caused. Fenberg was using the money to buy a new set
of custom boots and erect an efficient, cowboy-yet-rustic
architectural statement from the rubble of the old *Bugle*. He'd
have to sift through the dwindling pile of resumes and find a
replacement for Elaine Miilkitski. Hopefully, it would be
someone older, with a slight emotional or drinking problem.
The others, the college all-stars, tended to stay at *The Bugle*
only a few months, using it as a springboard to a bigger
paper. And of course, he had to compose another editorial
apology for Angry Joe wasting two pages of newsprint on a
risqué tribute to heavy metal music.

Fenberg hung a right at the park. He spotted Tuberski sitting on a park bench, alone.

"I take it you didn't find the creature last night. Again," said
Fenberg, sitting next to his brother.

Tuberski gave a tired, well-duh look.

"Just asking," said Fenberg, crossing his legs. "I tried calling
all last night. She wouldn't come to the phone."

Tuberski slapped the back of his head and rapidly
scratched, as if rousting for fleas. It was a new habit he'd
acquired since that night on Webster's Leap.

"I figure she's just confused right now, what with the
trauma and ordeal from those three days in the woods and

all," said Fenberg.

Tuberski was violently itching an invisible irritation on his chest.

"I think she just needs the proverbial 'time and space.' Then she'll be back." Fenberg's voice had a whistling-in-the-cemetery tone. "I think I'll give her another call this morning. Maybe under the pretense of asking where a missing story or file or something is. It's transparent, but it might work."

Tuberski rubbed his nose. "You don't need to call her. God, I've sure been itchy lately. I wonder if I picked up some poison oak somewhere. Funny." His head perked. "Kind of early for someone to be having a barbecue."

Fenberg twitched his nose. He couldn't smell anything. "Where?"

Tuberski looked at a distant mountain peak. "I think in a cabin, up there," he said, nodding.

Fenberg squinted at the range, a half-day away. He looked at his brother, askance. "What do you mean, I don't need to call her?"

Tuberski pulled out a wrinkled blue-and-white Express Mail envelope from his back pocket and handed it to Fenberg. It was addressed to Michael.

"It came this morning," said John.

"It's been opened."

"Well, of course. I read it."

Fenberg ravaged the packet. Inside was a wallet-sized photo of Elaine Mitikitski in a cheerleader outfit and a long blond wig. She was holding a doll in a blanket. A note was attached.

> *Dear Mike,*
>   *If you feel a morbid compulsion to stare at pictures of blondes and babies, it had better be at me and the forth-coming new arrival.*
>   *The doctors have been giving me dire warnings that I'm just not going to believe. One way or the other, if I have to sell my soul, I'm going to deliver our baby.*
>   *I've spent a small fortune talking on the phone with*

*your brother. He called me collect from a pay phone
from God knows where. You're right. Your brother is
truly an amazing fellow. He helped me see a lot of
things correctly, about me, about us. Want you and the
boys to come meet the family. Waiting to see you, handsome.*

> *Charmed, I'm sure,*
> *Elaine Mitikitski*

"Read the part again about me being amazing," Tuberski
asked, looking over Fenberg's shoulder. Michael smiled
broadly, screamed, and jumped in the air. He pulled Tuberski
off the bench and hugged him.

"Yippee coyote," said the razor-stubbled Tuberski dryly.
Fenberg danced and shadowboxed around his much larger
sibling, slipping in sharp jabs to the biceps. "Stop it," said
Tuberski, covering up.

Fenberg planted a big kiss on the picture and hugged Tuberski one last time. He ran from the park toward his temporary office above the drugstore. He was going to call Mitikitski.

"Hey!" Tuberski yelled. "Red Dog is looking for you. . . ."

But Fenberg had disappeared. Oh, well. He'd tell him later.
Tuberski sat back down on the bench, got up, circled it three
times, and sat down again. He stared narrowly ahead, wondering why he did that as he scratched the spot on his chest
where Behan had raked him.

Fenberg ran down the tree-lined main street, smiling and
yelling hello to a couple of passing merchants, mentally
pigeon holing them quickly as quarter-page and half-page
advertisers, respectively. He jogged past the charred remains
of *The Bugle* and was just two doors away from his temporary office when a stranger asked him for directions.

Fenberg skipped to a stop, torn between politeness and
the urge to talk with Elaine. The man was dressed funny—he
wore a full beard, sunglasses, tennis hat, and long trench
coat. He had a large head. Square. Almost blocklike.

A tourist. Fenberg impatiently listened, waiting for the
inevitable ". . . where's the snow in these parts?" question.

"The nice thing about being a werewolf is that when you're in your primeval form, you're virtually indestructible. See? Not a scratch."

Martin James Behan took off the sunglasses and fake beard and stuffed them into a shopping bag. "It's your time, Michael. I've come for you." Fenberg glanced down. Under Behan's shopping bag he held a large-bore revolver pointing at Fenberg.

Fenberg shook his head slowly. No. It struck him as patently unfair and certainly incorrect. Behan shouldn't be alive. Yet, there he was. And this was a lousy way to get revenge, considering that M. J. Behan was a bona fide werewolf, and werewolves shouldn't carry revolvers. Three shots snapped the air, hitting the newspaperman squarely in the chest and midsection. Fenberg flinched and held on to Behan's shoulder for support.

Tears filled Michael's eyes. It's not fair, he thought.

But tears soften, at least, Fenberg considered. Light flashed, and he was watching all this from out of his body. He saw Tracy, bathed in a white, loving glow, her arms stretched in welcome. The baby was peeking from the purest ivory crib, mischief etched on his face, and stepping from this spinning tunnel were his parents, Roy and Dale.

"Mike . . . Mike . . . I've got a poy-um for you."

Poy-ums were what Fenberg's mom called poems.

The picture accelerated, and Fenberg saw his life flash before him. He saw himself in the operating room, holding his newborn son. He saw Tuberski as a grinning teenager with a butch haircut. They were together, holding helmets and jumping up and down on the football field, triumphantly swinging a huge trophy over their heads. Everyone in Basin Valley was in the stands, cheering. Fenberg saw himself as an old woman, crushing olives in ancient Greece. Fenberg made a face. Crushing olives?

Malulu ran from the temporary *Bugle* offices, her rubber zories making that god-awful *ka-snappida ka-snappida* sound, and Fenberg thought, great. The last thing I'm going to see in life is a female Jack Webb running at me in thongs.

The pain.

Fenberg clutched his stomach and doubled over. He pulled himself away from Behan.

Elaine. He wanted Elaine. Fenberg reached for the picture. His hands probed for the red dampness he knew would soon be spilling from his mortal wounds. A curious expression filled his face.

Fenberg slowly straightened, patting himself down for bullet holes.

Maybe they were small bullets, he thought, checking. Fenberg looked down and noticed he wasn't bleeding.

M. J. Behan fell forward into Fenberg's arms, his gun clattering to the sidewalk. Fenberg steadied him.

"You know, it was I who sent you that silver bullet in the mail," Behan confessed, smiling wickedly. A coughing spasm wracked his body. One of the bullets had caught him in the lung.

"You? Why?" Fenberg asked. Behan was dying.

"After a couple of hundred years, I wanted a challenge." The crafty smile faded. "Who am I kidding? A long time ago, I made a very bad deal. I couldn't even pull the trigger now. I'd rather just roam the woods with the pain. I just don't think I can do this monster stuff anymore." Behan coughed again, and Fenberg gently guided him to the concrete. "I've got to warn you. . . ."

"Just rest up," said Fenberg, holding him.

Behan warned Fenberg of a dire Brotherhood, dark masters of the psychic three-dimensional world. Of a woman, an old and treacherous vampire. On the plus side, she was quite stunning and attractive. On the minus, she was very interested in obtaining not only the souls of Elaine and Tuberski, but that of the new Baby Fenberg as well.

Behan coughed. Michael could see three dark holes widening red on the frail man's chest. Behan began shaking from the cold that was creeping into him. "I'm scared. I'm so sorry. Someone please forgive me, I'm so sorry."

"I'll forgive you, if you'd like."

"I've got so many sins to pay for. . . ."

Fenberg nodded his head slightly. "You've already been forgiven, don't you remember?" With reassuring arms, Fenberg adjusted Behan's slipping body. Fenberg remembered something his brother had told him, years ago. It had been a great comfort. "Martin, I can't swear this is true. But I'll tell you, in some part of my heart, it feels very right. In a little while, you'll come right back again, as a fresh baby, with a clean slate, and you can try it all over again."

That seemed to give Behan hope. Before he died, Behan managed a smile of release and a sincere thank-you. He also asked Fenberg who the hell shot him. Fenberg didn't know.

Fenberg closed Martin's eyes and reflected. There were a lot of things he didn't know.

A few feet away behind Fenberg, Red Dog Rassmussen stumbled drunkenly out of an alley. He raised his revolver and took careful aim for another shot at the back of Fenberg's head. Red Dog lost his balance, and the gun went off in the air. The reaction sent him sprawling backward. He collapsed spread-eagled and quite intoxicated on the sidewalk.

There Fenberg sat, on Main Street, Behan's head cradled in his lap, a crowd beginning to gather. The first three months of the year had been rather interesting. What made Fenberg's brow furrow was that his brother, the one with the different last name who had it changed for career purposes despite the fact he didn't have a career, was acting strangely. It wasn't much, really. But since being scratched by Behan, Tuberski had been wolfing down his meals. And while Fenberg couldn't swear to it, he sensed his brother wanted to chase cars.

Fenberg sighed, then smiled. He was daydreaming, and it wasn't of Tracy. He had a rather clear picture of a tall brunette with a rounded stomach, clear complexion, robin's-egg-blue eyes, and a very bad attitude. Fenberg had to admit. He was a sucker for crazy women.

Red Dog Rassmussen protested lightly when the Basin Valley Sheriff's Department came to arrest him again.

"I really do hate reporters," Red Dog confessed.